Contents

Preface

This is a book about professional development. It is written specifically for teachers and educators who are interested in using information and communication technology (ICT) in their teaching or professional learning. As we all know, there has been great pressure on teachers to use ICT in their classrooms but unfortunately integrating technology in the curriculum is a difficult thing to do. Teachers lack the time, the resources, and sometimes the expertise to use technology effectively in their teaching. It is our hope that this book will assist teachers in dealing with some of the issues that arise in their long and sometimes lonely journey of using technology in their work.

The book falls into three sections, with a total of ten chapters. The first section discusses the ways the Internet (or ICT) can be used for the professional development of teachers. There are four chapters in this section. Chapter 1 is introductory, outlining the professional development needs of ICT-using teachers. The second chapter outlines some professional development models currently in use, with examples drawn from both New Zealand and overseas. Chapter 3 discusses the use of online learning networks for formal and informal professional development. Chapter 4 of this section describes how an ICT professional development plan can be developed.

The three chapters in the second section provide a guideline to the resources available on the Internet that can be used in both teaching and professional development. Chapter 5 is an Internet and Web guide, documenting resources both for teaching and teachers' personal professional learning. Chapter 6 investigates how websites can be developed and evaluated. Chapter 7 in this section discusses how online classroom-based projects can be designed and implemented.

The final section of this book focuses on the ethical, social, and health issues involved in the use of the Internet in the classroom. Chapter 8 is a general introduction, discussing issues such as Internet censorship, privacy, hacking, and copyright issues. Chapter 9 focuses specifically on the strategies that can be used by both teachers and parents in dealing with objectionable or inappropriate materials available on the Web. The final chapter deals with health issues encountered by teachers and school administrators.

I am particularly pleased that all of the contributors to this book are either my close colleagues at the School of Education, University of Otago, or my former or present postgraduate students. As teachers and students in a school of education that values highly professional development and research, we were clear right from the beginning when this book was conceived that writing the book would be a professional development exercise for ourselves. We are pleased that we can now share the outcomes of this exercise with the wider educational community.

Many people have worked closely with me in producing this volume. I am particularly grateful to the contributors who were committed to finishing their manuscripts on time. I also wish to extend my gratitude to Wendy Harrex, managing editor, and Fiona Moffat, production editor of the University of Otago Press, and their team, for their continued support in the last six years. Wendy has not only managed to publish three books for me, but has been my managing editor for *Computers in New Zealand Schools* since 1995. I also wish to acknowledge the support of my colleagues at the School of Education, University of Otago, particularly Professor Keith Ballard, Dean of the School of Education. I am also grateful to Philip Munro, who produced the index for this book.

Finally, I must thank my wife, Sook-Han, for her unfailing support and love throughout my career as a teacher and researcher. I also wish to thank my children, Shang-Chin and Keng-Yin, for their hugs and smiles. Without their support, this book would not have been possible. I am pleased to dedicate this book to them.

Kwok-Wing Lai
School of Education
University of Otago

Professional Development: Too Little, Too Generic?

1

Kwok-Wing Lai

There is no doubt that both computer accessibility and Internet connectivity in schools have been greatly improved in the last few years. For example, in the US, the student-to-computer ratio has reduced from 9.1 students per computer in 1995 to 4.9 students per computer in 2000, with 98 per cent of the public schools placing some computers in classrooms (Market Data Retrieval, 2000). Classroom Internet connectivity has increased from 14 per cent in 1996 to 63 per cent in 1999 (Web-based Education Commission, 2000).

Similar increases have been reported in New Zealand. For example, the ITAG report (2000) estimated an average ratio (excluding computers used solely for administration) of one computer to seven students in secondary schools and one computer to thirteen students in primary schools in 1999. In terms of Internet connectivity, in 1999, 96 per cent of 2,300 primary schools and 99 per cent of 340 secondary schools had access to the Internet from at least one computer. A more recent study (Lai, Pratt, & Trewern, 2001a) conducted in 2000 to evaluate the use of Information and Communication Technology (ICT) in all 27 secondary schools in the Otago region of New Zealand has confirmed the increase in computer accessibility. The findings from this Otago Technology Project were similar to the ITAG figures, with a computer-to-student ratio of 1:6.9 in secondary schools, and an average of 63 per cent of the computers connected to the Internet.

There has also been an increase in teachers accessing computers and the Internet. For example, in 2000, more than 75 per cent of the US schools reported that the majority of their teachers used computers daily. In New Zealand, Lai, Pratt & Trewern (2001a) reported that more than 70 per cent of the teachers and all the ICT co-ordinators in the Otago Technology Project used word-processing or desktop publishing programs at least daily or even more frequently in their work.

Teachers Aren't Using Technology

Even with such noted increases in computer access and Internet connectivity, both for teachers and students, classroom use of ICT has continued to be 'uneven, slow, and of decidedly mixed variety' (Cuban, 1999). Cuban observes that for teachers there are three groups of computer users. The first group he called 'serious users' who have 'incorporated the powerful machines into the very fabric of their lives in and out of school'. The second group is 'occasional users' and they are teachers who considered computing technology to be 'marginal rather than central to their classroom'. The last group is called 'non-users' where the use of the computer for teaching is 'minimal to non-existent'. He notes that in the late 1980s, the vast majority of the teachers were non-users, about 25 per cent were occasional users, and only 10 per cent were serious users. A decade later, after huge investments have been made in computer hardware, only 20 per cent of secondary school teachers have become serious users (merely 10 per cent in primary), about 40 per cent are occasional users (one-third in primary), and 40 per cent are still non-users (50 per cent in primary). Other surveys have also documented the limited integration of technology into the school curriculum. For example, according to the Market Data Retrieval survey (2000), only 8 per cent of the public schools in the US reported that the majority of their teachers could integrate technology into the curriculum in 1999. Similarly, the Otago Technology Project (Lai, Pratt, & Trewern, 2001a) reports that only 15.7 per cent of the secondary teachers could use technology as an instructional aid and integrate it into the curriculum. These figures show that the overall adoption of technology in teaching in the last few years has been slow, in spite of the huge investment in the purchase of technology hardware and software for schools.

Many explanations have been proposed for the lack of integration of technology into the school curriculum. For example, more than ten years ago, Sheingold and Hadley (1990), from the Bank Street College of Education, were already maintaining that three conditions need to be met before successful technology adoption could be expected. These conditions include: (1) accessibility of computers for teachers and students; (2) support for teachers in learning and planning to use technology; and (3) a school structure to encourage its use (Sheingold & Hadley, 1990). The Otago Technology Project (Lai, Pratt, Trewern, 2001a) asked principals, trustees, teachers, ICT co-ordinators of twenty-five Otago secondary schools to rank order a list of barriers to technology adoption. Findings from this study show that teachers' perceived barriers were quite different from the principals' and school trustees'. For example, principals and trustees have considered cost, of both equipment and technical support, as a key barrier of technology adoption in schools. However, for teachers, lack of knowledge of the equipment, understanding of the value of its use, as well as knowledge of integrating the technology into teaching were considered important barriers to using technology in schools. This study clearly shows that the lack of knowledge and understanding of technology and its value in teaching has greatly limited the use of technology by teachers. It thus highlights the need for professional development if teachers are to benefit from using technology. In this introductory chapter we will discuss some of the key issues involved if we wish to help teachers make better use of technology in their teaching as well as in their professional learning.

The 'Why' Before the 'How'

It is encouraging to see an increase in professional development opportunities for ICT-using teachers in the last few years. Unfortunately, the main focus of these professional development programmes is skill-based, emphasising technical skills (the hows) rather than pedagogical knowledge and understanding (the whys) (Lai, 1996). There seems to be an implicit assumption in these programmes that teachers should use ICT simply because it is there for them to use (the 'Everest Syndrome', as suggested by Maddux (1988)), without asking teachers to reflect on why they should use it in the first place. The 'why' question has long been taken for granted. For example, a report titled 'The Power of the Internet for Learning' (2000), recently submitted to the US president and Congress, has the following conclusion:

> The question is no longer *if* Internet can be used to transform learning in new and powerful ways. The Commission has found that it can. Nor is the question *should* we invest the time, the energy, and the money necessary to fulfil its promise in defining and shaping new learning opportunity. The Commission believes that we should ... (p.vi).

Unfortunately, similar to many other reports on the use of technology in education, few systematic findings, other than some anecdotal evidence, have been provided in this report to justify the use of technology in teaching and learning. As reported in the Otago Technology Project (Lai, Pratt, & Trewern, 2001a), teachers do not necessarily understand nor are they aware of the benefits of ICT use in their teaching. While teachers are under pressure from educational authorities, parents and the community, to use ICT in the classroom, they will be reluctant to invest the time and energy to facilitate computer-supported learning if they are unconvinced of its value in enhancing the learning process or in managing their teaching.

There is a need to provide teachers with credible evidence and exemplary practices and models to let them make professional judgements as to how technology should best be used in their own teaching. We should note that although researchers have tried very hard in the last twenty years to document the benefits of ICT use in the learning process, there is no conclusive evidence that it has universal benefits or that its use is appropriate in every learning situation. When looking for benefits, perhaps teachers should be more specific, asking:

> What evidence is there that the information technology we want to use in the ways we propose to use it, for the curriculum we want to teach in the time that we have, with the teachers we employ and with the professional development and technical support we can provide will help our students learn better? (International Society of Technology in Education, n.d.).

Research has documented positive outcomes of ICT use in a variety of learning situations. For example, Schacter (1999) has summarised seven major reviews on the impact of technology on student learning and he concludes that computer-assisted instruction (including integrated learning systems), simulation applications, and open-ended applications all have positive effects on learning. It is interesting to note that a range of computer applications have been included in Schacter's (1999) review. For example, one of the studies included was a meta-analysis of 500 individual research studies of the impact of computer-assisted instruction (CAI) on achievement (Kulik, 1994). Another study included in the review was Scardamalia and Bereiter's (1996) Computer Supported Intentional Environment (CSILE) (now known as the Knowledge Forum, refer Scardamalia, 2000), a project which creates a student-centred, constructivist learning environment to support in-depth knowledge acquisition and creation for young learners. This review shows that technology could be used to promote virtually any value system in the classroom (Pea, 1998). For example, the CAI applications (particularly the tutorial programs) reviewed by Kulik (1994) were often used to support a teacher-centred learning environment. Teachers thus have to be mindful that although ICT has great potential for enhancing learning, not every kind of technology application is appropriate to and compatible with their teaching philosophy or would be advantageous to student-centred learning. Current learning theories, however, support the use of ICT as a cognitive or mind tool to facilitate metacognitive and problem-solving skills in a learner-centred, authentic, and constructivist learning environment (Lai, 1993a; 1993b).

Teachers may wish to reflect on some fundamental questions before starting to use technology in their classrooms. Cuban (1998) suggests that we should ask three questions. The first is 'what do you want students and teachers to achieve in the classroom from the use of information technologies?' This question is about the goals of teaching and learning. We need to understand the nature and characteristics of ICT, what it can do for us, as well as how relevant it is as a justification or rationale (e.g., economic, social, learning effectiveness, efficiency rational as suggested by the Education Review Office (1997)). Once we are clear about the goals, the second question we should ask ourselves is whether ICT is the best option to achieve these goals. That is, 'can you reach the same goals at less cost without additional investments in technology?' Finally, if we are happy with the answers to these two questions, we can then ask the implementation question of 'what configuration of hardware, software, and Internet connections would best meet your goals and projected use of computers?'

Too Little Professional Development

It has been clearly documented in the literature that it is teachers' attitudes towards technology, their beliefs in teaching and learning, as well as their styles of teaching that affect how students use technology and what sort of learning experience they will have (Cuban, 1998; Lai, 1999; McCabe, 1998). The teacher matters most to the student's learning (National Commission on Teaching and America's Future, NCTAF, 1996) and thus professional development is essential when innovative practice such as computer-supported learning is to be implemented in the classroom (Fullan, 1990). A report (Wenglinsky, 2000) was recently published in the US examining the link between student achievement in mathematics and science with teaching. In this report it was documented that, in science, students whose teachers had professional development in laboratory skills outperformed their peers by more than 40 per cent of a grade level. Similarly, in mathematics, students whose teachers had professional development in higher-order thinking skills outperformed their peers by about 40 per cent. This report clearly shows the importance of professional development for teachers. Based on his findings, Wenglinsky (2000) suggests that teachers should be provided with more professional development opportunities, for an extended period of time, and the topics of professional development should be closely tied to effective classroom practices. The importance of professional development should not be underestimated. Cooley & Johnston (2000) have outlined eight major factors hindering the integration of technology into teaching and learning. Of these eight factors, half are related to the lack of or inappropriate teacher training and the changing role of the teachers in the learning process.

Although younger teachers very often know how to use application programs such as word-processing or emailing, they are not much better than their older colleagues at integrating technology into teaching. In fact, most beginning and experienced teachers feel unprepared to integrate technology into their teaching as little pre-service and in-service training has been provided. As reported by the National Centre for Education Statistics (2000), almost two-thirds of all the US teachers felt that they were not prepared or somewhat prepared to use technology in their teaching. According to another report (Moe & Blodgett, 2000, cited in Web-based Education Commission, 2000), 65 per cent of the teachers in the US had never used a computer before being introduced to one in the classroom. It is surprising to know how little professional development has been provided for teachers. For example, in the US in the 1998–99 school year, only 39 per cent of the teachers had received some basic computing training of one to five hours and another 19 per cent for six to ten hours (Market Data Retrieval, 2000, cited from Web-based Commission, 2000). In New Zealand, the situation is rather similar. For example, the Otago Technology Project (Lai, Pratt, & Trewern, 2001a) reported that 86 per cent of the teachers and 88 per cent of the ICT co-ordinators in the Otago region would like to be involved in professional development in ICT.

The lack of funding has greatly reduced the opportunity for teachers to participate in professional development. Schools very often do not have the funding to provide relief teaching. One report (Web-based Education Commission, 2000) documents that only 49 per cent of the professional development of US teachers occurs in paid time, compared to 90 per cent of all corporate and government training. Funding has instead been devoted mainly to the purchase of hardware and software. According to a study (Market Data Retrieval, 2000) surveying nearly 90,000 public schools in the 1999–2000 school year, only 17 per cent of the technology spending was devoted to professional development, but 63 per cent was spent on hardware and 20 per cent on software. The percentage spending on professional development is not even half of the 40 per cent recommended by the National Education Association (cited in the Web-based Commission, 2000).

The lack of financial support for professional development is particularly noted in New Zealand. A study conducted by Cowan and Diorio (1998) reports that schools in Otago and Southland spent on average only 5.3 per cent of their annual budgets on professional development in 1997, which was already higher than the 4 per cent documented in an earlier report published by the Education Review Office (1995). In the Otago Technology Project (Lai, Pratt, & Trewern, 2001a), it was reported that one of the biggest issues facing schools and teachers was the limited professional development systematically delivered for technology inclusion across the curriculum to support the increased level of technology assets. The lack of support can be seen from the low level of spending on professional development in these schools. Of the eight schools interviewed, the average spending per student was only NZ$8.5 (compared to US$45 per student per year being spent in the Digital High School project in California, Schiff & Solmon, 1999). The situation has somewhat improved in recent years with the injection of some central funding for professional development by the Ministry of Education for ITPD projects.

Pre-service Teacher Education

Teachers should begin their training in ICT when they are student teachers. Unfortunately, very little attention has been given to integrating technology into the existing teacher education programmes. A report was published by the Office of Technology Assessment of the US in 1995 about the need to prepare teachers for the technology era. In that report, titled *Teachers and Technology: Making the Connection*, the following statement was made:

> Despite the importance of technology in teacher education, it is not central to the teacher preparation experience in most colleges of education in the United States today. Most new teachers graduate from teacher preparation institutions with limited knowledge of the ways technology can be used in their professional practice. (p. 2)

Unfortunately, the situation has not much improved after five years. For example, in the US, fewer than 50 per cent of the colleges of education required students to 'design and deliver instruction-using technology' although states in the US already require 'computer education' for initial licensure (Web-based Education Commission, 2000).

To be sure, some basic ICT training is normally included in teacher education programmes. However, most of the training is provided through stand-alone courses and the learning outcomes are not effective. According to Moursund and Bielefeldt (1999), in a survey of all the teacher education institutes in the US, formal stand-alone IT coursework does not correlate well with scores on items dealing with technology skills and the ability to integrate IT into teaching. As well, although it was reported that IT was available in the classrooms where student teachers got their practical experience, they didn't routinely use technology in their teaching practice and were not advised to do so by the classroom teachers. Moursund and Bielefeldt (1999) suggest that teacher training institutes should increase their level of ICT integration into their training programmes and student teachers need more opportunities to use ICT in their teaching practice. Similar recommendations are made by Hunt (2000). After surveying eighty New Zealand student teachers, Hunt (2000) concludes that many beginning teachers had very few personal or pedagogical skills in the area of IT and many student teachers had little experience of using IT in their field practice.

Moursund and Bielefeldt's survey (1999) also reports that more than half (54 per cent) of the teacher education institutes in the US did not have a 'written, funded, regularly updated technology plan' (p. 2) and most teacher educators did not model use of IT skills in their teaching. Brownell (1997) echoes the same concern, after reviewing models of using technology in teacher education programmes, that it is important for teacher educators to serve as role models, as their attitudes and uses of technology in the classroom will greatly influence their students. This underlies the need to provide role models for teachers, not only in formal teacher education but in school-based professional development programmes as well.

The reasons for failing to provide a leadership role and model in integrating technology in teaching and learning are 'relatively easy to explain, if difficult to excuse' (National Council for Accreditation of Teacher Education, 1997, pp. 6-7). Cooley & Johnston (2000) have suggested five reasons for the lack of integration. They are: (1) inadequate infrastructure development and teacher educators having limited access to technology; (2) inadequate technical support; (3) lack of understanding of the role of technology by teacher educators as there is a lack of professional development for them; (4) insufficient incentives and rewards; and (5) some teacher educators viewing 'pressure to teach with technology as an infringement on their academic freedom'. Perhaps these reasons are equally applicable at the school level.

Leadership Role of the ICT Co-ordinator

To help change the beliefs and values of teachers in technology use, a strong and effective leadership at the school level (as contrasted to the national level) is needed (Lai, 1999). When we talk about school leadership we sometimes focus only on the role of the principal as the one who can inspire their staff. For example, in New Zealand, workshops such as Principals-Only Days have been routinely organised for such purposes. However, in the school setting there are other leaders, who may not have the same level of power or authority as the principal, but who nonetheless may be as influential in providing vision as the principal. The ICT co-ordinators, for example, could serve as school reform or change agents (Marcovitz, 2000).

Although not necessarily the sole drivers of school policies, the ICT co-ordinators have a great influence in formulating ICT-related policies in schools. For example, in the Otago Technology Project (Lai, Pratt, & Trewern, 2001a), the role and consequently the focus of the ICT co-ordinators in each of these schools appears to have been pivotal in the way ICT has been implemented within the school. The roles of ICT co-ordinators usually fall into two quite distinct categories, each one supporting different philosophies of learning. There are those roles that involve technologically driven decision-making and those oriented toward educational-needs decision-making.

In New Zealand, ICT co-ordinators do not usually have full-time positions. For example, in the Otago Technology Project (Lai, Pratt, & Trewern, 2001a), the ICT co-ordinators were either deputy or assistant principals (28 per cent) or department heads of ICT, mathematics, or technology (61 per cent). Only two of the ICT co-ordinators in this study had no teaching responsibilities. Very often, ICT co-ordinators are experienced teachers in positions of responsibility within the school. They also tend to have responsibility for the purchase, maintenance and support of ICT equipment, as well as for teaching others how to use it.

As a group, the ICT co-ordinators appear to be in a good position to act as agents of change in terms of the integration of ICT. In the school setting, we suggest that they can serve the following leadership roles:

As Planner and Manager. In the Otago Technology Project (Lai, Pratt, & Trewern, 2001a), the ICT co-ordinators had a high level of involvement in the planning and management of the purchase of large amounts of technology hardware, with 83 per cent of them involved in planning and 89 per cent in managing the project. The funding agency of this Technology Project required schools to submit a technology plan before funding could be accessed. Just over three-quarters of the ICT co-ordinators were involved in writing the applications and overseeing the implementation of the project.

As Envisioners. ICT co-ordinators are teachers who usually have a deeper understanding of how computer technology should be used in schools. Very often, they are early technology adopters and have used technology both at home and in school (e.g., using the Internet for communication). It should be noted, however, that

ICT co-ordinators tend to teach computer studies or programming courses and their focus is often on how best to teach computer skills. Even where ICT co-ordinators do have a vision of whole school integration, their focus tends to be general rather than subject oriented.

As Trainers. The Otago Technology Project (Lai, Pratt, & Trewern, 2001a) reports that schools used a variety of ways to provide professional development for their staff. The most effective and common way was in-school professional development, usually provided by the ICT co-ordinator. Although schools did make use of external consultants, very often the ICT co-ordinators were the ones who planned and provided professional development for their colleagues.

As Technicians. In order for teachers to gain experience in using ICT, it is important that the equipment is working. In some schools a great deal of this maintenance and repair work falls on the shoulders of the ICT co-ordinator. In most schools the ICT co-ordinator is required to be a technical whiz.

ICT co-ordinators are the people who could play a major role in the planning and implementation of technology integration in schools. They could serve as agents of change as they are the ones who could provide professional development for their colleagues. They could also be the drivers of technology development. However, there are a number of issues that must be dealt with before this can occur. The first one is the workload issue. The job of ICT co-ordinator is usually added to regular responsibilities, and very limited time or no time at all has been made available for these additional tasks. Many ICT co-ordinators find balancing the technical aspects of the job with teaching quite difficult. Very often ICT co-ordinators have to spend time dealing with students who abuse various aspects of network systems. For example, several network managers in the Otago Technology Project have considered this to be frustrating and time-consuming (Lai, Pratt, & Trewern, 2001a). Another issue related to workload is the time needed to keep up to date with technological innovation. Rapid technological development in the IT field is endemic and chronic. The lack of opportunity to gain networking knowledge and expertise in maintaining the school network is quite an issue for some ICT co-ordinators. In addition to dealing with technical issues, if ICT co-ordinators are to be the whole-school agents of change they also need professional development relating to school-wide integration of ICT. Although they may have the technical knowledge, if ICT is to be successfully integrated they also have to understand how it is being used, and how it can be used, throughout the whole school.

Ethical, Social, and Health Issues in Professional Development

While the importance of professional development has been readily recognised, social, cultural, and health aspects of ICT use are not normally included in these programmes (Lai, 2000b). We believe that social, ethical, and health aspects of ICT use in education are significant issues and therefore should be part of a professional development programme. Issues such as the following should be included (for a more detailed discussion, see Part Three):

Internet Addiction. Anecdotal evidence of addictive use of the Internet, similar to drug or gambling dependency, has recently begun to emerge (Chou, 2000; Young,

1999). It has been reported that some addictive Internet users spend up to 80 hours a week on the Internet, and up to 20 hours per session (Young, 1999). This is alarming, as it is not clear what the nature of Internet addiction may be. Also, we do not know whether and to what extent some of the addictive behaviours or pathological uses of the Internet reported in the literature are detrimental to long-term social and psychological development. As teachers, it is important to gain some understanding of how young people use the Internet both in school and at home and the aspects of the Internet (e.g., the characteristics of this medium and its nature of communication, and its contents, including pornography and games, etc.) their students may find addictive. Rather than focusing on the cognitive effects, the use of the Internet may have social, academic, psychological, cultural, and physical health effects and implications, particularly for heavy Internet uses.

Internet Safety. As, increasingly, students are using the Internet as an educational and research tool, teachers have to be aware of their custodial role in gatekeeping materials which may be considered objectionable to students. How teachers should assist students in using the Internet ethically is a key question, and issues such as Internet censorship, online privacy, freedom of speech, etc. should also be discussed in a professional development programme. These are important ethical issues to consider.

Health Issues. As both teachers and students are spending more time on the computer for their work, schools cannot ignore the health risks associated with computer use, and teachers have to be aware of these issues not only for their own well-being but for their students' as well. Increasingly, health and education professionals have suggested the need for teachers and students to be ergonomically conscious and they are concerned about a number of health risks involved with computer use which range from discomfort such as eyestrain, wrist and shoulder pain, and overuse syndrome, to musculoskeletal injuries (for example, refer Laeser, Maxwell & Hedge, 1998). The advent of laptop computers in schools, for example, where students are expected to use a small keyboard, trackball, or some pointing device for extended periods of time, has already posed a greater risk of developing occupational overuse syndrome (OOS) (Ministry of Education, 1998).

Digital Divide. The issue of accessibility should also be examined from an equity perspective. For example, attention should be given to the lack of accessibility of computing resources for students with disabilities. The gap between the haves and the have-nots in computer and Internet access, now termed the 'Digital Divide', has begun to draw some public attention and a critical awareness of the issues involved in accessibility is needed (Yoder, 2001). It should be noted that although Internet connectivity has been greatly increased, the increase mainly occurs in industrialised countries. Even in industrialised countries, higher income groups and better education mean improved chances of accessing the Internet. According to an United Nations Human Development report (1999),

> [I]ndustrialised countries, with only 15 per cent of the world's population, are home to 88 per cent of all Internet users. Less than 1 per cent of people in South Asia are online even though it is home to one-fifth of the world's population. The situation is even worse in

Africa. With 739 million people, there are only 14 million phone lines. That's fewer than in Manhattan or Tokyo; 80 per cent of those lines are in only six countries. There are only 1 million Internet users on the entire continent compared with 10.5 million in the UK (UN Human Development, 1999, cited from Yoder, 2001).

e-Learning

Although the Internet has already been used as an educational tool in the classroom, we have just begun to use it for professional development. In our information society, we believe that teachers not only need to know *about* the Internet but should learn *with* it to enhance their professional learning. The Internet is an ideal support for learning and professional development in a number of ways:

Situated Learning Opportunities. Professional development has to take into account the needs of the teacher as an adult. According to Putnam and Borko (2000), professional development should be situated in the teachers' work environment where teachers have opportunities to collaborate with their colleagues, and work on authentic tasks, in a continuous on-site learning community. Unfortunately, it is not always possible for teachers to work with their colleagues in a face-to-face manner, as it is well known that teaching can be an isolated profession. The Internet can bridge the distance and provide a medium for teachers to communicate and work with their colleagues on authentic tasks.

Collaborative Learning. The Internet opens up exciting opportunities for teachers to communicate not only as a group, but also with each other. There have been successful teacher networks both in New Zealand and overseas which were designed to enhance collaboration.

Building an Online Learning Community. There is no doubt that the Internet has already changed or will change the way people work, the way people learn, read, listen to music, etc. As noted by Stefik (1999), 'technological changes lead to cultural changes – especially changes in the social and legal institutions that are now co-evolving with the technology of the Internet' (p. 1). One great potential for using the Internet is to support the development of e-communities. The Internet can thus support ongoing learning communities for teachers. Using the Internet for community development serves at least the following purposes (Lai, 1996):

- Providing validation for pedagogical methods of teaching;
- Fostering intellectual stimulation and creating multiple perspectives;
- Facilitating peer–peer collaboration by sharing exemplary practices and course materials, and by co-constructing, reviewing, and publishing resources;
- Broadening teachers' learning horizons by discussing new beliefs and teaching practices.

Chapter 3 will provide a more detailed discussion on online learning communities.

Concluding Remarks

In this chapter we have highlighted the importance of professional development if technology is to be successfully integrated into teaching. However, we should not be led to believe that professional development, though important, is the only factor at work, so that 'once policy makers and administrators get a grip on organisational strategies to provide teachers sufficient access to the technologies, prepare them to use the technology, creatively, and secure sufficient technical help to maintain the machines, teachers will then do the right thing in their classrooms' (Cuban, 1999). We should remember that there are factors other than professional development at work that will affect teachers' decisions in the use of technology. These factors include cultural beliefs, organisational structures, political considerations, and individual factors such as learning styles. To be sure, professional development is a key factor for successful technology adoption but it should not be treated as the panacea for all the problems that we currently face in technology integration, and teachers thus should not be blamed for not doing the 'right thing', even if they are thought to have participated adequately in ICT professional development.

We have also argued in this chapter that too little professional development has been provided to ICT-using teachers. Whenever provided, professional development activities are too generic, and too much emphasis has been put on skill-based training, without paying adequate attention to the learning theories underpinning the use of technology in education. Teachers are not encouraged to examine the social, ethical, and health issues involved in the use of technology in education. We believe that it is now timely to critically examine the contents of our professional development programmes with a view to including a more balanced range of topics of what should be delivered to our teachers.

References

Baker, E. (1998). *Understanding Educational Quality: Where Validity Meets Technology*. Available at: <http://www.ets.org/research/pic/angoff5.pdf>.

Brownell, K. (1997). Technology in teacher education: Where are we and where do we go from here? *Journal of Technology and Teacher Education,* 5(2/3), 117-138.

Chou, C. (2000). *Research on Internet addiction: A review and further work.* Paper presented at the 8th International Conference on Computers in Education/International Conference on Computer-Assisted Instruction. Nov 21–24, Taipei.

Cooley, N. & Johnston, M. (September/October, 2000). *Why can't we just get on with it? Forces that complicate the integration of technology into teaching and learning*. Available at: <http://horizon.unc.edu/TS/commentary/2000-09b.asp>.

Cowan, B. & Diorio, J. (1998). *Using Computers in the Professional Development of Teachers: An Otago/Southland Survey*. Unpublished Manuscript.

Cuban, L. (1998). *The Pros and Cons of Technology in the Classroom. Part 2: Cuban Speech*. Available at: <http://www.tappedin.org/info/teachers/debate.html>.

Cuban, L. (1999). *Why are most teachers infrequent and restrained users of computers?* Report from the Fifth Annual Public Education Conference, Vancouver. Available at: <http://www.bctf.bc.ca/parents/PublicEdConf/report99/appendix1.html>.

Education Review Office (1995). In-service training of teachers: The responsibility of Board of Trustees. Wellington: Education Evaluation Reports.

Fullan, M. (1990). Staff development, innovation, and institutional development. In B. Joyce (Ed.). *Changing School Culture through Staff Development*. Alexandria, Virginia: ASCD.

Hunt, T. (2000). Exploring a new frontier: Beginning teachers' experiences with information technology. *Computers in New Zealand Schools*, 12(3), 33-46, 58.

International Society of Technology in Education (n.d.). *Information Technology Backgrounder*. Available at: <http://www.iste.org/research/background/FAQ01.html>.

ITAG (2000). *ICT in schools 1999*. Available at: <http//www.med.govt.nz/pbt/infotech. ictschools1999.html>

Kulik, J. (1994). Meta-analytic studies of findings on computer-based instruction. In E.L. Baker & H.F. O'Neil, Jr. (Eds). *Technology Assessment in Education and Training*. Hillsdale, N.J.: Lawrence Erlbaum.

Laeser, K., Maxwell, L., & Hedge, A. (1998). *The effect of computer workstation design on student posture*. Journal of Research on Computing in Education, 31, 173-188.

Lai, K.W. (1993a). Minimal computer technologies and learner-centred environments: Some New Zealand experience. *Computers and Education*, 20(4), 291-297.

Lai, K.W. (1993b). Lego-Logo as a learning environment. *Journal of Computing in Childhood Education*, 4,(3/4), 229-246.

Lai, K.W. (1996). Computer-mediated communication: A new learning context. In K.W. Lai (Ed.) *Words Have Wings: Teaching and Learning with Computer Networks* (pp. 1-18). Dunedin: The University of Otago Press.

Lai, K.W. (1999). Teaching, learning, and professional development: The teacher matters most. In K.W. Lai (Ed.) *Net-Working: Teaching, Learning, and Professional Development* (pp. 7-23). Dunedin: The University of Otago Press.

Lai, K.W., Pratt, K., & Trewern, A. (2001a). *Learning with Technology: Evaluation of the Otago Technology Project*. Dunedin: The Community of Otago Trust.

Lai, K.W. (2001b). Role of the teacher. In H. Adelsberger, B. Collis, & J. Pawlowski (Eds). *Handbook on Information Technologies for Education & Training*. Springer-Verlag.

Maddux, C. (1988). Preface to a special issue on assessing the impact of computer-based instruction. *Computers in the School*, 5(3/4), 1-10.

McCabe, M. (1998). Lessons from the field: Computer conferencing in higher education. *Journal of Information Technology for Teacher Education*, 7(1), 71-87.

Marcovitz, D. (2000). The roles of computer co-ordinators in supporting technology in schools. *Journal of Technology and Teacher Education*, 8(3), 259-273.

Market Data Retrieval (2000). *New Teachers and Technology*. Shelton, C.N.

National Centre for Education Statistics (2000). *Teachers' Tools for the 21st Century*. Available at: <http://nces.ed.gov>.

National Commission on Teaching and America's Future (1996). *What Matters Most: Teaching for America's Future*. Available at: <http://www.te.columbia.edu/~teachcomm/What.htm>

National Council for Accreditation of Teacher Education (1997). *Technology and the New Professional Teacher: Preparing for the 21st Century Classroom*. Washington DC.

Ministry of Education. *(1998). Safety and Technology Education: A Guidance Manual for New Zealand Schools*. Wellington: Ministry of Education.

Moursund, D. & Bielefeldt. (1999*). Will New Teachers Be Prepared To Teach In A Digital Age? A National Survey on Information Technology in Teacher Education*. Available at: <http://www.mff.org/publications/publications.taf?page=154>.

Pea, R. (1998). *The Pros and Cons of Technology in the Classroom. Part 1: Pea Speech*. Available at: <http://www.tappedin.org/info/teachers/debate.html>.

Putnam, R., & Borko, H. (2000). What do new views of knowledge and thinking have to say about research on teaching and learning? *Educational Researcher, 29*(1), 4-16.

Scardamalia, M. (2000). Social and technological innovations for a knowledge society. In *Proceedings of the 8th International Conference on Computers in Education/International Conference on Computer-Assisted Instruction* (pp. 22-27). AACE.

Schacter, J. (1999). *The impact of educational technology on student achievement: What the most current research has to say*. Available at: <http://www.mff.org/publications/publications.taf?page=161>.

Schiff, T. & Solmon, L. (1999). *California Digital High School: Process Evaluation Year One Report*. Available at: <http://www.mff.org/publications/publications.taf>.

Sheingold, D. & Hadley, M. (1990). *Accomplished Teachers: Integrating Computers into Classroom*

Practice. N.Y.: Bank Street College of Education.

Stefik, M. (1999). *The Internet Edge: Social, Technical, and Legal Challenges for a Networked World.* Cambridge: MIT Press.

U.S. Office of Technology Assessment (1995*). Teachers and technology: Making the Connection.* Available at: <http://www.wws.princeton.edu/~ota/disk1/1995/9541.html>.

Web-based Education Commission to the President and Congress of the United States (2000). *The Power of the Internet for Learning.* Available at: <http://www.ed.gov/offices/AC/WBEC/FinalReport/>.

Wenglinsky, H. (2000). *How Teaching Matters: Bringing the Classroom Back Into Discussions of Teacher Quality.* Available at: </teamat.pdf http://www.ets.org/research/pic/teamat.pdf>.

Yoder, M (2001, February*). The Digital Divide. Learning and Leading with Technology.* Available at: <http://www.iste.org/L&L/archive/vol28/no5/featuredarticle/yoder/index.html>.

Young, K. (1999). *Internet addiction: Symptoms, and Treatment.* Available at: <http://www.netaddiction.com/articles/symptoms.htm>.

Professional Development for ICT-using Teachers

2

Keryn Pratt, Kwok-Wing Lai, Philip Munro

In recent years there has been an awareness of the role and importance of teachers and of the role new reform activities, such as the integration of technology, can play in enhancing student learning. Professional development has been identified as playing a key role in ensuring teachers are able to incorporate these reform activities into their teaching. Unfortunately, most teachers have not yet been able to do this.

Teachers need to further their professional learning because they matter most in the teaching and learning process. A number of reports have been published in the last few years to document the importance of the teacher in the learning process. For example, the CEO Forum (1999) reported that the most critical factor in determining educational quality is the teacher. A number of studies have found that teacher quality, among other factors, has an impact on student learning. For example, Greenwald, Hedges and Laine (1996) found that the quality of teachers, along with the class size and the amount of resources the school had, were all related to student achievement. Darling-Hammond (2000) also found that teacher quality had a greater positive effect on student learning than socio-economic status, students' first language, their race or the spending levels of the school. Like Greenwald *et al.*, Darling-Hammond maintained that smaller classes also had a positive effect on student achievement, but this was most likely to benefit students when the class also had a good teacher.

Professional development enables teachers to remain up-to-date with their subject specialty, as well as with new and effective ways of teaching and assessing students. It also offers the opportunity for teachers to engage in collaborative planning, and to discuss their teaching and subject area with other teachers, as well as with specialists. According to Sparks and Hirsh (1999), the purpose of professional development is to change the culture of the school, and therefore the attitudes of the teachers, with the result that the school becomes a learning school. Given the current climate of change, professional development is needed to ensure that teachers are prepared to implement these changes.

A number of research studies would suggest that teachers are not as well equipped to implement these changes as they would like to be. For example, Lewis, Parsad, Carey, Bartfai, Farris & Smerdon (1999) found that, in the United States, only 28 per cent of teachers reported feeling very well prepared to implement the new student performance techniques, with 36 per cent feeling very well prepared to implement curriculum and performance standards. Forty-one per cent of the teachers reported feeling very well prepared to implement new teaching methods. These results are similar to those found by Alexander, Heaviside and Farris (1999) who reported that 35 per cent of teachers felt very well equipped to set or apply the new higher-standards system for their students. They also found that only 42 per cent of teachers reported understanding the concept of the new higher-standards for student achievement.

Alexander *et al.* also asked teachers to report the extent to which they were implementing new reform activities. They found there was a wide range, from 56 per cent of teachers who were using instructional strategies aligned with high standards to a great extent to only 7 per cent of teachers who reported using innovative technologies such as the Internet to a great extent. It appears that although teachers have a great impact on student learning, they do not all have the skills to maximise this impact.

Professional development is a necessary and accepted part of most jobs today, and there appears no reason why the teaching profession should be different. In this chapter we will discuss issues related to professional development in information and communication technology (ICT), what makes a professional development programme successful, and then we will focus on the professional development of ICT-using teachers, in both New Zealand and overseas.

Barriers to Technology Adoption
Lack of professional development

Lewis *et al.* (1999) found that fewer than 30 per cent of teachers reported that they feel well prepared to integrate technology into their classroom instruction. This finding is supported by Alexander *et al.* (1999) who found that only 7 per cent of teachers were currently using technology such as the Internet. They also found that nearly 80 per cent of teachers agreed that this area was one of three for which they most required information. A number of reasons have been given as to why so few teachers are able to integrate technology into their lessons. Hargreaves (1994) and the CEO Forum (1999) both believe that technology will not be used effectively in classrooms until teachers receive effective professional development on the best means of doing so. Although approximately 50 per cent of teachers had taken part in professional development sessions on how to integrate technology (Choy & Chen, 1998), the fact that fewer than 30 per cent felt prepared to do so suggests these sessions were ineffective and inadequate.

Lack of access

Lack of professional development is not the only barrier to successful technology adoption. Lawton (1994) points out that the issue of access is one of a number of problems. If teachers are to be encouraged to use resources such as technology, it is necessary for them to have adequate access. In addition, it is important that the technology that teachers have access to is working, as teachers with technical support on hand are more likely to use and continue using technology (Ringstaff, Yocum & Marsh, 1995).

Lack of support

Means and Olson (1995) found that readily available technical support was an important factor in determining the success of a school-wide change to incorporating constructivist teaching and technology use. As they point out, teachers are unlikely to use technology if they believe they are likely to encounter a technical problem that will take some days to be fixed. Types of support other than technical are also necessary to encourage teachers' effective use of technology in the classroom. For example, the Apple Classrooms of Tomorrow (ACOT) Teacher Development Center project found that teachers who had the support of the principal were more likely to use technology with their classes than those who did not (Ringstaff *et al.,* 1995). Support from the principal is necessary because integrating technology into everyday lessons may require adjustments to equipment purchasing or school scheduling, to allow teachers time to plan and collaborate on complex projects.

Lack of time

A number of researchers (e.g., Cook, 1997; Ang, 1998; Glennan & Melmad, 1996) and the National Education Association (NEA, 1999–2000) believe that lack of time is a crucial issue facing schools as they initiate a school culture of learning. The NEA believes that time is essential if teachers are to take part in effective professional development programmes and to work collaboratively, as time is needed for 'growth, preparation, and reflection' (p.1). It recommends that half of teachers' work time should be in student contact hours and half should be for professional responsibilities. As Ang (1998) pointed out, teachers need time to absorb what they have learnt, to plan how to implement it in their classrooms, and to evaluate this implementation. Cook agrees with Ang, acknowledging that when educational reform is undertaken teachers require time to plan, test and assess new ideas, and arguing that time for teachers' professional development should be a central part of their job. The ACOT Teacher Development Center programme also recognises the importance of time. Before teachers are accepted into the programme, their principals are required to agree to provide time for participants to plan new programmes and reflect on their success following their completion of the programme (Ringstaff *et al.*, 1995). Although recognising that time was an issue for teachers, Hargreaves (1994) pointed out that '[a]dditional time does not itself guarantee educational change. How that time is used and interpreted is also important' (p. 98).

Process of change

Perhaps the biggest barrier to teachers' integrating technology is the issue of change itself. According to the CEO Forum's (1999) stages of adoption (see Figure 1), integration occurs when teachers design tasks and even change their classroom environment to take advantage of the technology. In order for teachers to effectively integrate technology, they must change the way they teach. The ACOT project (Apple, 1995), which provided students and teachers with technology-rich classrooms, is a good example of some of the changes needed for technology to be used to its full potential. In the ACOT project, researchers observed teachers changing, over a period of time, from using the computer to deliver traditional forms of whole-class lessons through to changing the way they taught (Dwyer, 1994). Dwyer reported that after four years teachers in the ACOT project had changed the layout of the classroom and their daily schedules, while students were encouraged to collaborate on projects. Even with easy access to technology, this change was not simple. Teachers had difficulties finding ways to assess students' work, and began to team-teach to a greater degree to enable cross-discipline work. As well as adjusting schedules within classes, at times the schedule of the entire school was adjusted to ensure the technology was used to its fullest. Making these changes required the support of the principal, as well as time to develop new units of work, and to plan team-teaching work with other teachers. Dwyer identified the most serious problem facing teachers in the ACOT classrooms as assessment, as the skills students were learning were not always reflected in the district assessment methods.

From the ACOT example (Apple, 1995; Dwyer, 1994) it can be seen that for technology to be successfully integrated teachers need to change the way they teach, and the way they think about teaching. In addition, schools need to change the way they do things, and the way students are assessed by outside agencies must be adapted to reflect the new higher-order skills students are learning. Identifying these changes does not necessarily mean they will occur, however. As Hargreaves (1994) pointed out, '[a]t the heart of change for most teachers is the issue of whether it is practical' (p. 12).

Change is itself a complex issue, and a change in learning or teaching is perhaps the most complex. Fullan (1993) believes that,

> the hardest core to crack is the learning core – changes in instructional practices and in the culture of teaching toward greater collaborative relationships among teachers among students, teachers and other potential partners. Changing formal structures is not the same as changing norms, habits, skills and beliefs (p. 49).

In his two books on the issue of change in schools, Fullan (1993, 1999) has developed a series of principles that he believes lead to a successful process of change. In these principles Fullan recognises that change of this type is complex, because the power structures need to be changed, and because there are large numbers of people involved, including teachers, principals, school management, students and their families. Change cannot be forced by school management or the government, but support from these areas is essential. Fullan also points out that during the process of change, problems and conflicts will arise, and that these should be learnt from, rather than seen as negatives. Change requires collaboration, but this collaboration should also allow and even encourage individuals to ensure multiple points of view are considered. In addition, Fullan believes that although the overall process of change must be flexible, it will be most effective if there are some guidelines. Any changes made within a school should also be linked to educational outcomes and pedagogy. Finally, Fullan points out that just as schools and their situations differ, so too will their solutions and the process of change that works for them.

Fullan's (1993, 1999) principles emphasise just how complex the issue of change is, so perhaps it is not surprising that at this stage schools have not yet undergone the change necessary to enable teachers to successfully integrate technology into their classrooms. What is clear is that there are a number of barriers to teachers' integration of technology, including the change process and the lack of professional development, and until these are addressed students will not gain the full benefits of this new technology.

Effective Professional Development Programmes

Knowing that teachers should undertake some form of professional development over the course of their careers is only the first step. Fullan and Mascall (2000) define professional development as 'the sum total of learning through formal and informal experiences' (p. 38) and as such there is a myriad of different types of professional development programmes available. Given this range of programmes, it is important to discover what kind of professional development is the most effective. In determining the effectiveness of a professional development programme, it is necessary to decide what outcome is desirable. For example, very different results might be obtained if attendance at sessions or some specified improvement in students' grades were the criteria by which the effectiveness of a particular professional development programme was measured.

A number of success factors have been proposed for effective professional development. As suggested by Ang (1998), these factors include the necessity for programmes to be student oriented, having student-related outcomes associated with them. In addition, Ang believes that professional development programmes should be designed to be appropriate to the teachers who are involved in them, and that they should be at a time that suits them. Programmes should also be at held at the teachers' schools, and be interesting. Effective professional development, according to Ang, should also be integrative, involve technology and be collaborative. Finally, Ang believes that schools should have plans for professional development that is ongoing.

WestEd, a research agency based in the United States, has recently looked at the professional development programmes of eight schools considered to be exemplary in the National Awards Program for Model Professional Development (WestEd, 2000). A number of factors were identified by the schools and by the researchers as being the key to the successful professional development programmes in these schools. For example, all staff needed to agree on the learning goals for students, and these goals had to be clear, with a wide variety of measures of student performance assessed regularly. All staff members, including, but not limited to, teachers, needed to become part of a team that works together to achieve the learning goals and solve problems. Professional development programmes need to be designed with student's learning goals in mind. There needs to be a wide variety of such programmes for all staff, who need to be given time to both attend the programmes and put in place what they have learned. In addition, informal professional development is needed, with ongoing learning being part of the school culture. Examples of informal learning included talking with other staff members, writing papers for publication, being involved in committees and observing other teachers. Another key factor for these schools was leadership. In each school there was an identifiable and strong leader or group of leaders who provided good models through their own behaviour and by their expectations of, and support for, others. It should also be noted that although each of these schools has become successful, the process was not easy, requiring a staff-wide commitment of time and effort. In a number of cases some staff members chose not to be involved, and left the school.

Whole-school approach

A number of researchers believe that effective professional development requires a whole-school approach, with a school culture that is focused on the learning of all in the school community (e.g., Fine & Raack, 1994; Fullan & Mascall, 2000; National School Boards Foundation, 1999). To be effective, a whole-school approach should have programmes designed to address the needs of each individual school and linked to outcomes particular to each school (Sparks & Hirsh, 1999). Fullan and Hargreaves (1991) also emphasise the importance of staff members working together within a school, pointing out that, at the time of writing, there were not enough opportunities for staff to work together and learn with and from each other. They also recognise that if the school culture does not encourage professional development then any programme will not be as effective. The concept of a whole school working together can promote learning; however, it can also cause problems. For example, Little (1990) points out that groups may both promote change and also conserve the present status, depending on the group's nature. It is important to ensure that any collaboration occurs naturally as a result of the problems and circumstances that teachers are sharing, and not as a result of artificially created groups.

Although a whole-school approach or commitment to professional development is necessary, other researchers have highlighted the importance of the individual within a programme. Clark (1992) believes that teachers should have the responsibility for their own professional development because it will be more effective if it is something they have chosen to do, rather than something they have been forced to do. He also points out that teachers are all individuals and as such have different needs.

Jackson (1992) believes that whole-school and individual issues should be considered when developing professional development programmes, and that a somewhat wider view of professional development should be taken. He believes that while professional development should aid them in improving their teaching, it should also encompass things that enrich teachers' lives, and therefore their teaching. He also believes that programmes will be most effective if teachers' working conditions are improved, including giving individual teachers more say in what they do. Jackson also believes that professional development programmes should be designed to relieve teachers of psychological discomfort by acknowledging the demands of their work, and helping them to cope with these demands. For professional development to be effective, it needs to be linked to the curriculum and the assessment of students (Cohen & Hill, 1998). As pointed out by Fine and Raack (1994), many professional development programmes lack relevance to the classroom, and they believe programmes should be restructured so that the majority of professional development is school based.

Professional Development for ICT-Using Teachers

The increasing emphasis on ICT use in teaching has resulted in a corresponding increase in the demand for professional development. A number of research projects have aimed at determining what makes an ICT professional development programme effective. The characteristics of effective professional development programmes, as described previously, are likely to hold for technology-related professional development; however, there are a number of additional factors that must be taken into account.

What should be included?

One of the first issues is the topic. ICT professional development programmes could be designed to teach teachers how to use the equipment; how to turn on computers; and how to use the basic applications, such as word-processing, associated with computers. Teachers could also be taught how to use peripherals such as digital cameras, scanners, etc. Alternatively, programmes could focus on multimedia or Internet-based applications, with teachers learning how to use the Internet effectively. McDougall and Squires (1997) identify five areas on which technology professional development programmes typically focus. The first area is skills-based programmes, while the second involves the integration of technology into the existing curriculum. The third area is technology-related changes to curriculum, with McDougall and Squires providing the example of how the use of dataloggers in science has changed, or has the ability to change, the nature of science experiments. The fourth area they identify is the changing role of teachers, with the increased autonomy technology can make available to students. Finally, the fifth area of focus is underpinning theories of education.

Professional development models

Generally, there are four models through which professional development may be delivered to teachers. In some schools, a whole-school approach is taken while other schools train a few teachers, who are then responsible for helping other staff members. Another approach is for a group of teachers to undergo some form of external professional development, then return to the school with new skills and ideas to pass on to other staff members. The fourth and final model is through online learning, where teachers can undergo appropriate individualised professional development at their own pace (discussed in Chapter 3).

Williams (1993) argues that technology professional development programmes should not be focused on a single skill, but on the desired outcomes. He proposes three technology professional development models with this aim. His first model is *Outcome-based Staff Development*, where programmes are designed by first deciding on the learning goal, and then developing a programme that will enable this to be achieved. Specific skills may be taught, but always with a learning outcome in mind. Williams also believes that, as part of any programme, all staff members involved with the learning goal should discuss the goal and the best means of achieving it. Technology is not always the most effective means of achieving a goal.

The second technology professional development model proposed by Williams (1993) is *Innovation-based Staff Development*. He believes that teachers are often slow to find out about new technology that may have relevance or be useful for them. As a result, professional development programmes that involve looking at the technology that is available and then finding ways to use it in schools are another valuable means of staff development. Once again, it is outcome-based, with the goal being improving instruction generally, with specific outcomes related to each piece of technology.

Finally, Williams (1993) proposes that *Trainer of Trainers Staff Development* is an effective technology professional development programme. This programme relies on the knowledge of staff within each school, with high-end users gaining further training and sharing their knowledge with others. This system can be carried one step further with specialists being shared within districts. As well as proposing these three specific programmes, Williams also mentions the importance of keeping sessions enjoyable and appropriate to individual staff members.

McKenzie (1998) also talks about the importance of technology professional development being focused on student-learning outcomes rather than application-based training. Like Williams (1993), McKenzie emphasises the importance of recognising that teachers are individuals and as such need individual programmes, or at least a wide range to choose from. He also encourages schools to look at innovative forms of professional development, similar to the informal learning opportunities identified by WestEd (2000). McKenzie also feels it is important to address the emotional aspects of using technology in classes. Teachers often feel reluctant to use technology with their students because of fears they will not be able to make it work, and then look foolish. He says it is important to address this issue as part of any technology professional development programme. He also talks of the importance of involving all staff and for providing the necessary time. McKenzie views the availability of support as important. He believes a number of teachers and even students should be encouraged to develop strong technology skills so when other teachers or students need help it can be immediately forthcoming. Once again, like WestEd, McKenzie emphasises that change will take time, and it is important to have ongoing programmes, and to persist with them.

Following the success of the ACOT schools projects, Apple set up 'Teacher Development Centers' (Ringstaff *et al.*, 1995). Teachers attend one- or four-week programmes that involve observing and working with ACOT teachers and students, so that teachers are learning skills in the situation in which they will need to use them. The programmes also focus on activities that are learner centred and interactive, similar to the learning environments that developed in the ACOT classrooms, and include follow-up in-school visits from an ACOT coordinator. Ringstaff *et al.* found that the majority of teachers who attended these programmes reported a positive effect on their teaching. The programme's effect was affected by factors such as the access to technology teachers had in their own schools. Teachers who had access to technical support were also more likely to continue to try new approaches to learning than those who did not, while those who received support from programme advisers, and more especially from principals, were more able to sustain change.

The CEO Forum (1999) identified a series of stages that teachers undergo when using technology in their teaching (see Figure 1). In the initial stage it is not the classroom teacher who is directing technology use, but rather the students themselves, or a specialist teacher. By the second stage, teachers are using technology to enhance personal tasks, such as administration, and are encouraging students to utilise technology, for example, as an improved type of a typewriter. In the third stage teachers are beginning to use technology to enhance the curriculum, without changing the way they teach. At this stage teachers will utilise aspects of technology such as CD-ROM encyclopaedias and the Internet, rather than using traditional book forms of information. At this stage the use of technology has not changed the way teachers instruct their students, and the tasks still tend to be teacher-directed. By the fourth stage teachers have begun to understand the possibilities of the technology, and are designing tasks that take advantage of its capabilities. Students are beginning to direct their own learning, and technology is used to aid them in achieving higher-order thinking skills. The fifth and final stage is reached when teachers are changing the classroom environment to maximise the technology and its use in the classroom. Students are now using the technology to help them learn basic and higher-level thinking skills.

Stage 1: Entry – students learning to use technology
Stage 2: Adoption – teachers use technology to support traditional instruction
Stage 3: Adaptation – technology used to enrich curriculum
Stage 4: Appropriation – technology is integrated, used for its unique capabilities
Stage 5: Invention – discover new uses for technology

Figure 1: Stages of technology adoption (CEO Forum, 1999, pp. 14–15)

From the CEO Forum (1999) stages of technology adoption it can be seen that it is not until teachers achieve stages four or five that they are able to use technology in ways that Weglinsky (1998) found enhanced student learning. It is also apparent that using technology in the classroom to improve student achievement involves a change in the whole classroom environment.

ICT Professional Development in New Zealand

In 1998 the New Zealand government recognised the role ICT could play in education with the launch of the programme called *Interactive Education Strategies for Schools* (Ministry of Education, 1999). Since then the amount of ICT hardware in New Zealand schools has been increasing. However, simply having more hardware does not mean ICT is being used effectively. A recent report by the Education Review Office (ERO, 2000) suggests that 'many schools are unable to point to specific improvements in teaching and learning that have been brought about by the use of ICT' (p. 2). The report goes on to say that those improvements that were reported tended to be improvements in technology use, such as better standards of writing, presentation and the inclusion of graphics, rather than improvements in cognitive skills such as problem solving. In most secondary schools, it was still the 'computer' teacher who taught students to use computers rather than technology being integrated across the school curriculum. The ERO report and another New Zealand study (Capper, 1999) both acknowledged that although the amount of ICT hardware in schools has improved, it is still not sufficient, and that this has to some degree affected the lack of integration of technology in New Zealand schools.

It should be noted that, as well as increased access to hardware, teachers also need sufficient professional development in how to successfully integrate ICT into their classrooms, and this is not occurring in New Zealand. In contrast to the 30–40 per cent of technology budgets that schools in the US are recommended to spend on technology professional development (Riley *et al.*, 1996; Web-based Commission, 2000), New Zealand schools are spending, on average, only 8 per cent of their technology budgets for this purpose (Sullivan & Anso, 2000). Capper (1994) noted that most New Zealand schools appeared to hold the view that professional development was an annex to mainstream school practice, with its main function being to keep teachers up-to-date with externally imposed curriculum changes.

New Zealand teachers are in need of effective and widespread technology professional development. The government recognised this in October 1998, when the prime minister of the time launched the 'Interactive Education' Strategy. Six months later, in April 1999, the Ministry of Education let contracts to twenty-three schools to become Information and Communication Technology Professional Development (ICTPD) lead schools. Each school received $115,000 per year for three years. The lead schools were to form a cluster of local schools, varying in numbers, and provide professional development to the staff, and in some cases to the board of trustees of their cluster. These partnerships between the lead school and their cluster allowed for 'unique features and experiences' (Te Kete Ipurangi, p. 2) of the individual schools to be incorporated into the design and delivery of the professional development programmes. Further ICTPD contracts were let out to form more cluster schools in late 2000.

A vast array of professional development models are utilised by the clusters. Some clusters opted for a mentoring/buddying model whilst others found that workshops/ conferences best suited their needs. A few clusters noted that the 'just in time' model was also used, in some cases alongside other models. The integration of ICT into the classroom was noted by several of the ICTPD schools as being a key area. A smaller number identified skill- or technical-based professional development as their primary focus. Examples of some of these models are briefly described in the following sections. More information about the professional development programmes of these clusters can be found in their websites <http://www.tki.org.nz/r/ict/pedagogy/schools/ index_e.php>.

Mentor/buddy

Some clusters used a mentor/buddy approach to professional development. For example, the cluster led by Auckland Normal Intermediate has adopted Selby's work on mentoring in their professional development programme. In this model each school in the cluster chose staff to become mentors and these people attended a training day with Dr Selby. Schools wrote Mentor Training Programme Action Plans, which outlined such things as who the programme is for, how it is to be funded, and how the programme would be evaluated. At Auckland Normal Intermediate mentors then approached staff with whom they felt they could work alongside. Buddies set objectives they wanted to reach based on their individual needs, and the time frame for reaching these was mutually agreed upon by both mentor and mentee. Both parties kept logs of meetings and training. The lead teacher of this school monitored their school's programme. Regular contact between the lead teacher of Auckland North Intermediate and the other schools in the cluster was maintained, and once a term the cluster coordinator met with each mentor and mentee to reflect on their programme. Each school then evaluated itself against its Action Plan and made adjustments accordingly.

Workshops/conferences

In the Wellington region, two schools combined their experiences with programme facilitators Learning Enhancement Associates (LEA) to create the Porirua School/ Houghton Valley School/LEA cluster. LEA provided courses to the cluster schools, as well as technical and professional development follow-up visits. Along with the courses provided to all cluster school teachers, LEA provided further workshops for lead teachers to 'explore the options' <http://www.tki.org.nz/r/ict/pedagogy/schools/ prog_poriruahoughton_e.php>. Cluster schools also had the opportunity of attending information technology expos run by the lead schools. These expos gave cluster schools the opportunity to see what their lead schools were doing with ICT, and to see ICT being applied.

As another example, Papatoetoe Central School offered its cluster two four-day block courses within a one-year period. The following list shows some of the topics included in these courses:

• theory-based instruction/consideration on pedagogy of ICT;
• consideration of what student learning outcomes are desired/determined;
• teacher skill and application-based instruction/tuition/coaching to pass areas of core competencies in computing, word-processing, Internet, email, fax, online resourcing;
• small group work with sets of four to five students on course and Papatoetoe Central School related ICT work, taking students further through the existing Papatoetoe Central School integrated ICT curriculum;
• observation of related management practices at Papatoetoe Central School;
• access to view and consider Papatoetoe Central School related planning, documents, policies, etc;
• methodologies for whole-school development to include establishment of school-based pedagogy and teacher development … leading directly to actual teaching and learning with ICT to secure successful school-wide student learning outcomes. <http://www.tki.org.nz/r/ict/pedagogy/schools/prog_papatoetoe_e.php>

Internet-based

Only one of the twenty-three clusters focused their attention on providing professional development through the online medium. Cantatech cluster provides training to teachers in ten rural Canterbury schools. The major focus was to expand and improve the delivery of senior courses to students, and professional development to staff, both via the Internet and in real-time.

The Cantatech cluster stated their goals for 2000 as being to:

- work with selected teaching staff from each school on a project to improve the integration of ICT into their teaching work;
- work with distance education delivery teachers to enable them to make full use of the tools available to them under the new delivery system;
- work with staff with responsibility for network management to improve their ability to solve day-to-day problems;
- set up technical support systems suited to each school, using remote management where possible;
- trial the use of video conferencing to enhance course delivery, and
- establish, and promote the use of, a cluster website to improve course delivery and cluster administration. <http://www.tki.org.nz/r/ict/pedagogy/schools/9_e.php>

The Otago Technology Project

The ICT cluster schools were given funding specifically for technology professional development, and therefore are in a different position to most other schools. It is possible to gain an impression of the current situation in other New Zealand schools from findings reported recently in a research project (Lai, Pratt & Trewern, 2001). This project, the Otago Technology Project, was an evaluation of the use of ICT in twenty-five Otago secondary schools. These schools received a hardware grant from the local community trust but no additional funding for professional development. The majority of teachers (62.7 per cent) and ICT coordinators (72.7 per cent) surveyed had taken part in an ICT-related professional development activity over the previous three years.

Like the ICTPD cluster schools, Otago schools had a wide range of professional development programmes. Most implemented their programmes in-house, while some had used external experts, and others enrolled in outside courses. In those schools where professional development was run in-house, the ICT coordinator generally provided most of the training, although some schools were using other staff members, including administrative staff, who had expertise in the course being provided. In a few cases, selected staff took part in ICT professional development and were then expected to share their knowledge with other staff members.

In a number of schools ICT professional development was compulsory, in others it was optional, while in some it was optional although 'arms are gently twisted'. Most of the ICT professional development provided was skills based, with teachers learning how to do administration tasks as well as to use the Internet, email, word-processing, etc. In one school, this skills training was tied to student learning, as was mentioned by Williams (1993) as being effective:

> Our librarian ran excellent classes for staff to use CD Rom, Websites, Internet (next time it will be E-mail). We worked through tasks that we could use with the students.

Another school had staff from two curriculum areas develop an ICT-integrated unit for their third and fourth form classes as part of their ICT professional development. These types of programmes, however, did not appear to be common in Otago.

Schools generally didn't appear to have long-term professional development plans nor did they seem to evaluate their courses or tie them into student achievement. A number of schools had taken part in other forms of development, such as going on a bus tour around the region to see what other schools were doing. In a couple of cases a member of staff attended or gave presentations at conferences. Although some of the Otago schools met some of the criteria for effective technology professional development, none of the schools met all of them.

All Otago schools need to face the issue of time. As one teacher commented,

> Many courses for Professional Development are one day courses. NO time is ever given to allow you to write units or come to terms with the material. By the time the holidays come (when you can make time) you have forgotten what it was about and even your notes seem like double-dutch! I think Professional Development like this is a waste of time. Teachers are too busy during the term and under too much pressure to spend much time on new things then.

Only one Otago school appeared to have a long-term school-wide systematic approach to ICT professional development, and the effects of this programme were beginning to be evident throughout the school. The principal's vision included technology being integrated throughout the curriculum. In order to achieve this vision, a systematic approach to technology professional development has been taken. Staff have compulsory skills-training sessions once a term, with additional optional sessions available. This training is run in-house for reasons of cost. As the skill levels of the staff are increasing, the focus of this training is shifting from purely skills based to having a more pedagogical focus.

In addition to the skills-training that staff are receiving, they also have access to support staff who have been employed to provide teacher support, rather than purely technical support. The support staff are available for one-to-one just-in-time training sessions, and also to help develop integrated lessons plans, and to provide classroom support during these lessons if required.

This school does not rely solely on in-house professional development. The principal and ICT coordinator have been to conferences and visited other schools in New Zealand and overseas, while other staff members have received funding to attend courses at local tertiary institutions. In addition, an outside expert is invited to the school annually to discuss wider issues of technology and integration with staff members.

The school has a long-term plan with a vision, and is putting in place a culture of learning. All teaching staff are involved in at least some form of professional development, with a range of options available to them. A large amount of skills-based training is provided, and although there is no mention that this training is tied into student learning, training related to integration and pedagogy is also occurring. It doesn't appear, however, that student outcomes are measured or tied into the professional development programme. Although not meeting all the criteria of an effective development programme as described previously, this school is certainly well on the way to doing so.

Despite the limitations of the technology professional development programmes of Otago schools, they still seem to be having an effect on teachers' technology usage (the effect of teachers' professional development on student learning was unable to be measured, as this was not the original purpose of the research). Teachers and ICT coordinators who reported having received some technology professional development in the last three years were more likely to report that their personal usage had changed, and that they used the Internet and word-processing more (Lai *et al.*, 2001).

Concluding Remarks

Effective professional development does not consist of well-run succinct courses on specific topics, but rather is just one part of a school-wide change to a culture of learning. In this way professional development will not merely be confined to specific programmes, but rather teachers will gain knowledge through observing and conversing with others, and through all other aspects of their school life. More formal planned programmes are also necessary, but these need to be tied to schools' long-term goals and be associated with attaining specific student-related outcomes. A wide range of courses are necessary to take into account the individual teacher's needs, and the different subjects and levels they teach, and to allow each teacher to learn in the way and at the time that best suits them. The value and effectiveness of such courses should be evaluated regularly, both through systematic teacher evaluations and through tracking student achievements. These factors are important both to professional development in general and to technology professional development. Teachers may need to learn specific technology related skills, but even these, as Williams (1993) points out, can be taught in a way that relates to student and learning outcomes, rather than merely giving teachers a knowledge of an application.

References

Alexander, D., Heaviside, S. & Farris, E. (1999). Status of education reform in public elementary and secondary schools: Teachers' perspectives. *Education Statistics Quarterly*. Available at: <http://nces.ed.gov/pubs99/quarterlyapr/4-elementary/4-esq11-g.html>

Ang, C. (1998). *Evaluation report: The FY98 professional development days (PDD program)*. Available at: <http://www.palmbeach.k12.fl.us/9045/pdd.htm>

Apple (1995). *Changing the conversation about teaching learning and technology: A report on 10 years of ACOT research*. Available at: <http://www.apple.com/education/k12/leadership/acot/library.html>

Capper, P. (1994). *Participation and partnership: Exploring shared decision making in twelve New Zealand schools. Part One*. Wellington: New Zealand Post Primary Teachers' Association.

Capper, P. (1999). *Information technology strategies in schools*. Wellington: Ministry of Education.

CEO Forum (1999). *Professional Development: A link to better learning*. The CEO Forum school technology and readiness report. Available at: <http://ceoforum.org/reports.cfm?CID=2&RID=2>

Choy, S.P. & Chen, X. (1998). Toward better teaching: Professional development in 1993-94. *Education Statistics Quarterly*. Available at: <http://nces.ed.gov/pubs99/quarterlyapr/4-elementary/4-esq11-f.html>

Clark, C.M. (1992). Teachers as designers in self-directed professional development. In A. Hargreaves & M.G. Fullan (Eds), *Understanding teacher development* (pp.75-84). London: Cassell.

Cohen, D.K. & Hill, H.C. (1998). *Instructional policy and classroom performance: The mathematics reform in California*. CPRE Research Report Series RR-39. Available at: <http://www.gse.upenn.edu/cpre/docs/pubs/rr39.pdf>

Cook, C.J. (1997). *Critical issue: Finding time for professional development*. Available at: <http://www.ncrel.org/sdrs/areas/issues/educatrs/profdevl/pd300.htm>

Darling-Hammond, L. (2000). Teacher quality and student achievement: A review of state policy evidence.

Education Policy Analysis Archives, 8. Available at: <http://epaa.asu.edu/epaa/v8n1/>

Dwyer, D. (1994). Apple classrooms of tomorrow: What we've learned. *Educational Leadership*, *51*, 4-10.

Education Review Office (2000). *In-service training for teachers in New Zealand Schools*. Available at: <http://www.ero.govt.nz/Publications/pubs2000/InServiceTraining.htm>

Fine, C. & Raack, L. (1994). *Professional development: changing times*. NCREL Policy Brief: Report 4. Available at: <http://www.ncrel.org/sdrs/areas/issues/envrnmnt/go/94-4over.htm>

Fullan, M. (1993). *Change forces: Probing the depths of educational reform*. London: Falmer Press.

Fullan, M. (1999). *Change forces: The Sequel*. London: Falmer Press

Fullan, M. & Hargreaves, A. (1991, revised 1996). *What's worth fighting for in your school?* London: Teachers College Press.

Fullan, M. & Mascall, B. (2000). *Human resource issues in education: A literature review*. Wellington: Ministry of Education.

Glennan, T.K. & Melmad, A. (1996). *Fostering the use of educational technology: Elements of a national strategy*. Available at: <http://www.rand.org/publications/MR/MR682/contents.html>

Greenwald, R., Hedges, L.V. & Laine, R.D. (1996). The effect of school resources on student achievement. *Review of Educational Research*, *66*, 631-396.

Hargreaves, A. (1994). *Changing teachers, changing times*: *Teacher's work and culture in the postmodern age*. London: Cassell.

Jackson, P.W. (1992). Helping teachers develop. In A. Hargreaves & M. G. Fullan (Eds), *Understanding teacher development* (pp.62-74). London: Cassell.

Lai, K.-W., Pratt, K. & Trewern, A. (2001). *Learning with Technology: Evaluation of the effectiveness of the Otago Technology Project*. Dunedin: Community Trust of Otago.

Lawton, D. (1994). Defining quality. In P. Ribbins & E. Burridge (Eds), *Improving education: Promoting quality in schools* (pp.1-7). London: Cassell.

Lewis, L., Prasad, B., Carey, N., Bartfai, N., Farris, E. & Smerdon, B. (1999). Teacher quality: A report on the preparation and qualifications of public school teachers. *Education Statistics Quarterly*. Available at: <http://nces.ed.gov/pubs99/quarterlyapr/2-feature/2-esq11-a.html>

Little, J.W. (1990). The persistence of privacy: Autonomy and initiative in teachers' professional relations. *Teachers College Record*, *91*, 509-536.

McDougall, A. & Squires, D. (1997). A framework for reviewing teacher professional development programmes in information technology. *Journal of Information Technology for Teacher Education*, *6*, 115-26.

McKenzie, J. (1998). *Secrets of success: Professional development that works*. Available at: <http://staffdevelop.org/secrets.html>

Means, B. & Olson, K. (1995). *Technology's role in education reform: Findings from a national study of innovating schools*. Available at: <http://www.ed.gov/PDFDocs/techrole.pdf>

Ministry of Education (1999). *Interactive strategies for schools*. Wellington: Ministry of Education.

National Education Association (1999-2000). *It's about time*. From the 1999-2000 New Member CD. Available at: <http://www.nea.org/bt/3-school/time.pdf>

National School Boards Foundation (1999). Leadership matters: Transforming urban school boards. Available at: <http://www.nsbf.org/report/home.htm>

Riley, R.W., Kunin, M.M., Smith, M.S. & Roberts, L.G. (1996). *Getting America's students ready for the 21st Century: Meeting the technology literacy challenge. A report to the nation on technology and education*. Available at: <http://www.ed.gov/Technology/Plan/NatTechPlan/>

Ringstaff, C., Yocam, K. & Marsh, J. (1995). Integrating technology into classroom instruction: An assessment of the impact of the ACOT Teacher Development Center project. *ACOT Report #22*. Available at: <http://www.apple.com/education/k12/leadership/acot/library.html>

Sparks, D. & Hirsh, S. (1999). *A national plan for improving professional development*. Available at: <http://www.nsdc.org/library/NSDCPlan.html>

Sullivan, C. & Anso, M. (March, 2000). *ICT in schools 1999*. Report prepared for Information Technology Advisory Group (ITAG). Available at: <http://www.med.govt.nz/pbt/infotech/ictschools1999/ictschools1999/html>

Te Kete Ipurangi (n.d.). ICT professional development schools. Available at: <http://www.tki.org.nz/r/ict/pedagogy/schools/about_e.php>

Web-based Education Commission to the President and Congress of the United States (2000). The Power of the Internet for Learning. Available at: <http://www.ed.gov/offices/AC/WBEC/FinalReport/>

Wenglinsky, H. (1998). *Does it compute? The relationship between educational technology and student achievement in mathematics*. Available at: <http://www.ets.org.research/pic/technolog.html>

WestEd (2000). *Teachers who learn kids who achieve: A look at schools with model professional development*. Available at: <http://web.WestEd.org/online_pubs/teachers_who_learn/TeachLearn.pdf>

Williams, B. (1993). *Barriers to new technology – part two: Skill fixation in staff development*. Available at: <http://staffdevelop.org/sd6.html>

Online Learning: An Alternative Way of Providing Professional Development for Teachers

3

Ann Trewern and Kwok-Wing Lai

The Web has altered the nature of information and the way people communicate with each other (Duchastel, 1997), resulting in an accelerated growth in the number and modes of learning available. Many tertiary institutions now offer a wide variety of online courses, qualifications and degree programmes that utilise various modes of computer-mediated communication. Some offer Web-assisted options to supplement face-to-face communication between students and teaching staff and others offer Web-based options where the Internet is the sole means of delivery (Lai, 1999). Within a single institution it is common to find a plurality of Web delivery options available to learners. In many universities and colleges, learning via the medium of the World Wide Web has become a mainstream activity. In tertiary education, the term 'Webucation' has been coined, with e-universities – universities that do not inhabit the traditional buildings and spaces so necessary in the past – becoming increasingly common in a number of countries. In the UK, the Higher Education Funding Council for England has planned to create an e-university with a budget of £400 million. Even traditional universities are considering ways that telecommunications may expand their academic communities. For example, Oxford University is considering linking with the US universities of Stanford, Yale, and Princeton to create an online college for their alumni, and Cambridge is exploring possibilities of linking up with MIT in virtual-learning opportunities (*Financial Times*, 2001). These e-universities aim at providing students with maximum flexibility in where they learn and when they learn.

The electronic medium is widely recognised as being well suited to teachers who are often shut off from professional contact with their fellow teachers. Lack of professional contacts has been attributed by researchers to the nature of teaching (Hargreaves, 1992; Huberman, 1993) as well as to the physical architecture of schools and classrooms and the division of students into separate year-groups (Hargreaves, 1992). Telecommunications also allow teachers working in rural and isolated areas opportunities to link to colleagues and other educational professionals and to advance their professional development options. The potential for communication technologies to be an effective medium to foster knowledge-building and discourse between individuals and groups within any profession has begun to be recognised by the wider educational community (Lai, 1997; Collis 1996a, 1996b; Trewern 1999).

The Internet has been used not only to provide formal professional development for teachers, in the form of credited courses; increasingly it has also been used by teachers for informal professional learning. This chapter will discuss how the Internet can offer formal and informal professional development for teachers, as well as some design principles that are pertinent in developing online learning environments.

Online Learning

Although a variety of multimedia tools are now available on the Web, and video and audio communications have become increasingly common, most of the Web-based learning systems and environments are still text based. According to Harasim (1996), text-based communication can facilitate learning, as 'the written word is uniquely suited to the construction, group revision and sharing of knowledge' and 'practically all education is built around text books and written assignments' (p. 3). As argued by Feenberg (1999), writing should not be considered a poor substitute for physical presence and speech, but rather as another medium of expression. By adding selected interactive elements to the learning process, the Web can widen the educative experience and encourage groups to share information and build knowledge through text-based communication.

Jonassen (1994) argues that learning is best facilitated by the design and implementation of learning environments that foster personal meaning-making and discourse among a community of learners. The role of the online teacher thus shifts from creating prescriptive learning situations to designing environments that engage learners, requiring them to construct that knowledge which is most meaningful to them. A major attribute of the Web as a learning environment is that it can enhance interaction between learners as well as between learners and the teacher. A range of real-time (synchronous) and delayed-time (asynchronous) tools can be used to great effect in Web-based learning environments. As an alternative to face-to-face tutorial sessions in the traditional classroom, students can share their opinions and co-construct knowledge in asynchronous threaded and computer-mediated discussion forums. Many students have noted that the asynchronous environment allows them the opportunity to work at their own pace, taking time 'to read, reflect, write and revise, before sharing ideas and insights with others' (Harasim, 1996, p. 4). Students can also interact with classmates and teachers in chat rooms and through email. Designers of Web-based learning environments have to be mindful that opportunities for purposeful interactivity are created and that learning activities are engaging, interesting and stimulating.

It is important to decide whether a Web-based learning environment is mainly used by individual learners who are required to complete their work alone or by groups of learners. We believe that the greatest potential of the Web is its ability to support structured collaboration and conversation among a community of learners (Leiberman & Grolnick, 1996; Jonassen, 1994). There are various ways that collaborative learning can be facilitated. For example, online exercises and assignments can be set in ways that encourage learners in their collaborative efforts. The learning environment needs to include features such as private discussion forums and chat rooms so that collaborative working arrangements can be supported.

Formal Professional Development

In recent years the Internet has been increasingly used by tertiary institutions to deliver distance learning courses and programmes. For example, according to a recent survey (Market Data Retrieval, 2000) of about 2000 accredited colleges in the US, nearly three-quarters (72 per cent) reportedly offered distance learning programmes in 1999, compared to only 48 per cent in 1998. The same survey also reported that the three most common subject areas for distance learning were business, social sciences, and education. In New Zealand, quite a few universities and colleges of education have begun to offer formal professional development options to teachers at both the undergraduate and postgraduate levels. For example, at the School of Education, University of Otago, there has been a significant growth in Web-based postgraduate and professional development opportunities since 1997. Teachers can now gain fully accredited postgraduate qualifications in teacher education and in the theoretical and practical use of information technology in educational settings. Some ten or so individual papers are offered during any year as single-semester or full-year papers.

An Example of Web-based Learning

To illustrate how Web-based learning works, the main features of the Web-based papers offered by the School of Education at the University of Otago are described here as an example. A course home page is shown in Figure 1.

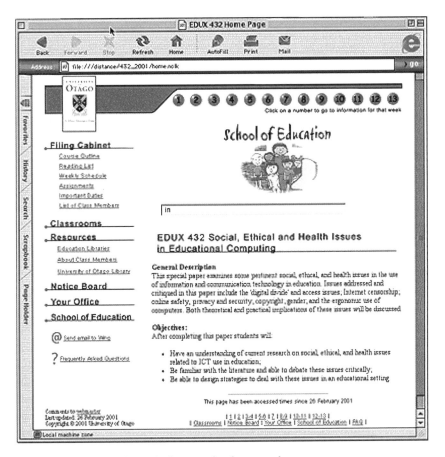

Figure 1: An example of a course home page

Classroom interaction. Traditionally, a distance learner is a lonely learner whose learning is very much individually oriented. With the use of the Internet, distance learning becomes interactive and classroom interaction can take place either by email exchanges or by synchronous and asynchronous conferencing. For example, in the Otago Web-based courses, asynchronous computer conferencing has been designed as the focus of all the learning activities. Instead of having face-to-face group discussions, students share their opinions and experience by participating in computer-mediated discussion forums. For a semester-long paper, there will be four two-week long virtual conferences. Each conference has a main theme. For example, in the 'Advanced Internet-based Learning' course, one of the conference themes is 'What is computer-mediated communication?' In 1997, when this paper was offered for the first time on the Web, this conference theme had five sub-topics, including (a) issues of technocentrism; (b) CMC and gender issues; (c) online persona/culture; (d) non-neutrality of technology; and (e) summary of conference papers. Before the conference, students are given background reading materials as preparation for participation. Then the conference moderators post questions to each sub-conference to kick off the discussion. Students discuss these questions and take their time to read and post their comments to the virtual classroom. They may initiate new topics as the discussion flows on (see Figure 2).

The effectiveness of the conferencing environment is well summarised by one student (Lai, 1997):

> While reading S's posting regarding the amount of territory (CMC and teacher development) covered – I doubt if this many ideas, or this depth of thought could have been presented in any other media. In FTF [face-to-face] the plot would have been frequently lost along the way, and the side issue not fully explored … the depth of thinking is greater. I'm guessing it is a function of the asynchronous nature of the media, and the suitability of writing for reflecting on thinking.

To maximise classroom interaction, synchronous chat sessions are designed as learning activities. Real-time communication is needed if students require urgent and immediate feedback from teaching staff or from their peers. There are frequent email communications between students and staff in this learning environment as well.

Collaboration. The Internet has great potential to foster collaboration. Students taking Otago Web-based papers are asked to work closely in groups, as well as with the teaching staff. We believe that mutual support is essential for adult learners, particularly when they learn at a distance. Activities are designed in this learning environment to encourage the exchange of opinions, ideas, and values.

Social interaction. It is believed that students learn best when they can socialise with other students. Earlier research on computer-mediated communication has criticised the lack of contextual and social cues of this mode of communication and therefore maintains that interaction and discussion, by and large, occur in a social vacuum in this environment (Baym, 1995). Our Web-based papers are designed to encourage social interaction among students. For example, a 'coffee lounge' has been included in the course website. This is a discussion area reserved for socially related matters and is maintained to enhance communication at the social level.

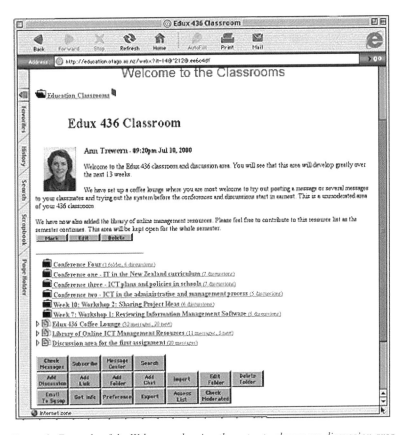

Figure 2: Example of the Web page showing the entry to classroom discussion area

Accessible course materials and databases. Lack of course information and reading materials could be a big concern for distance learners. In our online courses, a CD-ROM is provided for students, which contains a complete archive of course materials and student support information. The website provides a learning structure (discussed below) to assist planning. This allows students the flexibility to forward plan or work on material retrospectively if events or situations prevent them from devoting short periods of time to courses. Several local and international databases are linked to the site, and distance-students can access bibliographic databases purchased by the university central library from their home computers. A local searchable database allows students to borrow computer software from the School of Education resource centre for certain courses.

Learning structure. The course websites are structured to provide the best support for students to complete their studies on time. In each course website, weekly learning tasks are scheduled. There is an 'Introduction Page' for each week, which outlines the learning objectives. This page is linked to three others. The *What to Know* page gives students more detailed guidelines for the weekly learning programme. The *What to Read* page lists the weekly reading assignments and the *What to Do* page outlines the weekly hands-on activities (see Figure 3).

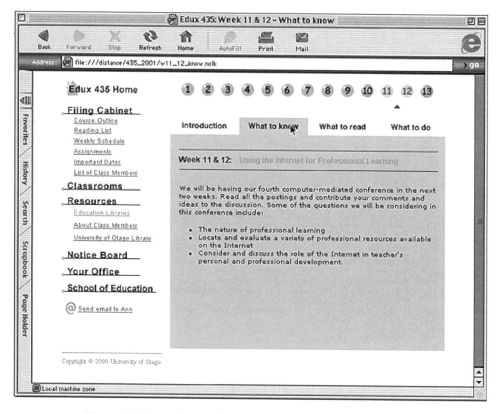

Figure 3: Web page showing how the students' course work is structured

Students' offices. A specific area on each course website is assigned to students as offices. Feedback and comments on student assignments are posted to individual offices. They are password-protected for confidentiality.

User control. A noticeboard with information about administrative matters relating to these papers is broadcast regularly. Students can also post information about course-related matters to the noticeboard or request collaborative partners in certain projects and assignments. A student directory is maintained, where students can post biographical details about themselves (see Figure 4).

The Roles of the Teacher and the Learner

While research (Institute for Higher Education Policy, 1999) in general suggests that there are no significant differences in terms of achievement between electronic and face-to-face modes of learning, it should be noted that taking a Web-based paper is rather different from taking an on-site paper. Web-based online papers impose cognitive and social demands on a learner. For example, students have to be able to master the communication technologies as well as the learning tasks that they have to complete on time. The workload may be an issue if learners are not sufficiently Internet literate. As suggested by Kazmer (2000), there are seven aspects potential students have to consider if they are to cope with the demands of studying at a distance. They include (a) planning; (b) technology; (c) workload; (d) social issues; (e) integrating life and study; (f) administrative adaptation; and (g) effort and rewards. In the Otago Web-based papers, additional support has been provided with voice communication and face-to-face visits for beginning learners.

As for the teacher, teaching in a Web-based learning environment is very different from teaching in a traditional classroom. For example, there is a fundamental change in the relationship with their students. Teachers are not there to impart knowledge and skills, but to provide guidance and support as coach and facilitator. Teachers also serve as moderators who organise and plan, establish and maintain social relationships, as well as providing intellectual stimulation and encouraging participation. For most teachers, the role of a moderator is quite new. They have to acquire the skills of 'defining the membership of the conferenc … keeping the discussion on track, and … scheduling the opening and closing of the discussion topic' (Kaye, 1992, p. 6) in order to guide and develop the discussion. The objective of the teacher is to give students as much control of their own learning as possible so that they can acquire the skills of learning independently (Lai, 1999).

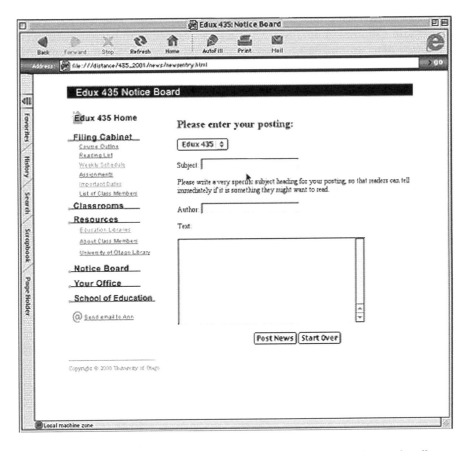

Figure 4: An example of the interactive noticeboard area where students and staff can post and read notices

Informal Professional Learning

Traditionally teachers have gleaned considerable professional knowledge in quite informal ways. Such knowledge is gained from colleagues, as a result of informal group interactions, and also from personal reading and locating resources and teaching materials. Many researchers consider this a valid and important way for professionals to advance their knowledge (Collis 1996b; Marchionini and Maurer, 1995).

Professional learning can be described as a self-directed adult activity where the individual decides on what to read, who he or she communicates with and what aspects of learning need be given most attention, and it is usually closely linked to job performance. Marchionini and Maurer (1995) define professional learning as

> the ongoing learning adults engage in to do their work and improve their work-related knowledge and skills. In fact for many professionals learning is the central aspect of their work. Like informal learning it is mainly self-directed but unlike formal or informal learning it is focussed on a specific field closely linked to job performance, aims to be comprehensive and is acquired and applied longitudinally (p. 68-69).

Collis (1996b) further describes professional learning as 'a blend of learning with one's on-going activities to allow context and experience to be utilised in a way relevant to the specific situation of the professional' (p. 153). Professional learning therefore does not take place in credited courses, or in training centres, but in the ongoing life of the professional. Collis (1996b) suggests there are two sources for professional learning. One source is learning media such as books, professional journals, and reports; the other source is informal interactions with colleagues and peers, who provide the necessary communication partners for the argument, debate, brainstorming and discussion that are crucial to the social construction of knowledge. The Internet, with its interconnecting informational resources and ability to allow connections between colleagues and peers, has expanded the possibilities for individuals to advance their professional learning. Specific online professional learning networks designed to support such learning opportunities as and when needed are effective sources for such learning.

Online Learning Networks

An electronically networked community is one that is bound by common use or purpose rather than by factors such as physical location, institutional affiliation, class level or subject area, which commonly define a face-to-face community. The members of networked communities communicate electronically via the Internet, which provides access to many resources that may not be readily accessible by other means. Electronically networked communities can have local, regional, national, or international participants who can join in network activities whenever or wherever it is convenient for them to do so. These communities offer enhanced opportunities for educational advancement to a wide range of users including educators, students, parents, researchers, business and industry. They can support a wide range of educational purposes including in-service professional development, pre-service training, collaborative project development, student learning, distance learning, and many others that link schools, homes, community organisations, and businesses (Kurshan & Wanamaker-Harrington, 1994).

Professionally oriented networks designed specifically for use by teachers are beginning to proliferate on the Internet. Groups of teachers can get together and make use of communications technologies to access teaching resources, source new ideas, use communications technologies to share ideas or innovative teaching practices, and reflect on aspects of classroom practice. Collis (1996a) describes electronic networks designed specifically for teacher professional learning as being able to provide,

> integrated access to a variety of resources and contacts. The resources can be local or distributed, of a time sensitive nature or related to lesson materials or models of successful practice. They may also include software resources, and reside in many different databases and servers, hyperlinked as in WWW sites or otherwise interconnected. The resources can also be focused on activities, with a prime focus on bringing teachers and their classes together for structured learning events. Finally the environment can provide teachers with the opportunity to participate in moderated discussions or more open newsgroups (p. 38).

For many researchers, such professionally oriented learning networks potentially offer quite radically different ways of providing professional development to teachers (Collis, 1996a, 1996b; Gordin, Gomez, Pea, & Fishman, 1997). Such learning environments are uniquely situated to provide the kind of learner control and independence which are key aspects of making ongoing and job-related learning meaningful for professionals. They can allow for combining learning with contexts and experiences that are relevant to the needs of the individual when those needs are most appropriate.

Professional Learning Networks for Teachers

Teacher-support networks can be found in many varieties and forms, and a number of examples can be found in New Zealand and overseas. The networks discussed in this section have been selected either for their relevance for New Zealand teachers or because they offer unique forms of knowledge-building and communication.

Many organisations offer a range of informal learning opportunities and ways of connecting teachers into networks and learning communities. In many countries ministries of education are involved in providing online policy documents and classroom resources specifically for teachers. Increasingly, professional support and professional development are seen as the primary roles of these support systems. Many other traditional education providers are also offering informal learning options through the Internet. These include schools of education and traditional educational textbook publishers such as Houghton Mifflin, and developers of visual educational resources such as Discovery Channel and Public Broadcasting Service (PBS), and museums and galleries (Collis 1996a; Trewern, 1999).

Several international initiatives in the area of teacher professional support and learning networks are worth a closer look. An interesting model for online professional interactive networks is TAPPED IN <http://wwww.tappedin.org/>. TAPPED IN is largely a communications network providing for both formal and informal collaborative activities, real-time (synchronous) communications and some delayed-time (asynchronous) activities. Network resources in this professional development network are centred on activities. A prime focus is on bringing teachers together for structured learning events. Real-time text communication is a feature of the network and is achieved technically by the use of a multi-user virtual environment (MUVE) or MOO. Asynchronous communications are achieved by email listservs. The network 'reception desk' is manned from 9 am to 6 pm so that anyone logging into the discussion areas from the web-entry pages will find a person to greet them on arrival. A calendar of upcoming events such as debates or discussions is available on the website or teachers can gather together for informal meetings.

A second and quite different example of a professional learning network is the *Sofweb* site which can be found at <http://www.sofweb.vic.edu.au/> and has been developed by the Victorian State Government Department of Education in Australia. This network offers integrated access to a variety of resources and contacts, and provides teachers with the opportunity to participate in moderated discussions. The network is an excellent example of a policy-dominated approach by a centralised authority. Professional services, classroom and professional information and discussion forums dealing with professional, curriculum and management issues are provided. These are specific to the Victorian educational community and functional for teachers looking for easy access to information resources and for areas to discuss educational issues with colleagues, and use language and structures that are entirely relevant to teachers.

Several networks have recently been established for New Zealand teachers. The development of an education portal site was identified as a policy infrastructure initiative in the *Interactive Education: An ICT Strategy for Schools* (Ministry of Education, 1998). Te Kete Ipurangi is the learning centre that has been developed and implemented over the past two years. It is, at this stage, predominantly an information and resource network providing integrated access to a variety of educational resources that are primarily New Zealand-based. A strength of the learning centre is its bilingual approach, which includes both English and Maori language Web resources.

As a portal, or umbrella, organisation operating as a central connecting point for New Zealand teachers to educational materials, the resources of Te Kete Ipurangi are largely archived in many different databases and servers. There is a strong emphasis on locally developed lesson materials and models of successful practice in several curriculum areas include links to websites such as *English-on-line, @science* and *New Zealand Maths*. Other resources provide local administrative materials, policy information on enhancing teaching and learning and on raising student achievement levels, as well as materials to support professional development for school management and teaching staff.

The New Zealand Learning Network (NZLNet)

The *New Zealand Learning Network* (NZLNet) <http://education.otago.ac.nz/NZLNet/home.nclk> was established in 1998 by the School of Education, University of Otago, as an information, service and discussion network for New Zealand teachers. The network is designed to expand the learning environment of the formal Web-based postgraduate and professional development programmes (described earlier in this chapter) into a larger online learning and sharing environment for all interested teachers. The network is designed as a hypertext learning environment that emphasises comprehensive interrelationships between information, concepts and activities that will assist teachers in pursuing learning that is work related and that can be accessed on a need-to-know basis. It is a learning environment that is designed to be explored by its users. The network organises online professional development activities and offers a range of tools and resources such as interdisciplinary information resources, services such as advice from experts, and opportunity for interaction and collaboration such as discussions and interactive projects.

The primary purpose of the network is to provide teachers who have access to technology with expanding opportunities to integrate technology within their classroom practice and to support their own professional learning needs. As an information network the *NZLNet* is designed to provide teachers with a one-stop shop for classroom and professional materials. It provides the following resources:

- filtered access to relevant Internet information for New Zealand classroom use;
- filtered access to relevant Internet access to teacher support materials in the form of background materials and theoretical readings;
- easy access to resources in ways that are logical and meaningful to teachers, e.g., matching resources to New Zealand curriculum strands and related topic sets;
- links to locally developed New Zealand-based materials wherever possible.

Extensive Internet libraries based on five of the seven curriculum areas (i.e. science, English, maths, social studies and technology) have been established to support the busy teacher looking for a direct link to that particular science unit or useful online article. Teachers do not have time to search the Web, or even a website, in the hope of finding information that might be useful. Important linkages between curriculum content and professional materials such as research papers, professional journals, mailing lists and conferences are provided. There are links to information about assessment practices, disability, and evergreen resources that are being developed by New Zealand teachers and network participants.

Many of the services provided by the network are designed to support teachers in ways that replicate their daily work. This is achieved by:

- sharing units of work, lesson plans and teaching resources online;
- providing professional materials contributed by a wide range of users, for example full text articles from a professional journal online;
- providing interactive projects to enhance online activities and interaction between network users;
- providing access to specialist and expert advice through the science departments at University of Otago;
- emailing a monthly newsletter to all network members informing them of updates and activities, professional opportunities that arise through Internet connections, and teaching strategies and good ideas for classroom use of the Internet;
- providing 'virtual wall spaces' for presentation of student online activities.

Although computer conferencing facilities have been designed as an integral feature

of the *NZLNet*, full development of the discussion areas is yet to come. There are a number of reasons for this. Teachers have been reticent about involving themselves in spontaneous discussion and the number of people with time available to promote and expand structured debate and discussion events to encourage teachers to participate has been limited. At present, discussion forums have provided opportunities for teachers and classes to work together in collaborative projects and in future it is hoped that forums will be available to encourage educators to share examples of good practice, teaching ideas and resources. The network provides opportunity to:
- link with colleagues and other professionals through message boards and online asynchronous discussion;
- link with colleagues and other professionals through the chat room (synchronous discussion).

Description of the New Zealand Learning Network
The *New Zealand Learning Network* utilises a range of interactive and communication elements similar to those used for the online papers but with different purposes in the informal environment of the learning network. Figure 5 shows some of the features available from the learning network home page.

Communication features include:
- *Forums.* The forums provide areas for structured discussions. Once teachers log on to the site, they will be able to post and respond to messages related to different discussion topics.
- *Chat room.* This is a collaborative work area or space for social interaction where network users can communicate in real time.

Interactive features include:
- *Notice board.* Any reminders or information relating to teachers, schools or the work they do can be posted by network participants to this news bulletin board area.
- *Ask an expert.* This is an area that links to the science departments at the University of Otago. Teachers can ask a question of a geologist, physicist, textile scientist, food scientist, etc., or search out already answered questions on aspects of science.
- *Interactive curriculum projects.* This is an area where structured curriculum activities are available for teachers to use with their students. Past curriculum project resources are archived and are available for teachers to use with their classes if they wish. More information about these curriculum projects is available in Chapter 7.

Resource features include:
- *Staffroom.* The staffroom is a resource area containing Internet links to professional materials. It also has links to professional materials provided by other network users. It is a slowly developing resource that focuses on teachers' needs for knowledge of assessment practices and ideas, and information about children with disabilities. It also contains classroom management issues and online links to many

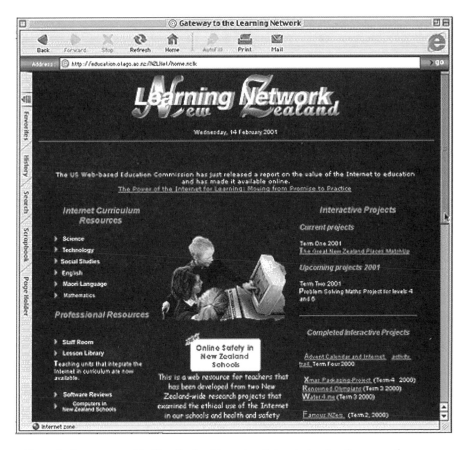

Figure 5: Home page of the New Zealand Learning Network showing the range of resources available to teachers

of the usual publications such as the *New Zealand Education Gazette* and other commercially oriented magazines for teachers.

• *Lesson library.* The resource exchange area requires input and development from teachers and network users. Users can access the online projects, evergreen lesson plans, and a list of school Web pages that are hosted on the site (see Figure 6).

• *Software reviews.* This is to be developed further. Teachers are often unaware what curriculum-related software is available for students for classroom use. Teachers will be able to submit comment and reviews about educational software they are familiar with and share teaching ideas about the use of software.

• *Curriculum areas.* Curriculum departments are also resource areas set up to support teachers using the Internet to locate content resources in science, technology, social studies, language, mathematics, the arts and music and in health and physical well-being for classroom use. Resources in these departmental areas also support curriculum content, providing background material for teachers as well as links to newsgroups, mailing lists, and conferences.

   • *Professional articles.* A sample of full-text articles from *Computers in New*

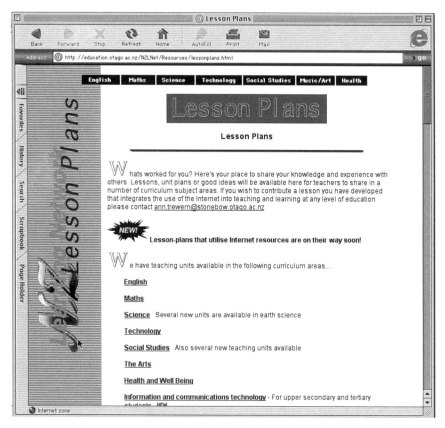

Figure 6: Links to useful 'evergreen' lesson plans and units of work that utilise the Internet. These are units of work developed by teachers in the postgraduate programmes.

Zealand Schools is available. This is a journal published for New Zealand teachers which has research papers and class-based activities in information and communication technology.

Principles of Designing Online Learning Environments

All online learning environments should provide desirable educational experiences for learners. As much as possible, the learning environments of both the Web-based papers and the *NZLNet* as described in this chapter have been designed to closely resemble a model of learning that teachers will feel familiar and comfortable to work with.

A familiar environment. It is important to create a familiar environment that users will recognise and feel comfortable with, especially if they are not used to this mode of delivery. A campus metaphor is used to represent the different resources for the online learning papers. When students log onto the course home page they can visit classrooms, browse library collections, open filing cabinets and check the noticeboards. They even have their own office on the website

To enhance feelings of familiarity for users, the *NZLNet* is designed to recreate as complete a model of teaching as possible. The information areas utilise a curriculum framework metaphor which is consistent with the way New Zealand teachers have been actively encouraged to model their knowledge domain since the New Zealand Curriculum Framework was first introduced in 1993. When teachers log onto the *NZLNet* homepage they can visit various curriculum departments (e.g. the social studies department), the staff room, subject discussion forums and an educational news area. Second-level information resources are divided according to the titles of separate curriculum documents. Third-level resources are divided according to curriculum strands or specific topics within the documents, where a plethora of Internet resources are available in a particular topic. Network colours are consistent with curriculum documents and easily recognisable for teachers across the compulsory education sector.

A structured environment. A most important issue in designing online learning environments is authenticity; i.e. the extent to which the environment faithfully represents the practices of the culture. A good management structure for learners includes clear and explicit information about tasks that are expected of them, and these tasks need to be kept within a structure that is familiar to learners. For university courses, an environment that replicates the features of university learning such as libraries, noticeboards, offices and classrooms is important. In the formal Otago papers, course information is archived in the filing cabinets, discussion occurs in the classrooms and additional information is obtained in the libraries.

A Web-based learning environment should also be a flexible environment, and a good management structure should be provided for learners. Structure and management of the learning environment for university course work is provided by pacing study contexts and assessment activities through a specified time period. A weekly learning schedule, with links to readings, learning activities, and learning objectives, is provided and students consider this to be a most important contribution to successful learning. Clear and specific information on assessment tasks is required, as well as just-in-time feedback for their assignments.

Interactive events offered by *NZLNet* also need to be well structured to support teachers. Online projects have successfully utilised a framework within which participating teachers are provided with a pacing structure for interclass interaction (see Chapter 7 for a more detailed discussion). This structure means that the learning environment is easy for online teachers to manage and students or users are not left confused about what it is they need to do and what they need to know.

The structure of the *NZLNet* information resources has a different purpose. The incidental learning resource structures are designed to replicate the organisational structures of teachers' work, so that users can move around the network structure effectively and locate specific classroom or professional Internet resources quickly. The network separates the functions of providing classroom resources, areas for teacher interaction, and resources to assist teachers to advance their own professional learning. Classroom resources are located under the curriculum subject headings. Links to subject associations and mailing lists are also categorised in this section. Teachers needing general background to topics, such as behaviour management, will find the material in the staffroom area. The lesson library is currently an area for locating locally created lesson plans. The online environment is structured so that those materials normally found in the school staffroom are also likely to be found in the online staffroom.

A learner/teacher-centred environment. Although a learning structure is provided, it is not intended to be restrictive for students, who are encouraged to set up their own learning goals and to explore issues that are interesting and important to them. Learning tasks and assignments are designed to be flexible and can be tailored to individual students' learning needs.

The *NZLNet* is designed first and foremost to be an environment that centres on the needs of teachers. It is inclusive of all educators who wish to participate and is not limited to a specific-interest group. Development of the network is a slowly evolving process where participants contribute and share teaching ideas, units of work, opinions and perspectives. Users can involve themselves in many different ways, depending on the time they have available. Some are low-level participants and others are very active in the network activity structures, sharing ideas and resources. Some become online leaders who design, develop and implement curriculum-based activities for colleagues.

User control. 'Users' refers to anyone using the learning environment, including teachers, moderators and other online leaders. There are different levels of user control in a Web-based learning environment. The user interface is the entry point for the user to communicate with the learning environment. The learning system should be designed to reduce the time required for users to learn how to find their way around, as well as to find relevant information and communicate with others. The system should to be easy to learn, easy to use, memorable, contain few errors and provide users with a sense of satisfaction (Nielsen, 1993). User control also refers to the ability of users to contribute to the generation of knowledge in the learning environment as well as the developing ownership of the environment. Issues of ownership are closely linked with the ability of the students to contribute and share knowledge with others, and to develop their own learning goals. Noticeboards and personal spaces such as virtual offices increase feelings of satisfaction with, and personal identification with, the learning environment.

The *NZLNet* has been designed to allow users to contribute to the website information systems and give them a feeling that they can share information rapidly with peers. The *NZLNet*'s noticeboards are an attempt to achieve that. Teachers can submit their own news items, as well as read items submitted, by filling out online forms and sending the information straight to the server for immediate viewing. Users can subscribe to online events and or subscribe to email news and information disseminated from the network whenever they wish.

Interactivity and collaboration. Collis (1996b) identifies three types of human networking that are necessary for professional learning. The first is personal networking, where individuals can establish contact with other individuals on a personal level. The second is project or structured networking. This occurs within the organisational framework of a project or online task. The third type is open networking, which also occurs within an organised structure such as moderated discussion forums, where one user can look for contact with another.

All three types of networking are successfully encouraged in these online environments. Students taking these papers are encouraged to network on a personal level. Email addresses are freely shared, biographical information is contributed by the students, and the encouragement to submit collaborative assignments means that personal networking is carried out extensively by participating students. Open networking, which occurs through the classroom discussions, allows for many group discussions that are easily archived and can be accessed at any time. For network participants these forums for developing ideas and contributing knowledge to the network are independent of time and place.

The communications areas of *NZLNet* are designed to actively support both structured and open networking, where participants can collaborate and interact with their colleagues and peers. Specific-project networking occurs through the structured interactive projects offered by the network and through organised informal courses and events which may be provided as part of future network services.

Concluding Remarks

In this chapter various online learning environments have been described and a range of principles underpinning the design of online learning systems have been discussed. Both formal and informal learning systems operating at Otago were used as examples of alternative options for teacher professional development. The principles by which these learning systems are designed are cognisant of constructivist learning theories. As such, the learning environments are primarily learner-centred and allow for high levels of interactivity and user control. Information structures are designed to closely resemble the actual world in which students or teachers function on a daily basis and to provide the classroom tool-kits and personal learning resources that support learning. Individuals can construct their own learning paths through the resources available. These learning environments are both exploratory and generative.

Exploratory learning environments are resource-rich systems in which learners can independently explore resources, or where support is provided for learners to use a range of communication tools and information resources in ways that promote deeper understanding of materials or concepts. Exploratory learning is a feature of both the formal courses and of the informal learning options available through the learning network at Otago, allowing learners an opportunity to 'identify, create, cultivate, pursue and satisfy their individual learning needs' (Hannafin, 1992, p. 54).

As generative environments, these online learning systems are designed for groups or individuals to ultimately create, elaborate and use the knowledge structures provided in ways that suit them. Teachers can connect with others, discuss issues that concern them, relate their classroom experiences, or simply use resources available in the learning environment to create new knowledge.

Although much material has been produced about the practical applications of Web-based learning environments, many questions are still to be answered about their educational value. Blanton, Moorman, & Trathen (1998) argue that a number of issues relating to the use of telecommunications as learning systems need to be resolved in further research. One of the issues is whether or not telecommunications provide desirable educational experiences for learners. A second issue by Blanton *et al.* (1998)

is whether or not telecommunications offer a sufficiently robust medium for the kinds of social interactions necessary for the joint construction of meaning and reflection which underpins the change of beliefs and practices that are inherent in successful professional development. The third issue is whether conflicts may exist between the usual way of providing inservice learning options for teachers and a proposed way that uses computers and telecommunications.

Many of these questions remain either fully or partially unanswered by research to date. The use of telecommunications as formal and informal learning systems is largely seen by both research communities and the teaching profession as an alternative approach that exists in the interstices and around the margins of the current system (Allen, Fitzgerald & Reeves, 1999), but this is a view that is changing.

References

Baym, (1995). The emergence of community in computer-mediated communication. In S. Jones (Ed.). *Cybersociety: Computer-Mediated Communication and Community* (pp. 138-163). U.K.: Sage.

Blanton, W., Moorman, G. & Trathen, W. (1998). Telecommunications and teacher education: A social constructivist review. *Review of Research in Education, 23,* 235-273.

Cochrane-Smith, M. & Lytle, S.L. (May, 1992). Communities for Teacher Research. *American Journal of Education*, 298-324.

Cochrane-Smith, M. & Lytle, S.L. (1999). Relationships of knowledge and practice: Teacher learning in communities. *Review of Research in Education, 24,* 249-305.

Collis, B. (1993). Evaluating instructional applications of telecommunications in distance education. *ETTI, 30* (3), 266-274.

Collis, B. (1996a). Telecommunications for teacher support and professional development. *Computers in New Zealand Schools, 8* (1), 31-39.

Collis, B. (1996b). *Tele-learning in a digital world. The future of distance learning.* U.K: International Thomson Computer Press.

Duchastel, P. (1990). Assimilatory tools for informal learning: Prospects in ICAI. *Instructional Science, 19,* 3-9.

Duchastel, P. (1994). Learning environment design. *Journal of Educational Technology Systems, 22* (3), 225-233.

Duchastel, P. (1997). A web-based model for university instruction. *Journal of Educational Technology Systems, 25* (3), 221-228.

Feenberg (1999). *Distance Learning: Promise or Threat?* Available at: <http://www-rohan.sdsu.edu/faculty/feenberg/TELE3.HTM>

Financial Times (January 5, 2001). Taking over the world by degrees. Available at: http://news.ft.com/

Fitzgerald, G., Allen , B. & Reeves, T. (1999) A scholarly review process for interactive learning and information systems. *Journal of Interactive Learning Research*, 10 (1), 59-65.

Gordin., D., Gomez L., Pea, R. & Fishman, B. (1996) Using the World Wide Web to Build Learning Communities in K-*12 Journal of Computer-Mediated Communication* 2, (3). Available at: <http://jcmc.huji.ac.il/vol2/issue3/gordin.html#s6>.

Hargreaves, A. (1992). Cultures of teaching: A focus for change. In Hargreaves, A. & Fullan, M.G. (Eds), *Understanding teacher development.* (pp. 216-239). New York: Teachers College Press.

Hargreaves, A. (1993). Individualism and individuality: Reinterpreting the teacher culture. In Little, J.W., & McLaughlin, M.W. (Eds), *Teacher's Work. Individuals, colleagues, and contexts.* (pp. 51-76). New York: Teacher's College Press.

Huberman, M. (1993). Model of the independent artisan in teacher's professional relations. In Little, J.W., & McLaughlin, M.W. (Eds). *Teacher's work. individuals, colleagues, and contexts.* (pp. 11-50). New York: Teacher's College Press.

Institute for Higher Education Policy (1999). What's the Difference? A Review of Contemporary Research on the Effectiveness of Distance Learning in Higher Education. Available at: <http://www.ihep.com/difference.pdf>.

Jonassen, D.H. (1994). Thinking technology: Towards a constructivist design. *Educational Technology, 34* (4), 34-37.

Kaye, A. (1992). Learning together apart. In A. Kaye (ed.). *Collaborative Learning through Computer Conferencing* (pp. 1-24). NY: Springer-Verlag.

Kazmer, M. (2000). Coping in a distance environment: Sitcoms, Chocolate cake, and dinner with a friend. Available at: <http://www.firstmonday.dk/issues5_9/kazmer/index.html#k5>.

Kurshan, B. & Wanamaker-Harrington, M. (1994). *An educator's guide to electronic networking: Creating virtual communities.* Revised by Milbury, P.G. (1994). (ERIC Document Reproduction Service No. ED 37 2772).

Lai, K.W. (1997a). Web-based learning: An example of two tertiary education papers offered on the Internet. *Computers in New Zealand Schools, 9* (1), 13-19.

Lai, K.W. (1997b). Interactivity in web-based learning: Some observations based on a web-based course about CMC in education. In Collis, B., & Knezek , G. (Eds). *Teaching and learning in the digital age.* (pp. 211-229). Texas Center for Educational Technology (TCET) and International Society for Technology in Education (ISTE).

Lai, K.W. & Trewern, A. (1998). New Zealand Learning Network: An online community for New Zealand teachers. *Computers in New Zealand Schools, 10* (2), 33-36.

Lai, K.W. (1999). Designing Web-based learning environments. In K.W. Lai (Ed.) *Net-Working: Teaching, Learning, and Professional Development* (pp. 123-141). Dunedin: University of Otago Press.

Lieberman, A. & Grolnick, M. (1996). Networks and reform in American education. *Teachers College Record, 98* (1), 7-45.

Marchionini, G. & Maurer, H. (1995). The roles of digital libraries in teaching and learning. *Communications of the ACM, 38* (4), 67-75.

Ministry of Education (1998). Interactive Education: An ICT Strategy for Schools. Wellington: Ministry of Education.

Nielsen, J. (1993). *Usability engineering.* Cambridge, Massachusetts: Academic Press Professional.

Rahm, D. & Reid, B. (1998). Tangled webs in public administration: Organisational issues in distance learning. Available at: <http://www.pamij.com/rahm.html>.

Trewern, A. (1999). Online professional interactive networks: Virtual professional learning communities for teachers. In Lai, K.W. (Ed.), *Networking: Teaching, learning and professional development with the Internet.* (pp. 157-177). Dunedin: University of Otago Press.

Wells, R. (1992). *Computer mediated communication for distance education; An international review of design, teaching, and institutional issues.* The Pennsylvania State University.

Developing an ICT Plan for Professional Development

Ross Alexander, Janice Wilson, Stephen Hovell

According to the Education Review Office (ERO, 1997), the need to incorporate information and communication (ICT) into our schools is driven primarily by four factors:

An economic rationale
New Zealand needs ICT skills to compete successfully in the global market place.

A social rationale
The education system should prepare students to participate fully in the world in which they live.

A learning effectiveness rationale
Information technology has the potential to raise student achievement across the entire student curriculum.

An efficiency rationale
Information technology can help to overcome problems of distance and isolation.
Under the heading of 'Learning', three possible impacts of using, or failing to use, ICT in schools could be:

1. That as students become more involved with the tools of the digital age their learning outside of school will seem more relevant to them, and by definition school (with its traditional curriculum) will become less relevant (Papert, 1980).
2. That the technology will open opportunities to teach and learn in new ways that will release us from the existing constraints of traditional school.
3. Because of the huge amount of information available, and the text-based nature of ICT, there will need to be a greater emphasis on all students being well equipped with the skills of information literacy, problem-solving, and the development of higher order thinking (Gawith, 1999).

Thus, there exists not only a sense of opportunity, but also a challenge. To face the challenge, schools need to plan and manage change for the use of ICT in schools. This chapter will give New Zealand teachers a guide for developing an effective information and communication technology plan to help manage these changes. It will begin with a discussion of some key issues in developing an ICT plan, and follow with a discussion of a specific plan for professional development.

The Process of Developing a School ICT Plan
Creating a vision
The first stage of developing an ICT plan is to create a vision that sets the focus for such a plan. The word *vision* means the conception of an image. A vision sets out a view of a realistic, credible and attractive scenario for a school that is better than the

existing situation. Bennis & Biederman (1997) describes vision as something like a mental picture of a possible and desirable future state of the organisation, and a condition that is better in some important ways than what now exists.

There is an expectation that New Zealand schools will incorporate ICT into their teaching and learning programmes. Schools are not in a position where they can choose whether to do this or not, but they are in a position to decide how well they can deliver the curriculum using ICT to enhance teaching and learning. In October 1999 the Ministry of Education's initiative, ICT in Schools, was launched, with the aim that by 2002 schools in New Zealand would be improving learning outcomes for students by using ICT to support the aims and objectives of the New Zealand curriculum and by providing ICT professional development for teachers and principals.

Carol Moffatt, Project Manager for ICT, Ministry of Education, likened integration of ICT into a school curriculum to a journey (personal communication, 2000). Every journey has a destination. The vision statement should capture the destination of a school's planning and implementation process, provide staff with an inspiring glimpse of where they are travelling, and keep the needs of the learners paramount. In order to motivate the staff to take this journey, the vision statement must be articulate and convincing, creative yet realistic, and, most important, connected to improved learning outcomes. It should contain:

1. A well-articulated statement of the overall vision of the school to achieve seamless integration of ICT into all of the teaching and learning within the school.
2. Information about the users of the technology and where and how they will use it.
3. A statement about the benefits (direct and indirect) that will ensue for teachers and students from the use of the technology.
4. An overview of how the school intends to make the vision a reality.

How should the vision be developed?

A strategic plan and vision should always be a group effort, owned by all and supported by all. A collaborative approach, as part of a well-established self-review process, will more readily lead to the vision being achieved and sustained, and there is less opportunity for one person or a small group to derail, impede or block change. Creating a vision will provide the school with an opportunity for important school development, a process whereby a self-reflective community increases the effectiveness of learning and teaching in its institution through commitment to the notions of collaboration, the school culture, data-gathering and mutual accountability (Prebble and Stewart, 1993). The vision should be developed in conjunction with staff, board of trustees and parents. There should be a sharing of ideas about ways in which ICT can enhance teaching and learning across the curriculum. A cross-curricular planning team could be appointed to help develop the vision.

The vision and leadership

Consideration must be given to the leadership issues in relation to the ICT vision and subsequent ICT plan. A motivated leader needs to share the vision, communicate it and encourage support for it because the vision will be the framework around which the ICT goals will be developed. The leader will be responsible for guiding the stakeholders in achieving the vision. Should this be the principal or the ICT co-ordinator? Whoever it is, that person needs to be a motivated leader, someone who can:

- set the direction and work in a team situation to develop the vision, assess the skill of the team and delegate tasks based on these skills, (the vision needs to be shared with the staff and agreement must be reached on the direction being taken);
- articulate the vision to staff for better teaching and learning with ICT;
- understand the basics of the hardware and software issues;
- lead by example with ICT.

We believe that a vision and strategic plan should be a group effort and the support of the principal is critical. As commented by Nick Billowes (2000), the National Co-ordinator of the ICTPD Schools Project for the Ministry of Education:

> The predominant and probably most obvious conclusion I have reached so far, is that there are many ways in which a successful staff development model can be generated. The backbone to whatever a staff or cluster undertakes in its ICT development programme however, is the level of commitment of the Principal and the degree to which his or her staff buy into the vision and dream.

The board of trustees has a role in the development of the vision. The trustees should take part in establishing the vision and selling it to the school community. It is critical that trustees should shift their thinking from the way ICT is used as a tool in a business environment. They must seek to understand the perspectives of an educational setting where ICT should be used to *support* teaching and learning (see Figure 1).

Conducting a needs analysis

For a school to travel along the journey to having a seamless integration of ICT into teaching and learning, it is vital to have appropriate data upon which to plan its professional development programmes. Thus, to ensure the effective use of resources, and that schools achieve their vision, a clear understanding of what data need to be gathered, why and for whom, has to be defined. First, there is a need to gather data about skill levels in order for schools to receive funding, or for accountability purposes. Second, the needs of the whole school must be determined, including those of management and the board of trustees. Third, the needs of individual teachers need to be determined.

Whole school needs analysis

Many New Zealand schools have collected data as part of their submissions for receiving funding from the Ministry of Education (e.g. the ICTPD contracts) or as part of Ministry of Education initiated reviews. In addition, data are also available as part of the teachers' appraisal process, evidence of effective use of Ministry funds, or in a school's self-review process. With ICT being the focus of these Ministry-funded developments, it was natural that most of the data-gathering using these questionnaires

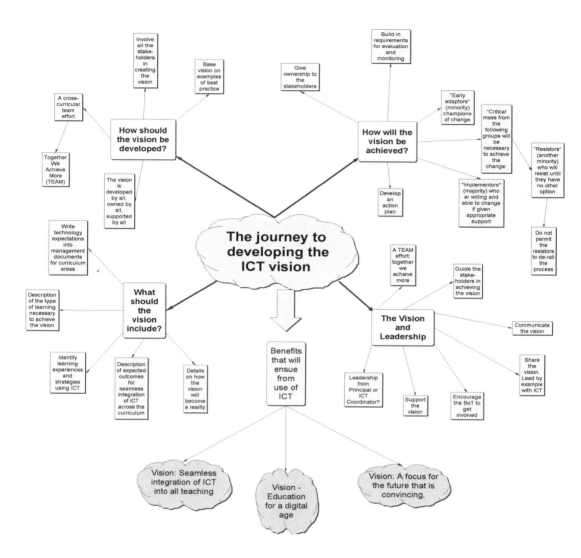

Figure 1: The vision in graphic form

involved the assessment of teachers' personal skills with IT, with some reference to their uses in the classroom. Whilst this data is of some use as a starting point, to base a school's journey toward its vision solely on it would, we believe, be insufficient. The questionnaires were often prepared within a short time-frame, in some cases by outside providers, and could be seen as a reactive approach based upon the desire to access much-needed funding, rather than to provide data for school-wide development in ICT, teaching and learning.

Determining the needs of the whole school on this journey involves the gathering of data, much of which is anecdotal, to determine the readiness of the organisation to move forward toward its vision. It could involve a review of what systems are in place for the implementing of change, how well the staff as a group is able to articulate the

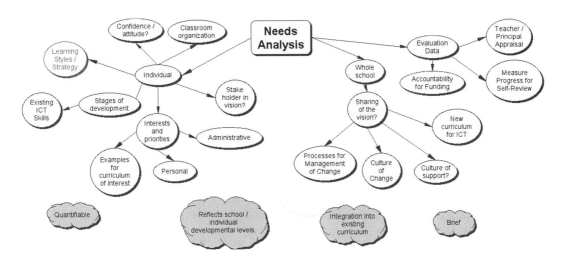

Figure 2: Needs analysis in graphic form

vision, what systems are already in place for mentoring and support, and what technical support is already available. It is also a time to ensure that the principal, while not necessarily the leader in terms of the technology, is committed to the journey. Similarly the board of trustees needs to be committed to the direction that the school is taking, and prepared to devote budget to this area of development (see Figure 2).

As well as accumulating data about the organisation of the school, information about the hardware and software will need to be collated. This could include the types of technology – their age, location and degree of use. It could look at how they are networked, what the life expectancy is and what upgrades may be likely. This is an area that many schools have frequently focused on in a needs analysis, believing that the realisation of the vision lies in having the right tools. Thus for many schools, because the focus is ICT, and because the technology is the most outwardly obvious sign of change, the needs analysis has focused on technology, not on the users and purposes.

Needs analysis for individual teachers

As teachers embark on the ICT journey they will of necessity focus upon learning the skills needed to use the technology. A needs assessment for individual teachers therefore should reflect this developmental stage, but should also provide some indication of teachers' needs in order to make best use of the technology in a classroom context.

Initially the analysis could find out the technical skills the teacher possesses in terms of using common technology applications. This would involve ascertaining how confident they are in using applications for their personal use (for example email), for administrative purposes (administrative or library databases or a word-processor for lesson plans), or to reinforce teaching and learning in the classroom. It should also reflect the fact that we are compiling data on a learner, and that each teacher is an individual. One of the major barriers or motivators in the learning process is attitude. What is the teacher's attitude to the technology? How do they feel about reflecting upon the way they see teaching and learning and realigning their practice towards an environment where ICT is an important component of their classroom programme? Equally important are questions such as how well are they able to articulate the school's vision, and do they see themselves as a stakeholder in this vision?

Information also needs to be gathered on each teacher's preferred learning style and preferences. For example, would they learn more effectively by attending a course out of school, working on their own, or with a mentor? What are the motivational factors? Do they want to learn a skill for personal reasons, or for their own classroom administration? With this approach the needs analysis is focusing not just on *what* the teacher needs to know but also *how* to learn best.

Whilst acknowledging the need to collate sufficient data to enable an effective professional development programme to be planned, it is also important that the questionnaire is kept as brief as possible, and is easy to follow without losing any quality in the information being provided.

Review of needs analysis documents
It could be argued that to adequately address their own professional development, a school should design its own needs analysis. The reality is that schools don't have time to do this, nor in many cases the expertise to do it. It is difficult to ask the questions about the ICT journey if you are unsure of where you are heading. Clearly some leadership is required, but at the same time we run the risk of trying to develop a generic 'one size fits all' analysis that fails to take into account the different organisations of schools, or their stages of development. Table 1 is a review of some of the needs assessment questionnaires available. It is not intended that any particular one should be used, but rather it illustrates the types of questions that could be asked when setting out on the journey.

Table 1: Examples of Needs Asessment Questionnaires.

Organisation	Details of needs assessment documents
Victoria Learning Technologies Survey Analysis programme (v1.1)	Available from: http://www.sofweb.vic.edu.au/pd/tchcap/survey.htm Developed as part of the Navigator Schools Project in Victoria and developed by Sofweb, the questionnaire is also supported by a CD-ROM (available for purchase outside of Victoria) as an aid for analysing the data.
From Now On Organisation	FNO (Jamie McKenzie) Available from: http://fno.org/techlife.html Described as a survey to assess the technological literacy and competency of teachers, this questionnaire looks at how teachers are integrating technology within the classroom and at their own levels of skill in using hardware and software. It also queries the teacher's attitudes to technology, and how they feel about the impact that it may have on their classroom practice.
E-resources	Available from: http://www.lea.co.nz/ICT/eResources/Questionnaire.htm Developed by Learning Enhancement Associates. It has a heavy focus upon the teacher skills using the technology, although does include sections on whether the technology is used in classrooms, and attitudes towards its use.
M.C.C.S.C. (Monroe County Community School Corporation)	Available at: http://www.mccsc.edu/survey.html Although focusing heavily upon the teacher's personal use of technology, it does survey their preferred learning format and time. With over 113 questions, many teachers would find this both time-consuming and threatening, especially if they are in the early stages of using technology.

Barriers in ICT adoption

In designing and implementing an ICT plan, schools need to be aware of the barriers to technology adoption. In the ICT journey, schools very often reach a plateau stage which many schools and teachers have trouble negotiating. These are so-called 'teething troubles' and 'uneven levels of uptake' or 'barrier' (ERO, 2000). While plateaus can come anywhere along the journey, perhaps the greatest plateau lies between the acquisition of skills, and the integration of those skills into the teaching and learning programme. Murray and Campbell (2000) have investigated barriers to the implementation of ICT in over 500 schools (almost 20 per cent of the total number of schools in New Zealand). From the 1,500 responses received, they have identified the following major barriers:

Lack of Professional Development (PD). The lack of professional development is the number one barrier identified in Murray and Campbell's report (2000). While acknowledging that considerable effort has gone into addressing professional development issues, the Education Review Office (2000) also concedes that low levels of teacher skills and confidence remain a concern for a large number of schools. Teachers' skill level and confidence are low.

Lack of Funding. It is often very difficult for schools to identify exactly how much they spend on ICT. Some purchases such as hardware, software, the direct cost of PD, etc., can quite readily be identified, but other types of funding, e.g. management release time to 'fix' hardware/software problems, time given to support curriculum initiatives in ICT integration, time spent by staff outside school hours studying or using ICT for preparation are much harder to identify. Hence the true 'cost' is often hidden and communities are often not aware of all that is involved. McKenzie (1998) claims the biggest reason for the failure of ICT to deliver in schools is the lack of funding for PD at a robust level. He suggests we should spend less on hardware and more on human infrastructure. Funding needs also to extend to providing staff with the tools for the job. Many teachers spend thousands of dollars on computers to learn and develop the skills needed for using ICT in the classrooms. For example, one New Zealand intermediate school leases computers to their teachers. This is one way of providing an incentive to staff. Moffatt (personal communication, 2000) sees the use of laptops by staff as a powerful tool for encouraging their adoption in the classroom. These can be taken home for teachers to carry out their preparation and planning, emailing, Web searching to support units of work, etc. Despite the relatively high number of computers in classrooms, a significant barrier for many schools was lack of finances to make improvements in the provision of ICT. A specific problem cited by several schools was the age of their equipment (ERO, 2000b).

School Organisation. Leadership was identified by Billowes (1999c) as being a critical issue in the process of change. The principal and board of trustees are in a pivotal position. Principals are often seen as too busy with management issues, or may have a lack of interest or vision in ICT. Time is often put forward by busy teachers as a barrier. The move towards integration of ICT across the curriculum is a genuine attempt to circumvent this barrier.

How to break through the barriers?

Policy Guidance. In using ICT in the classroom, the most difficult task is to integrate it into the existing curriculum to improve teaching and learning. Without adequate guidance in planning and resourcing, from the Ministry of Education, the process sometimes can be seen as having to reinvent the wheel.

School Leadership. Schools sometimes can take a significant step in promoting the integration of ICT and thus precipate change through self- review where the impact of ICT on student learning needs are to be investigated.

Teacher as Learner. The teacher needs also to see him/herself as a learner. By placing oneself in this situation, the teacher is not only providing positive modelling to students, but also providing a perspective that they might not otherwise have accepted. It also gives teachers an appreciation of the differing learning needs of their own students. McKenzie (1998) raises an interesting issue, which might be referred to as 'the 4-Cs'. His global experience has revealed that the best adult learning gives high priority to confidence, comfort, calm and competence. He suggests that emotions play a major role in blocking acceptance of ICT. One of the authors of this paper can remember sitting in front of a computer for the first time with a group of knowledgeable colleagues gathered around, feeling terrified and embarrassed, not knowing what to do. Teachers cannot be allowed to feel foolish in front of their colleagues, or further barriers to learning are erected. They will be wondering: when will I become an expert, if ever? A comfortable environment lends itself to better learning experiences.

Barriers as Opportunities. Nick Billowes (personal communication, 2000) suggests that rather than identifying barriers which have negative connotations, teachers can define a constructive process to help the school move off plateaus and towards using ICT effectively.

Peer Support. Short bursts of learning onsite are perfect for busy teachers, as suggests McKenzie (1999). He recommends that trusted colleagues can become in-house technology coaches offering brief lessons in comfortable small group settings. Teachers can be helped a great deal by seeing examples of what other teachers have created and viewing top-quality interactive projects. An example of these would be the WebQuest series which can be found at: http://edweb.sdsu.edu/webquest/webquest.html.

Time Matters. McKenzie (1999) also considers that quality time out of the classroom must be provided for teachers to translate new ideas and strategies into practical classroom lessons and unit plans. He suggests that this should be at least one week a year if the school wishes to see robust integration of ICT into the curriculum.

Developing an ICT Plan for Professional Development

The term 'professional development' can be used to refer to 'any activity that develops an individual's skills, knowledge expertise and other characteristics as a teacher' (ERO, 2000a, p. 3). Butler (1992) suggests that when teachers are involved in professional development they are 'seeking and taking advantage of opportunities to improve their professional skills and increase their effectiveness.' ERO (2000a) accepts that one of the aims of professional development is to 'improve … practice' in order to 'impact on student learning and achievement.' (pp. 2-3) So while professional development is aimed at the teacher, its purpose is to bring about better quality learning for students. It is our belief that ICT can serve as an agent of change in schools and, as a consequence, professional development must be integral to that change.

Go beyond traditional practice

All too often what has been offered as professional development to teachers in the past has been courses on computer skills, e.g. basic word-processing, how to set up a spreadsheets, organising databases, Kid Pix slide shows, designing a Web page, etc. In discussing professional development in ICT, the Education Review Office (2000a) suggests the need for 'not just the acquisition of new skills but a fundamental change in teaching practice and the culture of classrooms' (p. 20). Stratford (2000) relates how many teachers in attending professional development in ICT are mainly developing skills and not learning how to integrate the computer into classroom learning contexts. Lai (1999) also notes that professional development needs to go beyond training in skills. Similarly, Ringstaff, Haymore & Dwyer (1992) acknowledge that to achieve long-lasting change in teacher behaviour in the classroom, there must be a corresponding shift in their beliefs about the purpose and nature of instruction, suggesting that 'these belief systems are remarkably resistant to change' (p. 6). In a similar vein, the US Consortium for Policy Research in Education (CPRE) (Corcoran, 1995b) suggests that much professional development uses 'unfocused, fragmented, low-intensity activities that do not lead to significant changes in teaching practice'. They recommend that a change in mindset is needed if professional development is to be used to initiate change in schools.

As suggested by Little (1994), current 'training' models used for teacher professional development use a 'repertoire of well-defined and skilful classroom practice' that is no longer adequate. McKenzie (1991) maintains that traditional methods for the delivery of professional development (PD) need to be reviewed. He even suggests that 'at worst, staff development is a waste of time and resources' with minimal transfer of skills to the classroom. He submits that one of the reasons for this poor record is 'a lack of understanding of research identifying the elements required to launch a successful program.'

There is no evidence to show that this has not been the case in New Zealand as well. In the past the focus has often been on '"quick fix" strategies [which] have met with limited success' (ERO, 2000a, p. 15). ERO (2000b) supports McKenzie's view in stating that the most difficult component of the Ministry's ICT strategy is the integration of 'ICT into the curriculum and using it to improve learning and teaching.' It is perhaps appropriate to draw on a metaphor from de Bono (1999, cited in Cooper 2000) in considering the flawed logic that what succeeded in the past will succeed in the future.

> The lights keep going out. The engine is faltering. The rudder is unreliable. The first mate is drunk. The crew is very demoralised. The service is appalling. The passengers on the ship are very dissatisfied. Then a new Captain and first mate are brought in by helicopter. Very quickly everything changes. The morale of the crew is lifted. Service improves. The engine is fixed. The lights stay on. Everything is fine. But the ship is still heading in the wrong direction.

If professional development is to be a vehicle for change, the old ways can no longer be put forward as a successful model. It is appropriate to herald a new paradigm which draws upon best practice of past success but is flexible enough to adapt to merging trends brought about through the introduction of ICT in the school environment.

Effective models of professional development

It is acknowledged that the transition from caterpillar to butterfly is not an easy one. In fact CPRE (1995) believes that 'reforming teacher professional development may sound like an impossible task' but agrees that 'engaging all teachers in discussions of good practice and supporting their efforts to learn and to use more effective pedagogy may be the first real step towards higher standards for all children' (p. 1). We endorse the views of Stratford (2000) who argues that best use of ICT will only be achieved through a melding of three ingredients – 'contemporary learning theory, teacher development, and models of institutional change.'

While conceding the lack of impact of many forms of PD in the past, McKenzie (1991) does acknowledge that 'staff development *can* make a powerful difference in performance of both students and teachers'. But for some teachers this is a difficult and daunting prospect. McKenzie (1991) likens the transition from 'transmitters of the old [to] pioneers, inventors and shapers of the new culture' to the metamorphosis of a caterpillar into a butterfly.

Ringstaff *et al.* (1991), through the Apple Classrooms of Tomorrow (ACOT) project, identified an evolutionary process in teachers' beliefs about teaching and thinking in relation to a technology-intensive classroom: Entry, Adoption, Adaptation, Appropriation and Invention. These can be shown graphically on a continuum (see Figure 3). They can also be used to illustrate stages in the acceptance, internalisation and application of elements of professional development. Lai (1999) presents a further model of professional development based on the work of Somekh (1998). This is presented in a manner similar to the ACOT model to enable comparisons to be drawn more easily (see Figure 4).

Entry	Adoption	Adaptation	Appropriation	Invention
Technology is seen as a problem and an inconvenience. i.e. no change in teaching style.	Technology is seen as having some limited utility. There is sometimes a degree of banner mania present at this level.	Technology is embraced and used for traditional instruction. There is a consistent use of technology to do what has always been done – technology at this level is an add-on.	Technology becomes a powerful tool for learning. The teacher asks: What will this powerful tool help us to do? There is powerful use of technology by the student and changes to teaching practice begin.	Teachers at this level allow technology to transform teaching and learning through the development of non-traditional classrooms and a powerful use of technology that is student-centred.

Figure 3: Instructional evolution in technology-intensive classrooms (ACOT in Middleton 2000, p. 14)

Orientation	Preparation	Routine	Refinement	Integration	Creative Integration
The focus in these first three stages is more on the teachers' personal and professional skills using ICT, e.g. specific software			The focus will be more on how ICT can integrated into the existing curriculum well as enhancing it		
Participants seek out information about the innovation	Participants are getting ready to introduce the innovation	First stage when participants have established low-level routine use	Participants seek to refine and improve their use of the innovation	Participants take steps to integrate their use of the innovation fully into their practice	Participants seek more effective ways of using the innovation, going beyond what has been achieved by others

Figure 4: Stages of development in introducing innovation (Lai 1999 p. 16 after Somekh 1998).

The arrows are shown in the above two diagrams as an acknowledgement that just as the implementation of ICT in schools can be thought of as existing along a continuum (ERO, 2000b), so too can professional development. There is no clear-cut boundary between the different stages shown in the above two models.

As well as identifying that professional development is an evolutionary process, the ACOT model also showed that, at each stage, teachers focus on different things, and this leads to the supposition that different types of support are needed to address the various stages, i.e. 'one hat does not fit all'. Clarke (2000) talks about a 'multi-layered support strategy', a term which acknowledges that staff are often at different stages in their development. Somekh's model also confirms that there are stages that teachers need to work through in adopting a new process such as ICT. Lai (1999) confirms that professional development should be aimed at the appropriate stage the teacher is at. He asserts that there is a twofold aim in professional development, to scaffold (strengthen and support), and also to extend. The Ministry of Education (1999) suggests that quality professional development can be achieved when based within the school where staff work together and call upon external providers if necessary. The report states that teachers can no longer operate as though they were in 'private practice'. ERO, in its 1997 ICT review, deplores the concept of reinventing the wheel, and so to use ICT as a vehicle for change we need to build on elements of best practice, for example from the twenty-three lead school project and from other schools that are successfully using ICT in the classroom. Teachers are adults and methods that capitalise on adult learning strategies must be used to maximise the effectiveness of any development programmes.

Thus quality professional development in the information age needs to take into account each of these three features as identified by ERO (2000a). They are research about adult learning; information on principles of effective inservice training; and roles of teachers in the knowledge society.

Key features of good ICT professional development

The following key features of professional development have been extracted from research and examples of best practice (see Figure 5). In extracting these key features, cognisance must be taken of the statement by Heppell (1999, cited in Billowes, 1999d) that 'best practice has been with us for years.' This is not a licence to 'throw out the baby with the bath water' but rather to take that which is good and build upon it.

Vision and Planning. Billowes (2000) advises that a critical issue in successful professional development is the need for quality visioning and careful planning. As national co-ordinator of the ICTPD project, he warns schools that they must look at their core beliefs about learning and teaching and continuously evaluate these as they move through the process. ERO (2000b) also supports the need for 'careful and systematic planning' in order for ICT to be used to support effective teaching and learning in schools. ERO suggests that planning for PD begins at the place where the teacher is in their own learning.

Needs Analysis. Donnelly (1996) notes that professional development needs to be aimed at the 'level of competence [of the individual teacher] and move forward from there.' This is why the needs analysis should be comprehensive, in order to identify exactly where each teacher is at. Following the needs analysis the State of Victoria DEET (2000) suggests teachers set up their personal PD plan which could include goals, professional development strategies, resources, timelines, and evidence of achievement. A completed sample sheet can be seen online <http://www.sofweb.viv.edu.au/pd/pdplan/personal.htm>. could be used quite satisfactorily if ICT is selected as one of the appraisal goals for the year.

Links between Theory and Practice. Relevant theoretical underpinnings are a must. Some teachers felt such references were a waste of time and that the real issue was learning how to use software. This view is not supported but current research on professional development and in fact effective change requires elements of both. McDougall and Squires (1997) point out that any PD that begins to examine theory may require additional readings and suggest that short courses do not really offer the possibility for indepth consideration of relevant issues. They report that as a rule courses that offer opportunity 'for such sustained examination and reflection on the underpinning principles in education are most typically provided for teachers through enrolment in formal courses at places other that the school, typically at post-graduate levels in tertiary institutions' (p. 4). But this is changing. The Auckland Education Advisory Service, for example, has been offering two-term courses in strands of science. They have a built-in theoretical component which then allows practice to be built on supporting theory. Not only does this type of course give teachers the 'what' but also the 'why'. We need to see it being augmented at the school level.

Relevance and Ownership. ERO (2000a) notes that good professional development needs to relate to where a teacher is at in their development (refer to stages of development as proposed by ACOT and Somekh). Reference has been made earlier to the importance of sharing the ICT vision. As teachers participate in the development of the vision, their ownership ensures that they will become more involved in the change process and they will take greater responsibility for their own learning. Cooper

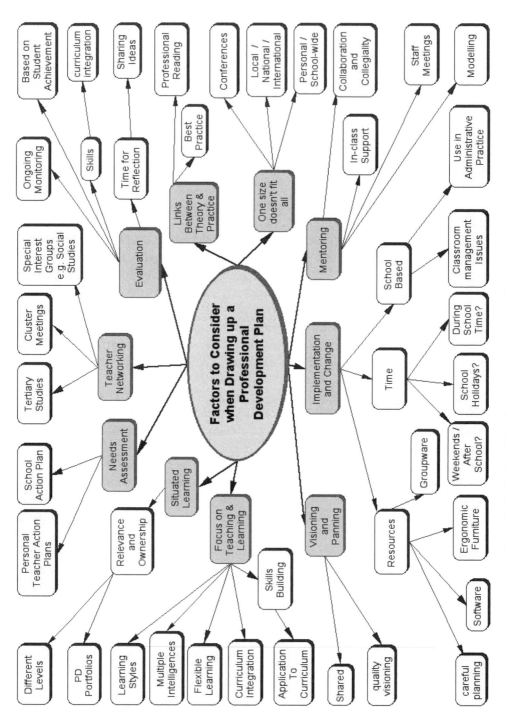

Figure 5: Professional Development summary in graphic form.

The diagram is centered on the node "Factors to Consider when Drawing up a Professional Development Plan" with the following connected elements:

Evaluation
- Based on Student Achievement
- curriculum integration
- Sharing Ideas
- Ongoing Monitoring
- Skills
- Time for Reflection

Links Between Theory & Practice
- Professional Reading
- Best Practice

One size doesn't fit all
- Conferences
- Local / National / International
- Personal / School-wide

Mentoring
- Collaboration and Collegiality
- In-class Support
- Staff Meetings
- Modelling
- School Based
  - Use in Administrative Practice
  - Classroom management Issues

Implementation and Change
- Time
  - During School Time?
  - School Holidays?
  - Weekends / After School?

Teacher Networking
- Special Interest Groups e.g. Social Studies
- Cluster Meetings
- Tertiary Studies

Needs Assessment
- School Action Plan
- Personal Teacher Action Plans

Relevance and Ownership
- Different Levels
- PD Portfolios

Situated Learning

Focus on Teaching & Learning
- Learning Styles
- Multiple Intelligences
- Flexible Learning
- Curriculum Integration
- Application To Curriculum
- Skills Building

Visioning and Planning
- Shared
- quality visioning
- careful planning

Resources
- Groupware
- Ergonomic Furniture
- Software

70 e-Learning

(2000) suggests teachers need to accept more responsibility for their own professional development. He discusses the concept of professional development portfolios as a means of achieving this, especially when they are based on classroom practice. He outlines a six-step process for developing such portfolios based on Gawith's action learning model (Gawith, 1999). He concludes by recognising that if teachers are true to their own beliefs, they should be using themselves what they expect in their students as far as learning goes.

Situated Learning. A good teacher will demand that any form of development relates to them and to their own classroom situation. 'In the case of teachers, the particular characteristics of their students and their school must be considered directly if change is to occur' ERO (2000a, p.16).

Beliefs about Teaching and Learning. ERO (2000b) made a pertinent observation based on reviews of 285 schools in the six months from October 1999 to April 2000. Although high emphasis is being given to planning, infrastructure and PD in ICT, their reviewers had difficulty in seeing any concomitant improvement in teaching and learning. They further suggested that there must be a 'planned match of pedagogy with the identified purpose of ICT activities and learning outcomes.' This can only be achieved if teachers are clear in their understanding of how children learn and the learning process itself. There must be provision for teachers to reflect on and to re–examine their own beliefs about teaching and learning. If the professional development is to initiate change, it must begin here. However, ERO (2000a) notes that this is often 'time consuming and can be threatening.' Teachers have a responsibility to up-skill themselves in the use of ICT. In the UK 'teachers will be expected throughout their careers to continue to improve their skills in using IT for professional purposes and keep up to date with the use of IT in the subjects they teach' (DFE 1995, cited in Reynolds & Dick, 1998). Billowes (2000) advises that this element should be a linchpin in quality PD. He also noted that across the twenty-three lead schools in New Zealand, commonalities have merged in PD being offered. These include 'pedagogical change, focus on learning styles, multiple intelligences, new classroom practice, [and] the concept of flexible learning' (Billowes, 1999a). Reference can also be made to the New Zealand curriculum framework, the essential learning areas and the essential skills.

Implementation and Change. According to ERO (2000a) 'key factors that impact on educational change at the school and community level [include] support from and involvement with colleagues, *sufficient time and resources* allocated at the school level to support change, and leadership issues.' Should courses be offered after school (when teachers are tired); or during the holidays (boards can require staff to come back for professional development)? Other options include purchasing release time using relievers, teacher-only days, and restructuring timetables (maybe not an option in primary schools). It has been shown that geographically *school-based* learning is more effective (Fordyce, 1999 in ERO, 2000a). Gutsky (1995) also talks about the importance of relating professional development and technologies to a particular setting. The implication is that such a programme will be relevant to that organisation.

Clarke's (2000) 'multi-layered support strategy' or McDougall and Squires' (1997) 'eclectic mix' are useful adages when it comes to determining not just the level at which PD needs to be delivered, but also the type of PD available. Will teachers have the opportunity to attend conferences? Will PD be school-based, local, national or international? Can teachers participate in tertiary study? Will PD be online or offline? Will it be compulsory or voluntary or a mix? Where should it occur? McKenzie (1991) reminds us of businesses who hold their training in comfortable conference centres, while teachers are often squashed into classrooms with student-sized desks and chairs after a full day's work. McKenzie also acknowledges that teachers come to PD at different levels, and one way of meeting these needs is to offer a menu of courses that reflect those levels. Other options (McKenzie, 1998) include:

- visits to other schools and IT centres,
- study groups,
- tutorials,
- summer reading, and
- free at-home access to computers and online information.

Just as we cater for differing learning styles in the classroom, there needs to be an acknowledgement of the different learning styles of teachers in professional development. Good PD should reflect the same values that we expect of our teachers in their classroom practice.

Collaboration and collegiality are also key ingredients (Fordyce, 1999). Selby and Ryba (1999) agree that 'the key to success of professional development is that it becomes an empowering collaborative process within the school community.'

Teacher networking (and online communities). One of the main strengths of computers and the Web is the ability to communicate with others in a way that has not been possible before. This has largely been because computers can be networked, ranging from intranets within a single institution to the Internet which is actually a global network. Trewern (1999) acknowledges that such professional networks can create new ways for teachers to work in a professional capacity. They can play a significant role in transforming teaching and learning practices. We see the advantages of such networking, for example, in the professional development courses being offered through the University of Otago School of Education ICT programmes. Tapped In (http://www.tappedin.org) is another prime example of networking where over 8,000 teachers, mainly from the USA but also from around the world, connect together for interactive professional development. This site emulates a real teachers' centre, offering a visual interface as well as text.

Mentoring. Prebble and Stewart (1993) note that teachers do not teach as well as they know how to and that they use only a fraction of the skills they possess. They suggest that rather than being filled with more ideas, 'they need support and guidance of a group of colleagues who know where they are going, and who share some commitment to helping each other get there.' Selby and Ryba (1999) suggest one 'promising approach' to the integration of ICT across the New Zealand curriculum is through the process of mentoring. They define a mentor as a person 'who assists staff to self-assess their skills and performances and to identify their future goals, formulate action plans, implement and evaluate these'. A strength of mentoring is that it involves a change in the school culture in such a way as to 'capitalise upon the skills and experiences of staff'. This comment by Selby and Ryba (1999) endorses our initial premise that ICT can be used as an agent of change.

Evaluation

Although PD is aimed at the teacher, according to Billowes (1999a) it needs to be monitored and evaluated in terms of the effect it has on teaching and learning and the way it enhances outcomes for students. This reinforces several of the key elements identified above, e.g. beliefs about teaching and learning, and links between theory and practice.

There is also a responsibility to share successful ideas with the profession and students. The strength of networking lends itself to this application. Billowes (1999a) notes that a significant effort is being made in the lead school project to doing exactly this so that schools can build on the successes of others.

McDougall and Squires' (1994, 1997) 'Perspective Interaction Paradigm' was developed for the evaluation of ICT-related educational activities. It involved taking a situated approach, which is based on authenticity, and therefore had credence for the practising teacher. The authors believe this allows it to be applied as a 'useful framework for evaluative thinking in the teacher professional development context.' Davis (1997) has enlarged on their paradigm and proposes that it would be an excellent tool for the evaluation of any professional development. The foci for evaluation should be:

- skills with particular application;
- integration into existing curricula;
- related changes in the curricula;
- changes in the teacher role;
- changes in the manager role;
- underpinning theories of education;
- evaluation of development and this framework.

McDougall and Squires (1997) give an example of an analysis on a PD programme in terms of their paradigm. As well as considering the above seven foci, they use three perspective interactions – teacher-designer; teacher-student; and student-designer – so that the programme is continually being related back to the classroom to ensure authenticity. Schools could take this and apply it to their own PD programme.

Jamie McKenzie (1999) suggests we will know we have made significant progress when the characteristics noted in Table 2 are abundantly evident:

Table 2: Characteristics of Progress

Invention	Much of the school programme is dedicated to problem-solving, decision-making, exploration and the creation of new ideas.
Fluency	Teachers move back and forth between an array of instructional roles and strategies. *'Sometimes they are the sage on the stage. Other times they are the guide on the side.'*
Support	The school provides ongoing support for all learners to develop thinking and information skills. These opportunities are rich, frequent and embedded in the daily life of the school.
Navigation, searching and	Learners find their way with boolean logic; search with appropriate syntax and know how to separate the reliable from the unreliable source. They recognise propaganda, bias and distortion.
Questioning	Learners know how and when to employ dozens of different types of questions.
Planning	Learners are acquiring planning and organisational skills.
Interpretation and deep thinking	Learners process information – translate, infer and apply what they have gathered to the issue at hand.
Commitment	All curriculum documents include clear statements regarding the information literacy expectations that are appropriate for each level.

Conclusion

Whether from the Ministry of Education, the Education Review Office, prospective suppliers of ICT, or from parents concerned to have their children become part of the digital age, there is a growing desire to have schools incorporate ICT into their learning programmes. In an effort to plan for this development, schools have chosen, or been required, to develop ICT plans. For many, this plan has focused largely on the technology – what needs to be bought, when and how. In this chapter we have documented the steps that a school should consider when embarking on this journey, and included a discussion of the issues that will ensure schools reach the ultimate goal – of incorporating ICT into learning programmes for the betterment of teaching and learning.

References

Bennis, W. & Biederman, P.W. (1997). *Organizing genius: The secret of creative collaboration*. Reading, Mass: Addison Wesley.

Billowes, N. (08/10/2000). Pers. comm.

Billowes, N.R. (2000). *ICT/PD 23 Lead Schools Project interim observations*. Wellington: Ministry of Education.

Billowes, N. (1999a). *23 ICT/PD schools lead the way*. Report: 02/09/1999. Available at: <http://www.tki.org.nz/ICT/curriculum/initiatives01_e.php>.

Billowes, N. (1999c). *National conference*. Report: 02/12/1999. Available at: <http://www.tki.org.nz/ IT/curriculum/initiatives01_e.php>.

Billowes, N. (1999d). *Y2K–wise teaching and learning*. Report: 16/12/1999. Available at: <http:// www.tki.org.nz/IT/curriculum/initiatives04_e.php>.

Billowes, N. (2000a). *Quality staff development?* Report: 10/07/2000. Available at: <http:// www.tki.org.nz/IT/curriculum/initiative_e.php>.

Brown, M. & Ryba, K. (1996). The information superhighway: A teacher's guide to the Internet. In K.W. Lai (Ed*.). Words have wings: Teaching and learning with computer networks*. Dunedin: University of Otago Press.

Butler, J.A. (1992). *Staff development, school improvement research series close-up #1* Available at: <http://www.nwrel.org/scpd/sirs/6/cu12.html>.

Clarke, R. (2000). IT and learning: the professional development journey. *Good Teacher*. Term 3 2000. Available at: <http://www.theschoolquarterly.com/good_teacher/gt_00_t3/5_prentice_clarke.htm>.

Cooper, A. (2000). Easy peasy PD portfolios. *Good Teacher*, Term 3 2000. Available at: <http:// www.theschoolquarterly.com/good_teacher/gt_00_t3/4_alan_cooper.htm>.

Corcoran, T.B. (1995a). *Helping teachers teach well: transforming professional development*. June 1995. Available at: <http://www.ed.gov/pubs/CPRE/t61/index.html#1>.

Corcoran, T.B. (1995b). *Helping teachers teach well: transforming professional development Conclusion: Going to Scale*. June 1995. Available at: <http://www.ed.gov/pubs/CPRE/t61/t61e.html>.

CPRE (Consortium for Policy Research in Education) (1995). *CPRE policy brief: Helping teachers teach well: Transforming professional development – June 1995 Conclusion: Going to Scale*. Available at: <http://www.ed.gov/pubs/CPRE/t61/t61e.html>.

Donnelly, J. (1996). *IT and Schools*. Kingston-upon-Thames: Croner Publications Ltd.

ERO (October 1997) *The Use of Information Technology in Schools*. Education Review Office Publication. Available at: <http://www.ero.govt.nz/Publications/eers1997/itsch.htm>.

ERO (2000a). *Inservice Training for teachers in New Zealand schools*. Number 1, Autumn 2000, Education Evaluation Reports.

ERO (2000b). *The implementation of information and communications technologies (IT) in New Zealand schools* (June 2000). Available at: <http://www.ero.govt.nz/Publications/pubs2000/ implementationIT.htm>.

Fordyce S. (1999). The significance of social support on school-based inservice transfer of training in New Zealand. Unpublished M.Ed thesis cited in ERO (2000). *Inservice Training for teachers in New Zealand schools*. Number 1, Autumn 2000, Education Evaluation Reports.

Gawith, Gwen (1999). Thinking in New Zealand schools: graphic metacognition. *Good Teacher*. Auckland: Metacog Limited.

Gusky, T.R. (1995). In search of the optimal mix. In T.R. Gusky & M._Huberman (Eds), *Professional development in education: New paradigms and practices* (pp. 114-131). New York: Teachers College Press. Cited from *IFETS Discussion Digest* 49, 6 October 2000.

Lai, K.W. (1999). Teaching, learning and professional development: the teacher matters most, in K.W. Lai (Ed.) *Net-working teaching, learning and professional development with the internet*. Dunedin: University of Otago Press.

Little, J.L. (1994). *Teachers' professional development in a climate of educational reform systemic reform: Perspectives on personalising education – September 1994*. Available at: <http://www.ed.gov/pubs/ EdReformStudies/SysReforms/little1.html>.

McDougall, A. & Squires, D. (1997). A framework for reviewing teacher professional development programmes in information technology. *Journal of Information Technology for Teacher Education*, 6(2). Available at: <http://www.triangle.co.uk/jit/pdf/06-2-am.pdf>.

McKenzie, J. (1991). Designing staff development for the information age. *FNO*, 1(4)

McKenzie, J. (1999). *How teachers learn technology best*. Washington, USA: From Now On Press.

McKenzie, J. (1998). Secrets of success: professional development that works. *eSchool News March 1998*. Available at: <http://staffdevelop.org/secrets.html>.

Ministry of Education. (1989). *Teach Learning Strategies*. Wellington: Ministry of Education.

Ministry of Education (1999). *Report of the length of the school day and the school year (The Austin Report)*. Wellington: Ministry of Education.

Murray, D. & Campbell, N. (2000). Barriers to implementing IT in some New Zealand schools. *Computers in New Zealand Schools*. 12(1), 3-6.

Papert, S. (1980). *Mindstorms: Children, computers and powerful ideas*. New York: Basic Books.

Prebble, T. & Stewart, D. (1993). *School development – strategies for effective management*. Palmerston North: Dunmore Press.

Ringstaff, C., Haymore, J. & Dwyer, D.C. (1992). *Trading places: When teachers utilise student expertise in technology-insensitive classrooms*. ACOT.

Selby, L. & Ryba, K. (1999). Mentoring: A model for information technology professional development (ITPD) in schools. *Computers in New Zealand Schools*, 11(1), 11-14.

State of Victoria Dept of Education, Employment and Training (DEET) (2000). *Personal PD planning for learning technologies*. Available at: <http://www.sofweb.viv.edu.au/pd/pdplan/personal.htm>.

Stewart, D. & Prebble, T. (1993). *The reflective principal*. ERDC Press.

Stratford, R., (2000). Professional development and the barriers to successful IT integration in classrooms and schools. *Computers in New Zealand Schools*, 12(1), 7-12, 19.

The World Wide Web: Educational Resources for Teachers and Students

5

Ann Trewern

> Students conditioned by the dynamic imagery of communication media, particularly television and digital games expect to learn in an environment that takes advantage of visual and auditory stimulation and interaction. (WBEC Report, 2001, p. 85)

As public interest in the Internet continues to grow, there is an increasing expectation that it will be used in schools and growing pressure on teachers to integrate appropriate Internet resources into classroom programmes (Laferrière *et al.*, 1999, McKenzie, 1998) in exciting and creative ways. While the Internet offers opportunities to expand teachers' access to resources, the effective integration of Internet information resources and online interaction and collaboration with others in ways that provide dynamic and worthwhile learning opportunities for students can be challenging for teachers.

There is evidence that the implementation of information and communications technologies is not happening in a widespread way in the average classroom (Cuban 1999; MacKenzie 1998). The information and interactive aspects of the Internet are not that easy to use in current school settings. There are classroom management issues for teachers in allowing their students access to the Internet, especially where there may be only one connection in a classroom or in a school. There are instructional issues for teachers in encouraging effective student use of the Internet. It can be difficult to find content that fits closely with curriculum objectives (Gray, 1997). It can also be difficult to locate quality resources that are relevant, and are child-centred with suitably graded reading levels for younger students.

Teachers essentially have two driving needs for locating good Internet resources – the primary need is to expand their resource base for classroom use and a secondary need is to grow professionally. The Internet can be a very effective medium for meeting both needs. The purpose of this chapter is to provide a starter kit, an aid to those teachers who are newly connected and who are trying to develop some familiarity with the huge range of educational resources that are available through this medium. This chapter is filled with examples of different types of resources that can be used to support teachers professionally and in the classroom. Web addresses or URLs are provided with brief evaluative comment about selected sites and examples of some of the exciting and practicable ways these resources can be effectively used in the classroom to support student learning are also provided.

Resources to Support Teachers Professionally
Background information for teachers
Teachers are often on the lookout for materials that will support them in advancing their knowledge of curriculum delivery methods, pedagogy, classroom management, assessment practices and many other areas that will support everyday practice as well

The World Wide Web: Educational Resources for Teachers and Students 77 as understanding the theories that underpin that practice. The Internet can be a goldmine for teachers looking for research resources whether they be academic articles that are made freely available by many online journals or accessible by subscription, educational comment in national and international education periodicals and newspapers such as *Education Week,* or the nationwide *New Zealand Infotech Weekly* publication, or research reports published by central educational agencies such as the Education Review Office.

Many educational research journals now provide online materials designed to support teachers' professional background needs, creating new opportunities for teachers to keep abreast of recent developments and educational research. Some of these online journals are listed in Table 1.

Table 1: Examples of international journals to support teachers

Phi Delta Kappan	http://www.pdkintl.org/kappan/kappan.htm	A good teacher publication that is not solely about technology. Some articles are readily available, others are for those who subscribe to the magazine.
Educational Leadership	http://www.ascd.org/readingroom/edlead/0005/frame0005el.html	A limited number of articles are published online from each volume, but there are some good ideas that are available and the online version is worth a look.
Educational Researcher (AERA)	http://www.aera.net/pubs/er/	Full text articles from leading researchers in a variety of educational fields are available to read online or to download in pdf file format since the beginning of 2000.
Electronic Policy Analysis Archives	http://epaa.asu.edu	EPAA has published original scholarly articles since 1993. It is an excellent source about issues in education in the United States, and has grown recently to include internationally related educational issues.
Triangle Journals	http://www.triangle.co.uk/	A range of good articles are provided in full text online from a number of journals that include (a) *Contemporary Issues in Early Childhood,* (b) *Teacher Development,* (c) *Journal of Information Technology for Teacher Education* and many others.

Some specific teacher journals and magazines are also available online. Some worthwhile journals and magazines are listed in Table 2.

Table 2: Examples of teacher journals and magazines to support classroom practice

Learning and Leading with Technology	http://www.iste.org/L&L/index.html	This is an excellent publication for teachers interested in using technology in the classroom. Not all articles are available to non-members but some are and it is worth a look.
From Now On	http://www.fno.org/	This collection of articles and news-letters about the use of information technology and need for information literacy in the classroom is by Jamie McKenzie.
ASCD	http://www.ascd.org	The Association for Supervision and Curriculum Development (ASCD) online website provides access to professional articles (some of which are online, and resources for teachers.
Good Teacher	http://www.theschoolquarterly.com/	Good articles published in *Good Teacher* are archived online. Articles are of general interest with an emphasis on information literacy and lots of recom-mended links for New Zealand teachers.
Starters and Strategies (Teaching Online)	http://www.teachingonline.org/lessons.html	Many of those successful lesson ideas you have used from *Starters and Strategies* are available for this Web page online.

Many educational periodicals and newspapers designed to inform teachers about national policy issues and current international, national and local educational issues are listed in Table 3.

Table 3: Examples of online educational periodicals and newspapers for New Zealand teachers

Infotech Weekly	http://www.stuff.co.nz/inl/ index/0,1008, 0a28,FF.html	Weekly newspaper with technology information published for New Zealand readers. Some useful material for teachers is published regularly.
TheSchoolDaily .com	http://www.theschooldaily.com/	An online newspaper that keeps up with the news on a daily basis. There are lots of articles for teachers, parents and others interested in education.
Education Week	http://www.educationworld. com/a_news/	Although this is an international publication there are some good articles available here that would be of interest to New Zealand teachers.
The New Zealand Education Gazette	http://www.edgazette.govt.nz/	All articles in the print publication that goes out to New Zealand schools are available online.

Providing research reports and other research information online is increasingly common. Many research institutes now provide summaries and presentations of data collected for public use. There are a number of research organisations both in New Zealand and overseas which provide reports of educational research online. Examples of New Zealand-based research resources that would be of interest to teachers are listed in Table 4 with some interesting overseas research organisations listed at the end of Table 4. Good research resources are normally located in various university websites, journal publishing organisations and under the body of work of individual people. However, there are some useful collections that are worth browsing.

Table 4: A sample of research and educational report sites

Education Review Office (ERO)	http://ero.govt.nz/Publications/index.htm	ERO produces Evaluation Reports on topical educational issues. These are based on the information gathered through reviews of individual schools and early childhood centres.
Te Kete Ipurangi	http://www.tki.org.nz/e/community/	There are links from this page to a variety of useful background information and articles relating to curriculum integration, assessment, NCEA and other areas of interest to teachers.
National Monitoring Unit	http://nemp.otago.ac.nz/welcomFr.htm	Reports and some exemplars used can be found at: http://nemp.otago.ac.nz/reportMe.htm It is really worth teachers having a browse here. Keep a watch for the latest reports for Art, Graphs, Tables and Maps and Science for 1999. The hard copy versions have just been published and distributed so the Web pages should not be too far behind.
Royal Society of New Zealand	http://www.rsnz.govt.nz	Material of interest to science and technology teachers is available here.
New Zealand Council for Educational Research	http://www.nzcer.org.nz/	The purpose of NZCER is to support educators through quality research, resources, and information. There are a number of books, journals, and research reports available online.
New Zealand Principals Federation	http://www.nzpf.ac.nz/	Some good articles available from this website for all educators whether a principal or not.
The Educational Resources Information Center (ERIC) Clearinghouses	http://www.accesseric.org/sites/barak.html	A wide range of ERIC clearinghouses for research information are listed here. Whole clearinghouses exist for assessment and education, urban and rural education, science and mathematics and many more. Many of the articles are online and are presented as full-text versions, as Web pages or downloadable as pdf files.

Table 4 continued

Milken Exchange	http://www.mff.org/edtech/	This link takes you straight to the Milken Exchange section that provides information on educational technology. The exchange is involved in publishing research and reports of research into educational technology and these are available online.
Office of Technology Assessment USA	http://www.wws.princeton. edu/~ota/ns20/alpha_f.html	Some of the articles in this archive are beginning to be older now as this office was closed in 1995. However there is still some very worthwhile material stored here.
British Columbia Education	http://www.bced.gov.bc.ca/irp/	Some good assessment material and other useful information is available at this website. The integrated resource packages http://www.bced.gov. bc.ca/irp/irp.htm are well worth a look.

Table 5: A sample of online catalogues and bibliographic databases

ERIC database	http://www.accesseric.org/ searchdb/searchdb.html	This freely available database contains more than one million abstracts of documents and articles in the field of education. Articles are submitted from around the world. Articles can usually be easily obtained by the Interloan system that operates through your University or College of Education library.
New Zealand University, other tertiary institutions and public libraries online	http://www.library.otago.ac.nz/I nternet/catalogues.html	Most New Zealand university library catalogues are now available on the Web and you are able to search the collections. There are also a number of colleges for education and public libraries with online catalogues available. This website provides an extensive list.
Amazon Book Store and Barnes and Noble	http://www.amazon.com http://www.bn.com/	Both organisations provide an extensive database of books and other resources currently available for purchase. Search tools allow for searching by subject and author. Both organisations provide for a second-hand trade in some sought-after books as well.

Increasingly library catalogues and other bibliographic databases are becoming available through the Internet. Bibliographic databases such as ERIC and INNZ provide lists of published material with supporting abstracts which can be obtained from local libraries for those enrolled for study at a tertiary institution. Many city council public libraries also have Internet access to catalogues available. Check with your local library. Table 5 lists some useful bibliographic databases of different types.

Central education authorities now commonly sponsor official collection sites for teacher support material. The New Zealand Ministry of Education is providing a leading support service for New Zealand teachers with the *Te Kete Ipurangi* (TKI) website <http://www.tki.org.nz> and associated satellite websites. A number of other international education authorities such as the United States Department of Education and in Australia the Victorian and New South Wales Departments of Education are providing some excellent educational support and resource sites. Examples of central government educational support websites are listed in Table 6.

Table 6: Administrative, curriculum and classroom management resources

Te Kete Ipurangi (TKI)	http://www.tki.org.nz/	Provision of resources to support governance and school management, curriculum content and delivery and classroom support in non-curriculum areas is provided. Administrative resources are available in the governance community area of the website.
Learning Media	http://www.learningmedia. co.nz/index.html	Provides a range of links to interesting resources for teachers. Updates to the CD-ROM version of the 'School Journal catalogue' are available and so are several learning modules called Immigration and Publishing a School Journal.
Sofweb	http://www.sofweb.vic.edu.au/ LEADERS/index.htm	A variety of resources are provided for a number of school leadership and management areas of interest. This website is managed by the Victorian state government of Australia. The website contains a considerable amount of background material that would be of interest to New Zealand teachers.
EDNA	http://www.edna.edu.au/EdNA	EDNA is an umbrella website that links various educational websites throughout Australia. There is some interesting background material listed here for teachers.

Internet resources for preparation of lessons and curriculum units

Websites providing lesson plans abound on the World Wide Web. Many sites ask teachers to provide lesson plans and often offer small rewards to encourage teachers to submit good lessons. Some international lesson plan websites are listed in Table 7. Provision of lesson plans for particular curriculum areas and achievement levels is a common feature of centralised education authority resource sites. The New Zealand Ministry of Education *Te Kete Ipurangi* (TKI) website <http://www.tki.org.nz> is a leading support site for lesson plans for New Zealand teachers. These curriculum sites are listed in Table 8.

Table 7: Online collections of lesson plans

AskERIC lesson plans	http://www.askeric.org/ Virtual/Lessons/	The AskERIC Lesson Plan Collection contains more than 1,100 unique lesson plans which hve been written and submitted to AskERIC by teachers. Plans can be browsed under subject headings or a search function can assist to find quite specific lessons.
Explorer	http://explorer.scrtec org.explorer/	Large numbers of lesson plans are available here that could be very useful to New Zealand mathematics and science teachers. Many of the resources require Adobe Acrobat.
Blue Web'n	http://www.kn.pcacbell.com/ wired/blue/webn/	There are a wide range of lessons here from all curriculum areas that can be browsed by content, subject area, or by grade level.
Graphing Calculator Activities	http://www.ti.com/calc/docs/ activities/html	This is a collection of ready-to-use lessons from the Texas Instruments (TI) calculator support site for the family of TI products from the TI 15 through the TI 82/83 Graphing Calculators and the CBL/CBL2. Activities are easily organised by class level and topic, and a search engine function is also included.
Encarta schoolhouse	http://encarta.msn.com/ schoolhouse/default.asp	A large number of good online lesson plans that support the encyclopaedic Encarta CD-ROM. Lesson plans are available for all curriculum areas.

Table 8: Online units and lesson plans for New Zealand teachers

NZMaths	http://www.nzmaths.co.nz/	This website provides units of work for the various strands of mathematics in the New Zealand Curriculum from level 1–4.
English Online	http://www.english.unitecnology.ac.nz/	English units written by New Zealand teachers are provided for Year 1–13. A range of other activities and projects are also available here.
Sunshine Online	http://www.sunshine.co.nz/	A not-to-be-missed site for the junior reading teacher that has a particular section of the website specifically for New Zealand children, parents and teachers. Lesson plans and online activities are available.
Social Studies Online	http://socialstudies.unitecnology.ac.nz/	The Web address given here will not remain the same and during 2001 will become part of the social science community on TKI. There are some excellent New Zealand based social studies units available here.
@ScienceSchool.NZ	http://www.science.school.nz/	Groups of lessons are provided for levels 1–4 and for three of the major strands of the New Zealand science curriculum. These include, Making Sense of the Material World, Making Sense of the Physical World, Planet Earth and Beyond.
The New Zealand Learning Network (NZLNet)	http://education.otago.ac.nz/NZLNet/Resources/lessonplans.html	A number of lesson plans and curriculum units utilising Internet resources have been written and developed by New Zealand primary and secondary teachers in a variety of curriculum areas as part of postgraduate course work by teachers.

There are many websites that provide extensive, well-designed educational resources and these frequently include specific units of work for teachers. A number of traditional educational providers are involved in the development of these resources and include such groups as museums, publishers of commercial educational materials, city and regional councils, and other organisations and institutions. Many science museums, for example, have received funding to specifically develop Web resources for educational use and a list has been published previously (Trewern, 1999a), or is available online at <http://education.otago.ac.nz/NZLNet/science/ science_museums.html>. Examples of some of the organisations providing units of work for teachers and their classes are available in Table 9.

Table 9: Examples of collections of quality online curriculum units

NASA		
Examples of some of the excellent educational sites available through the NASA network are listed below:		
Science@NASA presents Thursday's classroom	http://www.thursdaysclassroom.com/	The aim of Thursday's Classroom is to provide a lasting connection between NASA's latest research and the class-room environment. There are some fun activities for children that link night sky events such as lunar eclipses to the interests of children.
Imagine the universe	http://imagine.gsfc.nasa.gov/docs/teachers/lesson_plans.html	Lesson plans in science and mathe-matics for secondary level (age 14+).
Spacelink online educational activities	http://spacelink.nasa.gov/Instructional.Materials/Online.Educational.Activities/	Using these Online Educational Activities, students can explore NASA through guided research, building models, planning space food menus, or tracking a hurricane through the Caribbean. The activities are ready for use in the classroom or computer lab and require minimal teacher prep time.
StarChild- A learning centre for young Astronomers	http://starchild.gsfc.nasa.gov/docs/StarChild/StarChild.html	Some excellent units of work available at this website.
How things fly	http://www.aero.hq.nasa.gov/edu/	Online tutorial or unit of work on understanding flight for junior primary students.
National Geographic Kids @national geographic.com	http://www.nationalgeographic.com/kids/	These are delightfully designed websites that are packed with information and activities for children. Two examples are: **Tower of London – A Haunted House** http://www.nationalgeographic.com/world/0101/tower/index.html **Ghosts in the Castle** http://www.nationalgeographic.com/castles/enter.html

Table 9 continued

National Geographic.com	http://www.nationalgeographic.com/	**Ice Treasures of the Inca** http://www.nationalgeographic.com/features/96/mummy/ **Kaikoura** http://www.nationalgeographic.com/kaikoura/index.html There are many more interesting interactive articles in the features section as well as maps, photographs and educational aspects.
Public Broadcasting Service (PBS)	http://www.pbs.org/teachersource/	There are hundreds of high quality lesson plans listed under various subject headings. Two excellent examples are:
(a) PBS History	http://www.pbs.org/neighborhoods/history/	There are many examples of excellent resources like those selected for listing here. **Conquistadors** http://www.pbs.org/opb/conquistadores/ **Napoleon** http://www.pbs.org/empires/napoleon/flash/flash_intro.html or http://www.pbs.org/empires/napoleon/home.html
(b) Nova Online	http://www.pbs.org/wgbh/nova/onlinelibrary.html	**The Vikings** http://www.pbs.org/wgbh/nova/vikings/village.html. This site includes quick time video sequences.
ThinkQuest library	http://www.thinkquest.org/library/search.html	The ThinkQuest Library of Entries is the collection of educational websites designed by participants in the ThinkQuest Contests. Teachers and learners can explore many topics of excellent quality by browsing or searching the library.

Internet resources for preparation of teaching and learning resources

Access to Internet resources for the purpose of preparing teaching resources such as worksheets and overhead transparencies is one way of developing classroom materials.

Many sites produce student worksheets as part of the teacher resources. Some are provided as pdf files which keeps the formatting of the document intact when it is downloaded.

If you have access to a colour printer, picture resources can be used in a variety of interesting ways to support the curriculum. The ability to produce many paper copies of images means they can be used for group discussion or manipulative activities and games. The ability to download copies of images means they can be incorporated into children's project presentations, such as word-processed documents, Powerpoint presentations, and Hyper-studio presentations. The NASA websites, for example, produce some wonderful images and information relating to planet earth and beyond that can be very successfully used in the classroom from year one and upwards.

Some sites are now providing access to making individualised puzzles such as *Puzzlemaker* at Discovery Channel <http://puzzlemaker.school.discovery.com/>. Table 10 is a list ofwebsites containing ready-made resources for students.

Table 10: Ideal sites for preparation of teaching resources

Puzzlemaker at Discovery Channel	http://puzzlemaker.school. discovery.com/	Puzzlemaker is a puzzle generation tool for teachers, students and parents. Create and print customised word search, crossword and math puzzles using your word lists. A great website to develop extra puzzle activities for early finishers or even to have students develop puzzles for their classmates.
English Basics – free worksheets from RHL School	http://www.rhl2school.com/ english.htm	A site that provides printable worksheets that deal with a range of grammar activities from parts of speech to kinds of sentences to antonyms, synonyms and homonyms may be useful for work cards for early finishers, general work cards and homework activities. Also reading comprehension activities and reference skills worksheets available at this site. A great site for freely available and downloadable worksheets.
Earth Observatory	http://earthobservatory.nasa.gov/	An interesting website from NASA that uses information gathered from various 'above Earth atmosphere' satellites to image the Earth's changing weather, atmosphere, land and sea conditions. Useful to include images and information in teaching presentations, for assessments or tests, or student worksheets.
Nineplanets	http://www.seds.org/nineplanets/ nineplanets/nineplanets.html	There is a great collection of space images available from this site that can be down-loaded, printed and used for games and classroom activities. Also lots of useful information. Still one of the best sites available for primary children.
NZHistory.Net	http://www.nzhistory.net.nz/ GalleryFrameset.html	Online exhibitions of New Zealand history are available here that include biographies, military history, politics and government, and social history.
Timeframes	http://timeframes1.natlib.govt.nz/	This wonderful image collection is 'a treasure' for social studies teachers.

Internet resources for professional communication

Electronic professional interactive networks (PINs) are a growing feature of the Internet and are a product of increasing use of groupware software that allows people to maintain discussions on the Web for a period of time. These are networks designed to meet the professional learning needs of teachers, using the Internet to improve work-related knowledge and skills. The unique feature of these networks is their intention to provide a form of professional development allowing opportunities for teachers who are geographically dispersed to get together to discuss aspects of teaching with colleagues. These networks achieve this in a number of ways such as archiving good links to other websites, providing an educational news service, providing research reports, lesson plans and giving professionals a range of ways to contact other professionals. Many of these networks are worth spending some time exploring (Trewern, 1999b). Table 11 provides a list of professional interactive websites.

Table 11: Websites focusing on professional development

Tapped In	http://www.tappedin.org/	The purposes of this network are to provide teachers with communication tools for social exchanges. Real time text communication is a feature of the network. The network reception desk is manned from 9 am–6 pm. The synchronous or real time environment is achieved by use of a Multi-user virtual environment (MUVE) or MOO. This is an interesting model of online teacher support.
Oz teachernet	http://rite.ed.qut.edu.au/oz-teachernet/	This is a general purpose service network providing teachers with online support for using the Internet in the curriculum and for professional development. It is supported by the Queensland University of Technology and provides information resources and publications relevant to curriculum, project archives, email lists for teachers, education departments and teacher professional associations.
Access Excellence	http://www.gene.com/ae	This is a special-interest network for biology and biotechnology teachers that has been supported by Genentech, a pharmaceutical company. The network provides lots of interactive features such as discussion boards for biology teachers and teacher mentoring features, interactive activities and fact-sheet information.

Table 11 continued

Sofweb	http://www.sofweb.vic.edu.au/	This is an example of an extensive and well-organised network developed and maintained by the Victorian Department of Education in Australia. This is intended as a one-stop shop for Victorian teachers providing a wide range of archived information resources for teachers and classroom use as well as some excellent communication opportunities.

Other excellent ways to find colleagues to contact are through discussion lists. Finding worthwhile discussion lists is not always easy. Table 12 lists some catalogue sites for discussion lists. Often websites provide a discussion list option which allows interested individuals to join through the website.

Table 12: Sources for discussion lists

Tilenet	http://tile.net/lists/	This catalogue site provides a search tool as well as categories of mailing lists to browse.
Catalist	http://www.lsoft.com/lists/ listref.html	There is a search tool available at the second level as well as a directory function where you can choose to search by size of membership, host country.
Liszt, The Mailing List Directory	http://www.liszt.com/	Another combined mailing lists cata-logue site providing a search function as well as an extensive directory function.

Many producers of education resources offer a newsletter service notifying registered users of changes, updates and new resources. If a resource looks interesting it may be worth subscribing via the email newsletter. This is usually free and involves submitting your name and email address via an online registration form. For example, teachers can submit a request to receive the monthly *New Zealand Learning Network Newsletter* 'Teach-IT' that provides good links to online resources as well as advising of online projects and activities at <http://education.otago.ac.nz/NZLNet/ Register/ Reg.html>.

Classroom Resources to Support Student Learning
Online exhibitions
The range of websites available for exploration and enjoyment that can be utilised in the classroom is extensive. Examples of exploratory sites include geographical explorations, online exhibitions, explorations through particular environments, or

explorations of particular events or times past. Some of the best of these are produced by such publishing companies as National Geographic, television programme producers such as Discovery Channel, and PBS, museums and education faculties, among many others, and may not have specific educational support materials available. Some of the websites listed in Table 13 are superb.

Table 13: Examples of some well developed exploration websites to support student learning

Coast	http://www.coast-nopp.org/	This is an example of an exploration through an ocean environment and is a beautifully designed website using visualisation techniques. The topic is oceanography and content is suitable for Year 7 upwards. Lessons and resources for students and teachers involve being able to interact with various ocean species, visualise coastal and undersea terrain, investigate navigation, and more. This site does require Internet version 4 browser capability and a special plug-in for VRML viewing called Cosmo Player. However obtaining and installing the player is straightforward and well worth it.
Discovering Lewis and Clark	http://www.lewis-clark.org/	This online exhibition covers the historic journey across the USA that led eventually to the westward population expansion. This beautifully designed website includes examples of original journal entries, as well as photographs, maps, movies, and sound to bring this historic journey to life.
Salem Witchcraft Hysteria	http://www.nationalgeographic.com/features/97/salem/index.html	This is an excellent production of the National Geographic online team that would be a worthwhile resource for senior secondary history teachers. This is an extremely well developed interactive presentation that would generate a high level of discussion at the senior secondary level as it looks at these events from a number of different perspectives. A well-crafted example of an exploration of a theme relating to a particular event in times past.
Solemates: The Century in Shoes	http://www.centuryinshoes.com/	This site presents shoes as fashion statements and cultural icons through the 20th century. This site utilises Quick-Time, Flash and Javascript™ technology.

Table 13 continued

In the Footsteps of Alexander the Great	http://www.pbs.org/mpt /alexander/	This is the website to accompany the television programme of the same name. There is a teachers' guide with this wonderful online exhibition at http:// www.pbs.org/mpt/alexander/guide/ index.html

Interactive games

With the recent development of virtual reality software such as Shockwave™, VRML, Quicktime™, Flash™ and others, there are increasing opportunities for students to interact with visual and text information resources while they are online. Resources utilising these softwares can range from problem-solving activities, manipulative activities, tutorials, simulations and games. These activities can be motivating for learners in the way they can capture students' attention and encourage them to feel they are in control of their learning. However, they can also require considerable computer power and bandwidth capability and can be slow to download and frustrating to use where Internet connections are slower. These activities usually require students to be online in order to complete the activity.

Problem-solving activities

Problem-solving activity structures are beginning to be found on the Internet. Sherman (1988) defined problem-solving activities as those that created a context for the problem, and provided a sequence of activities that involved some form of cognitive activity to find a solution. Examples of good problem-solving resources that would be useful in the classroom are listed in Table 14.

Table 14: Examples of interactive online problem-solving resources

Math Never Dies	http://library.thinkquest.org/17932/	This Think Quest simulation has a problem-solving orientation that encourages participants to save the world or at least New York from villainy. The time-honoured game introduction is as follows 'You have infiltrated the secure site of the Hex Agency. Your mission, if you choose to accept it, is to track down international criminals using your Math skills'. Great for upper primary and lower secondary students and covers algebra, geometry and trigonometry. Various modules provide additional information to assist 'agents' with both the maths required and the game.
Carmen Sandiego's Great Chase through Time	http://www.carmensandiego.com/products/time/time1.html	Student research information for this website is provided by *Britannica Online* and the website has been developed by The Learning Company – educational software publishers. There are 18 cases beginning with Case 1: Queen Hatshepsut in Egypt in 1490 BC (her Book of the Dead has been stolen) and Case 2: Caesar in Rome in 50 BC (The Forum is stolen) to Case 10: Columbus in 1493 (who has a problem with stolen charts), right through to Case 18: Yuri Gagarin and the Space Race 1961 (it seems Yuri's right to be first has been stolen!). Lots of great information here. Highly recommended for middle and upper primary classes for use in English or Social Studies areas.
Ace on the Case: Secrets @ Sea	http://www.secretsatsea.org/	This interactive online mystery game explores an ocean theme. It is hosted by the Vancouver Aquarium and is free for classroom or individual use.
Access Excellence – River of Venom	http://www.accessexcellence.com/rov/	This is a problem-solving activity to test students' scientific sleuthing. See also: **The Blackout Syndrome** http://www.accessexcellence.com/tbs/ **Arctica** http://www.accessexcellence.com/arc/

Drill and practice activities

These activities provide exercises where students repetitively work an item to practise and gain confidence with successfully completing the activity. Basic drill and practice activities, such as timed flash card activities using multiplication tables, or manipulating letters and sounds, are quite common on the Internet, especially in maths and English-based word and spelling exercises. Students generally receive feedback on their level of correctness in the activity, most commonly a fairly simple 'OK' or 'try again' text message. Students are often free to decide what level of activity they wish to embark on, with many sites providing junior and senior levels of access. Some examples of drill and practice activities that would be useful in the classroom are listed in Table 15.

Table 15: Examples of drill and practice websites

Astronomy puzzles for children	http://linux.rsp.lv/astro/puzzles/index.html	This is an interactive website requiring children to guess the name of the constellation pictured from a multi-choice list. Some of these are northern hemisphere constellations that New Zealand children will not see but the information is testing and quite fun for those interested. The users can choose three levels of difficulty for guessing the name of constellations from astronomical outlines and three levels of difficulty for naming bright stars in particular constellations or groups of constellations. Lots of uses for the images in making up your own educational games for children.
Funbrain.com	http://www.funbrain.com/kidscenter.html	This website provides a series of inter-active games especially for primary-level students that includes maths and word games, and games relating to culture, universe and other topics. Game titles include 'Paint By Idioms', 'Grammar Gorillas', 'Spelleroo',' Fresh Baked Fractions' and so on. There is also an option for students to make up their own games and to print them out.
Quai! Mathematics Games	http://www.quia.com/dir/math/	This site provides online interactive drill and practice games – Flashcards, Match-ing Games and Concentration practice activities from simple addition to more complex fraction to decimal equivalents. A good resource for primary students.
Funbrain.com The piano player	http://www.funbrain.com/notes/index.html	Activities relating to learning to play a keyboard for primary level students. There are various levels of difficulty. From beginner to virtuoso.

Tutorials

Online tutorials offer information in an instructional sequence in much the same ways as a classroom teacher would deliver instruction on the topic (Roblyer & Edwards 2000). The information is usually complete enough to stand on its own so that the student does not need to refer to other materials for support. There are many online tutorials available. Some can be used by the students as a learning sequence that will substitute for teacher explanation. A good example is *Kids Click* <http://www.world ofsearching.org/ >, a site that assists children through the process of deciding on an Internet search and then developing a systematic process for carrying it out. The *Kids Click* website and others such as the *Physics 2000* < http://www.Colorado.EDU/ physics/2000/index.pl > may be able to be used by teachers using a data projector as part of the teaching sequence as well as for independent student use. Examples of tutorial-type websites that would be useful in the classroom are listed in Table 16.

Table 16: Examples of tutorial websites

Kids Click	http://www.worldofsearching.org/	This tutorial encourages children to think carefully about the type of research they are trying to undertake when using the WWW for information searches.
Physics 2000	http://www.Colorado.EDU/ physics/2000/index.pl	An excellent example of a tutorial website for secondary physics students that incorporates many interactive elements into the design. The website aims to make physics more accessible to students and people of all ages and to counter its current negative image.
Mathematical Ideas in Science	http://www.7stones.com/ Homepage/Publisher/Tut02.html	This is an online tutorial which uses flash technology to convey information about a vast array of mathematical and physical principles for secondary students. Topics include vectors, and linear geometry, wave motion, relativity, astronomy that includes ideas about the expanding universe and the Doppler shift. This is an interesting site for physics teachers.
Electronic Music Interactive	http://nmc.uoregon.edu/emi/ emi.html	Electronic Music Interactive is a multi-media tutorial for electronic music that prepares students for more advanced study (needs Shockwave™).
Frog Dissection	http://curry.edschool.virginia. edu/go/frog/menu.html	The purpose of this lab activity is to help students learn the anatomy of a frog and provide a better understanding of the anatomy of vertebrate animals in general. This program provides both still and motion visuals of frogs, in addition to text.

Table 16 continued

Cow's Eye Dissection – Exploratorium	http://www.exploratorium.edu/ learning_studio/cow_eye/	A step-by-step tutorial about the dissection of a cow's eye with images and text explanations of parts.
From the think quest library comes the Online Cat Dissection	http://library.thinkquest.org/ 15401/learn.html	Here students can 'virtually' dissect a cat, view labelled diagrams, or even see live dissections to expand their knowledge of cat anatomy.

Simulations

Simulations are models of real systems or imaginative situations designed to teach how a system works (Roblyer & Edwards, 2000). Simulations on the World Wide Web are still in their infancy. Because of the huge information and feedback requirements of simulations and the quite restricted bandwidth capability of the Internet, these simulations tend to be relatively simply constructed compared to many simulations found in CD-ROM presentations. This is, however, an area where real growth and change can be expected to occur over the next few years. The examples of online simulations presented in Table 17 represent a range of different types of simulations that could be incorporated into class work.

Table 17: Examples of online simulations

Escape from Knab	http://www.escapefromknab.com/	This is an online situational simulation that encourages participants to take a one-way trip to the Planet Knab but they have to pay for the return trip – costing $10,000. Participants need to earn the cash to come home and in the process are required to choose a job, save their monthly earnings, and complete tax forms to keep everything above-board for the planet Knabian IRD. This is a great activity for learning about finances and money management, writing cheques, transferring money from savings and cheque accounts, paying Knabian tax on purchases and so on. Recommended as an activity that will appeal to upper primary and lower secondary students.

Table 17 continued

Absurd Math	http://www.hrmvideo.com/abmath/	Four interactive adventures are provided. Each simulation has a mathematical objective and a game objective and both objectives need to be accomplished in order for participants to progress further into the game. Game participants are asked to identify flesh-eating bacteria, capture dissolving solvent and challenge the Powers 2B, all with the help of problem-solving skills and the agents from the 'Society of the Half-Closed Eye' Teacher lesson plans in support of the online missions help make Absurd Math a great resource. The activities for these problem-solving simulations come from a computer gaming tradition and will be appealing to the upper primary and lower secondary age group.
Interkinetic haunted house	http://www.interkinetic.com/haunted/	Interkinetic Haunted House requires Shockwave™ and the Flash™ plug-in to run the animations, great graphics and spooky sounds, and therefore good bandwidth capability. The simulation takes the form of an interactive journey of exploration. Some really interesting written work could arise out of this presentation, especially for Years 3 to 6+ students, and could include group development of pick-a-path stories around the house, developing class audio narratives to go with the presentation. This website would be useful to incorporate into English curriculum activities relating to writing and viewing and presenting.

Publishing school and student materials

A number of websites encourage the presentation and publication of student work. Publishing students' work online can motivate students to lift their level of presentation. When students write for publication they often care more about their final presentations and are willing to spend more time working on them. McCullen (1999a) suggests that computer-supported publishing projects, ranging from multimedia reports to Web 'zines, are some of the best ways to get teachers and their classes enthusiastic about reading, writing and technology. Examples of children's published work and Web 'zines are listed in Table 18.

Use of programs like Hyperstudio™, Powerpoint™ and Kai's Powershow™ are becoming common classroom activities and much of this software now includes html converters that allow teachers to put student work on the school internal network or intranet. There are some examples of student work published online that has resulted from material developed from several collaborative projects offered through the New Zealand Learning Network. One example of student online presentations is images submitted by students taking part in the *Christmas Packaging* Project in term four 2000. These are available at <http://education.otago.ac.nz/NZLNet/xmas_project/solutions.html>.

Sunshine Online provides an option in the project activity centre where students can access a template which works in conjunction with the user's *Powerpoint™* application and guides students through the development of a project on penguins using the Web. This can be found in the creative production section <http://www.sunshine.co.nz/nz/kia/creative/penguin2.html>.

Table 18: Examples of websites that publish student work

English online – Writers Window Homepage	http://www.english.unitecnology.ac.nz/writers/home.html	There are opportunities to write stories and poems, research topics and write reviews and have them published online. The best of these are online at http://www.english.unitecnology.ac.nz/writers/showcase_stories.html Students can add to a continuous story or read a completed collaborative story at http://www.english.unitecnology.ac.nz/writers/continu.html
Midlink Magazine	http://www.cs.ucf.edu/~MidLink/	Midlink is a Digital Magazine published for Kids, by Kids. There is a range of organised projects and submissions from students. To submit materials to Midlink have a look at http://www.ncsu.edu/midlink/call2000.html where the submission topics are available. The Web'zine is published quarterly.
Kidlink	http://www.kidlink.org/	Kidlink is a multinational website that publishes children's art and written work.

Communication resources and collaborative projects

The Internet is an ideal way of making email contacts with geographically distant students. Often referred to as keypals, this form of communication is the modern version of penpals and usually comprises student-to-student communication, although it can also be group-to-group. Good keypal exchanges can be hard to sustain long term, but where these work they can be extremely worthwhile. There are a number of websites that provide opportunities for teachers around the globe to make contact and establish student-to-student and class-to-class links. Examples are listed in Table 19.

Table 19: Finding people for Communication Links

CWA Education Web	http://www.cwa.co.nz/eduweb/edu/email.html	An extensive list of New Zealand schools' email addresses is available here.
Web 66	http://web66.coled.umn.edu/	This is an international directory of schools with email addresses.
The Penpal Box	http://www.ksconnection.org:80 /penpal/penpal.html	A site that offers opportunities for class connections as well as for individuals with listings in age groupings. If your children are looking for US pen pals then there are plenty here to choose from.
ePALS Classroom Exchange projects	http://www.epals.com/esearch/	A searchable database of registered participants interested in email contacts.

Interactive projects are another way of establishing class-to-class contact with a purpose. Many such project sites available on the World Wide Web offer a range of different types of curriculum projects. In an excellent online publication called Virtual Architectural at <http://ccwf.cc.utexas.edu/~jbharris/Virtual-Architecture/> Harris (2000) describes three general types of collaborative projects that are available:

(a) Interpersonal exchanges are activities in which students communicate electronically with other individuals, individuals communicate with groups or groups communicate with other groups. Interpersonal Exchanges include: keypals, global classrooms, electronic appearances, telementoring, question-and-answer activities, and impersonations.

(b) Information collection activities are those which involve students collecting, compiling, and comparing different types of interesting information. Projects include: information exchanges, database creation, electronic publishing, tele-field trips, and collaboratively gathered data analysis.

(c) Problem-solving activities generally promote critical thinking, collaboration, and problem-based learning. Examples of problem-solving projects: information searches, peer feedback activities, parallel problem-solving, sequential problem-solving, telepresent problem-solving, simulations, and social action projects.

Table 20 lists some of the websites that offer online, interactive, collaborative projects for teachers.

Table 20: Websites that provide links to or offer their own curriculum-based interactive projects

Houghton Mifflin Education Centre – Projects	http://www.eduplace.com/ projects/index.html	Large number of listings of tele-communications projects for teachers and their classes of all kinds and types.
Kidlink	http://www.kidlink.org/ KIDPROJ/projects.html	Kidlink is a grassroots organisation aimed at getting youth from age 10 to 15 involved in a GLOBAL dialogue and works through a system of mailing lists. The network offers some very good projects.
The Global Schoolhouse is now a part of Lightspan.com	http://www.lightspan.com/ teacher/pages/projects/default. asp?_prod=LS&_nav=T2_proj	Lightspan.com provides access to collaborative projects, discussions including classroom conferencing, mailing lists, discussion boards and professional development activities. The Global Schoolhouse is where teachers can search an index of over 500 projects by grade level, date, curriculum area, technology used, and complexity of project. Global SchoolNet calls this 'the one central place on the Internet where you can find projects from across the globe to bring into the classroom.'
Intercultural Email Classroom	Connections http://www.iecc.org/	In operation since 1992, the IECC has distributed over 19,000 requests for email partnerships. There are more than 7,300 teachers in approximately 73 countries participating in IECC lists.
Electronic Elementary	http://www.inform.umd.edu/ EdRes/Topic/Education/K-12/ MDK12_Stuff/homepers/emag/	This sites offers and provides links to Internet projects, activities, and creations of elementary students around the world.
New Zealand Learning Network	http://www.education.otago. ac.nz/nzlnet/home.nclk	Past and current projects are available for viewing. See Chapter 3 for more details about the projects offered specifically for New Zealand teachers through this network.
English Online	http://www.english. unitechnology.ac.nz	Some good projects for New Zealand teachers with an interest in English. See 'Book backchat', 'What's Hot', and Writer's Window for examples of ongoing projects.

Stepping beyond using the Internet for student information searches

The mechanics of integrating Internet information resources effectively into teaching and learning is one that many teachers can find frustrating. An important aspect of integrating the Internet effectively into the curriculum requires teachers to have access to successful strategies and structured curriculum units that successfully engage students in meaningful and purposeful enquiry (McKenzie, 1998). There are many examples of both simple activity structures and more complex enquiry-based research structures available on the Internet that teachers can use. One site worth a visit is the *Filamentality* website at <http://www.kn.pacbell.com/wired/fil/formats.html#Hotlist> where a number of examples of supportive classroom learning activities are provided with examples. These structured activities range from simple activities for those teachers who may be less confident Internet users to quite complex structures. They are all activities that

> … require higher level thinking, problem solving and fresh thought. They also provide plenty of scaffolding – supportive structures that help guarantee that student time will be spent productively. There will be little wandering about or 'surfing.' Teachers can rest assured that students will be challenged and motivated. They will be directed toward reliable and developmentally appropriate Web resources. (McKenzie 1998).

Table 21 provides examples of websites that contain some good activity structures for teachers to use or adapt as they need and to encourage use of the Internet for student learning.

Table 21: Examples of websites with good activity structures for classroom Web use

Filamentality	http://www.kn.pacbell.com/ wired/fil/formats.html	*Filamentality* is an interactive website for teachers that guides the user through the process of picking a topic, searching the Web, gathering good Internet sites, and turning Web resources into learning activities. There are also links to some good examples of different activity structures for using the Internet in the classroom that encourage enquiry learning.
Teaching history with technology	http://www.caryacademy. pvt.k12.nc.us/historytech/	This online journal is designed to help intermediate and high school social studies and history teachers.
ICT teaching ideas for primary teachers	http://teachingideas.co.uk/ ict/contents.htm	This includes ideas to set up within your own class and with other classes that include sending email pictures, talking books, electronic comics, shared writing and lots of others.

Table 21 continued

The Webquest Page	http://edweb.sdsu.edu/ webquest/webquest.html	This site developed by Bernie Dodge provides a great deal of information about Webquests and there are many examples for all levels of the school that are also categorised into subject areas.
Spartanburg District 3 County Schools – using scavenger hunts	http://www.spa3.k12.sc.us/ Scavenger.html	This site has been set up by the Spartan- burgh school district (US) to explain how to use the Web in various ways. This set of pages introduces teachers to templates for scavenger hunts, as well as examples and why they can be a useful strategy for Web use in the classroom.

Strategies for using the Internet in the classroom

The following section includes some simple ideas for teachers who are relatively new to Web use in the classroom; they are particularly useful where there is limited class access to computers.

Hotlists

Creating a hotlist is a way of collecting together a variety of particularly useful resources for students. This can be a timesaving strategy that also serves to keep student searches on track when there is limited class time for searching. Hotlists can be provided for your students in the form of a printed worksheet, as a Web page left on the school intranet or as a word-processed file on the classroom computer hard drive, for students to access sites directly from the links created.

A number of teacher-based websites regularly provide hotlists of topical sites for teachers. The New Zealand Learning Network <http://education.otago.ac.nz /NZLNet/ home.nclk> provides hotlists of topics both from the homepage and through the regular monthly TEACH-IT email newsletter. *Te Kete Ipurangi* <http://www.tki.org.nz/> also provides regular hotlists in the 'Hot Topics' section of the website, and through the *New Zealand Education Gazette Web Guide*. It is worthwhile checking out recommended sites and adding any potentially useful ones to the class hotlist.

A multimedia scrapbook

Multimedia scrapbooks can be created by the students once some searching has been carried out and some good material found. Students can download text headings, photographs, maps, sound clips, video clips and clip art, or copy and paste interesting text pieces or quotations into a word-processor, desktop publishing package, *Hyperstudio*™s presentation, slide show, or Web page. Scrapbooks can be kept for a short-term project and relate to a specific topic being studied or can be kept by students over time as an eclectic record of their own particular interests. This can also be an interesting way of keeping a current events scrapbook, portfolio or diary of world, national, local or personal events of interest to an individual child. It can also be used as a weekly reading group activity. Students should be encouraged to acknowledge the sources of their quoted material. For an example of quite a structured approach to students' developing a multimedia scrapbook, see 'Democracy Online in America Today' <http://www.kn.pacbell.com/wired/democracy/scrapbook.html>. This example provides some good ideas that can be adapted and used for different classroom situations.

Treasure hunts, scavenger hunts and activity trails

Hunts and trails are for those teachers who feel they are more 'web-savvy'. Web pages essential to a specific topic are gathered and a question or questions are posed for each Web page. Students need to be given direct access to the page to search for the answers, rather than be given the homepage of a huge website, which would mean they need to search through the whole website for the answer/s. Carefully constructed treasure hunts or activity trails can extend students' thinking, especially if they include good searching questions and an overarching final question where students need to synthesise the information they have gathered and so develop a broader understanding of the bigger picture. A good example of an Internet Treasure Hunt is *The Treasures of China* available at <http://www.kn.pacbell.com/wired/fil/treaschina.html>. Quite a range of treasure/scavenger hunts and activity trails already exist on the Web. Some of these require online responses and others do not. Teachers might like to try several of those listed in Table 22 before developing their own.

Table 22: Examples of Internet treasure hunts, scavenger hunts and activity trails

Museum Mania	http://www.museummania.com/treasure.htm	There is a series of quite general treasure hunts available here that are interactive, in that participants can select answers and receive feedback on their answers.
History Mystery Game (scholastic)	http://teacher.scholastic.com/histmyst/index.asp	The treasure hunts listed here have been developed by Scholastic. Some are specifically for students in the US but those under the following headings are recommended. Have a look at the list under the headings of Exploration, Inventions and Technology, World Civilisations.

Table 22 continued

Advent Calendar Activity Trail (NZLNet)	http://education.otago.ac.nz/ NZLNet/advent/advent.html	This Internet activity trail covers a different theme relating to Christmas for each of the 24 days of Advent. Themes cover Christmas icons from holly and bells to Father Christmas and The Nativity. The trail provides links to many Internet sites providing information about Christmas traditions, interactive puzzles, stories, worksheets, listening to songs, jokes, recipes and works of art and is designed to be a fun activity for the last days of the school year.
The Great New Zealand Scavenger Hunt	http://www.teachingonline.org/ Scavenger.html	Quizzes and questions about New Zealand with lots of links provided for you to find the answers.

Subject samplers

Students are presented with a small range of interesting specific topic websites. Each site needs to offer students something interesting to do, read or see. Students are asked about their perspectives on topics, to compare experiences read about with personal experiences, provide interpretations of images, artworks and so on. Subject samplers are ideal when a teacher is wanting students to feel 'connected' to a topic and to deepen understanding of curricular content (*Filamentality*, 1997). An example of a subject sampler is *My China* available at <http://www.kn.pacbell.com/wired/ China/sampler.html>.

Webquests

Webquests are enquiry-based activities that generally provide a scenario, challenging task or problem for students to solve using listed or linked Web resources and an opportunity to organise the information gathered to produce some form of presentation. Most suitable topics for this type of activity are those that provide opportunities for varying perspectives to be investigated. Although Webquests are usually highly structured, these are also open-ended activities that promote higher-level thinking, problem-solving and fresh thought. Webquests are a popular form of information collection inquiry activity on the Web and can now be found for younger as well as older students and in a variety of topics that can range from lunar Webquests to investigating volcanoes, and can range from simple short-term study projects to lengthy in-depth themes. Some examples of actual Webquests are listed in Table 23.

Table 23: Some examples of Webquests

Who are the Heroes? WebQuest	http://powayusd.sdcoe.k12.ca.us/ dhogan/heroes/herohome	This Webquest explores the topic of heroes – both ancient and modern day heroes and heroines. Team members gather information and then nominate a hero who has made significant contributions to humanity, either publishing information about the hero of their choice or designing a suitable monument or commemorative object in their honour.
New Moon! Why Did You Leave So Soon? Moon Webquest	http://schools.wcpss.net/ Root/moonwebquest.html	This Webquest explores the phases of the moon and allows younger students (Year 4) to explore and learn about the changes that occur in the moon's shape each month.
Ancient Egypt Webquest	http://www.iwebquest.com/ egypt/ancientegypt.html	A Webquest about ancient Egypt in which students undertake various missions and learn about daily life, mummies, hieroglyphics, King Tutankhamen, games, and archaeology. Students are set a task in which they must locate the burial mask of the ancient Egyptian Pharaoh, Tutankhamen. On the inside of the mask is written a message that, if successfully decoded, could solve our earth's environmental crisis. Your quest is to decode the ancient Egyptian message and return to our time.
A Genealogy Quest	http://www.ultranet.com/ ~olmckey/quest.html	A Webquest that allows students to explore the processes involved in building and developing a family tree.
Eruption Update	http://education.otago.ac.nz/ NZLNet/lesson-plans/Roddy/ Main.html	Although not listed as a Webquest, this teaching unit essentially fits the criteria for a Webquest and is a very good example of a Webquest that utilises Internet information for New Zealand students. This unit was designed for use in a Year 10 class. See a similar unit 'Eye on Earthquakes: A news team report' from *The Encarta Schoolhouse* at http://encarta.msn.com/schoolhouse/ default.asp.

Conclusion

The range of resources available on the Internet that can be used in the classroom continues to grow. Many of these resources are fun and are of exceptionally high quality. This chapter is designed to whet the appetite of the classroom teacher with the exciting range of resources available and the unlimited possibilities that the World Wide Web has to offer both at the classroom level and as background material for the professional educator. As more and more funding is poured into supporting information and communication technology in schools and as more evidence becomes available that our students are highly motivated to learn through this medium, it behoves us as teachers to harness this resource creatively and effectively. Teachers are and will remain 'critical filters' through which learning opportunities are realised for students. The need to design learning environments, teaching resources and learning strategies that will make the most effective use of these opportunities is important.

Note: All sites mentioned in this chapter were checked and found to be available at the time of writing. However, the World Wide Web is a dynamic resource and sites can be subject to change for a variety of reasons. If a link does not work, try typing the name of the site into the search engine of your choice.

References

Collis, B. (1996). Tele-learning in the K-12 classroom: The teacher's view. *Tele-learning in a digital world: The future of distance learning.* International Thomson Computer Press.

Cuban, L. (1999). *Why are most teachers infrequent and restrained users of computers?* Keynote for 5th Annual Public Education Conference. The British Columbia Teachers' Federation. Available at: <http://www.bctf.bc.ca/parents/PublicEdConf /report99/appendix1.html>.

Filamentality website <http://www.kn.pacbell.com/wired/fil/formats.html#Hotlist>.

Gray, T., (1997). Does virtual teacher support yield real benefits? In B.Collis & G. Knezek (Eds) *Teaching and learning in the digital age: research into practice with telecommunications in educational settings.* The Texas Center for Educational Technology and International Society for Technology in Education, pp. 69-85.

Harris, J. (2000). Virtual Architecture's Web home. Available at: <http://ccwf.cc.utexas.edu/~jbharris/ Virtual-Architecture>.

Laferrière, T., Breuleux, A., Baker, P. & Fitzsimons, R. (1999). *Inservice teachers professional development models in the use of information and communications technologies.* A report to the SchoolNet National Advisory Board. Available at: <http://www.tact.fse.ulaval.ca/ang/html/pmodels.html>.

McCullen, C. (March 1999). *Author! Author!* Available at: <http://www.sasinschool.com/resource/pages/ techlearn_author.shtml>.

McCullen, C. (November/December, 1999*). Midlink Magazine: The Quintessential Collaborative.* Available at: <http://www.infotoday.com/MMSchools/nov99/mccullen.htm>.

MacKenzie, J. (September 1998). Grazing the Net: Raising a Generation of Free Range Students. *Phi Delta Kappan.* Available at: <http://www.fno.org/text/grazing.html>.

Pea, R. (2000). *Pros and cons of technology in the classroom.* Available at: <http://www.tappedin.org/ info/teachers/debate.html>.

Roblyer and Edwards. (2000). *Integrating educational technology into teaching.* New Jersey: Prentice-Hall.

Sherman, T. (1998). A brief view of developments in problem solving. *Computers in the Schools* 4, (3-4), 171-178.

Trewern, A. (1999a). Using Internet resources in the classroom. In K.W. Lai (Ed*.). Net-working: teaching,* *learning and professional development with the Internet,* pp. 57-106. Dunedin: University of Otago Press.

Trewern, A. (1999b). Online professional interactive networks: Virtual professional learning communities for teachers. In K.W. Lai (Ed.*). Net-working: teaching, learning and professional development with the Internet.* Dunedin: University of Otago Press.

Warner, M. (2000). *ICT teaching ideas for primary teachers* [online]. Available at: <http://teachingideas.co.uk/ict/contents.htm>.

WBEC (Web-based Education Commission). (2001). *The Power of the Internet for Learning: Moving from Promise to Practice* [online]. Available at: <http://www.ed.gov/offices%20/AC/WBEC/FinalReport/WBECReport.pdf>.

Development and Evaluation of Websites: A Case Study

6

Stephen Hovell, Sharon Nicholson, Stephen Fletcher

Almost every school in New Zealand is connected to the Internet, which is increasingly used to support student learning. Also more schools are now developing their own websites. Whether the aim is to use the Internet to access or to publish information, there are guidelines both for evaluating the quality of any site and guiding the designer in producing a site. The classroom teacher needs to carefully examine what is chosen as well as how it is to be used. This chapter looks at the effectiveness of Web-based materials from both a user's and an author's perspective. It looks at the material itself and the pedagogical beliefs underlying its method of use. Factors that would facilitate purposeful and active engagement by learners is also considered. As an example, reference is made to the development of the science website Landforms (http://www.crosswinds.net/~taumarunui/landforms/) which supports the Planet Earth and Beyond section of the New Zealand Science curriculum (see Figure 1).

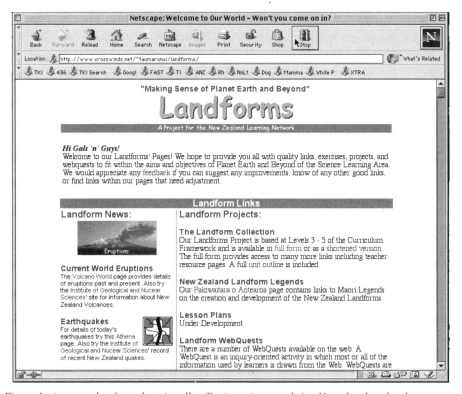

Figure 1: An example of an educationally effective science website. Note the clear level statements

The Internet and Science Education
Information from the Internet
The task of locating suitable information is not easy and is compounded by the need to authenticate material obtained. Generally, reputable sites from recognised sources (such as museums, or large research organisations such as NASA) contain sound content, and are stable in terms of availability over repeated visits. However, sites still need to go down for maintenance and upgrading. When more than one suitable site is available, their inclusion may assist to minimise the inconvenience associated with down-time and encourage students to actively seek information.

Pedagogy and the Internet
Information and communication technology (ICT) as a medium of instruction can be used to support a variety of teaching approaches, but '... technology, in and of itself, contains neither pedagogical nor content bias.' (Zhao and Campbell, 1995). The 'effectiveness with which ICT is used as an instructional tool ... relates to the educational objective in which it will be used' and should be 'congruent with one's beliefs about how people learn.' (Dufresne *et al.*, 1996).

Teachers are more likely to implement those activities and learning styles which relate more closely to their own philosophies. Thus, not only do they need assistance with the technology itself, but with understanding their own teaching styles and those that enhance the inherent characteristics of this medium. Professional development and continuing internal support is therefore required to aid teachers in implementing new technology-reliant approaches effectively (Bowman, 1997; Dufresne *et al.*, 1996; Zhao and Campbell, 1996).

Behavioural perspective
Traditional learning theories are readily supported through the use of ICT. For example, elements of programmed learning and positive reinforcement are evident in a variety of programs and sites (Palumbo, 1995). Elements of surprise and reward add variety to a site and would be described by behaviourists as positive reinforcement. An example of this would be the clapping sound clip we have included on our Landforms picture when students discover the cave (see Figure 2).

However, mastery of information and 'extrinsic rewards' do not necessarily promote understanding. For durability and retention, information needs to make sense to the learner. Mestre (1998) reinforces this by explaining that if new information 'conflicts with knowledge already possessed ... then the individual either will not be able to accommodate in memory the process learned in any meaningful sense or will construct parallel, conflicting knowledge structures.' Of concern is the regularity with which Dufresne *et al.* (1996) note the inadequacy of existing knowledge structures, and the failure of traditional teaching practices to address and correct these misconceptions. Also, Mestre (1998) asserts that the cognitive mechanism by which individuals learn is also neglected by the behavioural approach.

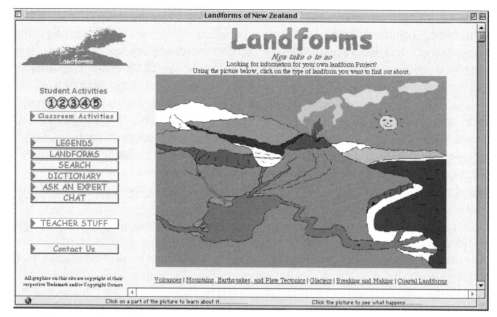

Figure 2: The Landform Locator uses elements of surprise. The small cave on the picture contains a hidden link to a Treasure Cave page with a cheering sound

Cognitive perspective

Examples of activities that emphasise the cognitive elements of learning are also found on the Internet. Wordfinds and questions (both appearing on the Landforms site) serve as examples by which information is processed and applied. However, reprocessing of isolated chunks of information does little to address misconceptions or flawed assumptions that students might have relating to large concepts, or underlying assumptions of knowledge and understanding. As such, they do provide some benefit, in that they offer the opportunity for students to work with the language of the topic but do little to address the more global aspects.

Constructivist perspective

The potential for the Internet to assist learning needs to be examined within the context of the present views of learning.

'Traditional methods for teaching science courses ... employ a lecture format of instruction in which the majority of students are passively listening to the instructor ... and jotting down notes' (Dufresne *et al.*, 1996). This view assumes that learners have the ability to passively absorb and understand material being presented (Mestre, 1998). But to understand information, the learner is required to be actively involved in information processing.

March (1999) acknowledges that hands-on, problem-solving activities are in short supply on the web. Landforms is an attempt to draw on information from an extensive range of sources to provide such activities. March sees 'creating activities [as] a main strategy for classroom teachers to integrate the Web with their students' learning' (p. 4).

Zhao & Campbell (1995) suggest that many teachers agree with a more interactive view of learning, an approach that has been identified by Palumbo (1995) as more time-consuming. To further compound the time perspective, Mestre (1998) identifies that many teachers 'feel under pressure to cover an ever-increasing amount of material.' It is suggested therefore, that there may be an over-reliance on the 'chalk-and-talk' technique, as a familiar and convenient method to transmit a large factual component of work.

The National Science Education Standards (NRC) have identified learning science as an 'active process' (Snyder, 1997) involving activities such as enquiry, reflection, interpretation, modelling and guided practice. Through this process, students 'construct meaning via cognitive experiences and activities focused on meaningful acquisition' (Fletcher *et al.*, 1999, p. 9). Meaningful and individual construction of knowledge 'stands in stark contrast to the view of learning in which individuals passively receive well organised knowledge' (Dufresne *et al.*, 1996, p. 2).

A constructivist view of education is 'fairly recent' (Isernhagen 1999), as is the implementation of ICT as a means of instruction. Yet, effective application of ICT has the potential to address concerns relating to the constructivist view of education. ICT may be used to facilitate a 'co-operative group-based learning style which is well-suited to the characteristics of the Internet' (Zhao and Campbell, 1995). It also has the potential to assist students with the ability to access and process vast resources of information (Palumbo, 1995; Snyder, 1997).

Interactive classrooms
Teacher
To apply the technology effectively, teachers need to have a working knowledge of 'instructional strategies for promoting and monitoring students' conceptual understanding' (Mestre, 1998, p.8). For teachers to 'become effective facilitators of active student learning' (Bowmann, 1997) a change in role is required from 'Sage on the Stage' to that of 'Guide on the Side' (OTA, 1995). These interactive approaches encourage students to become more actively involved in constructing and using knowledge (Dufresne *et al.*, 1996; Fletcher *et al.*, 1999).

Technology
Resources must be considered and should be chosen to emphasise and enhance conceptual knowledge rather than facts. The view of learning as a process of enquiry can be supported by the teacher asking (but not answering) questions organised under a few powerful principles (Mestre, 1998). Information presented in a non-linear fashion also facilitates an enquiry-based process and allows students to explore information to meet their own requirements. There is still a place for facts in science and these can be addressed through the careful use of questioning by the teacher and searching websites by students.

In an effort to address the requirements for factual information, and to facilitate enquiry, we have presented a range of questions on our Landforms site. Questions are organised under different headings or concepts. But often a choice of hyperlinks is provided, and students (either individually, or in groups) can present a range of suitable answers (see Figure 3).

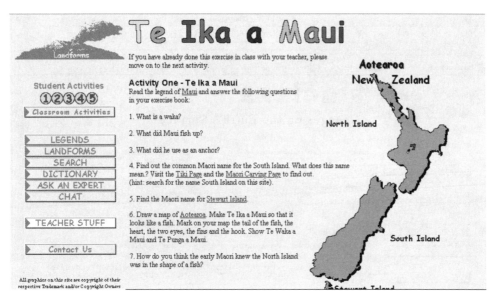

Figure 3: A range of questions along with a choice of hyperlinks facilitates enquiry

Practical

Fletcher *et al.* (1999) emphasise the value of true concrete learning experiences over that of simulated experiments found on the Internet. A concern relating to the value of real science practicals is raised by Isernhagen (1999) who identifies poor teacher training and confidence as a major barrier to implementing enquiry-based experimentation in the classroom. We believe that the Internet may also provide an avenue for addressing this concern, albeit at an introductory level.

Practical activities can be found on the Internet and we have identified and applied some to our Landforms site. We have chosen practicals that we believe support an inquiry-based approach as the emphasis lies in the process rather than a 'right' answer. We have also included objectives and explanations which we hope would provide an uninitiated teacher some support and background (see Figure 4).

The cookbook approach to experimentation overlooks the need for meaningful engagement to help facilitate knowledge construction. Nor can it identify and address misconceptions and mistaken beliefs held by students (Palumbo, 1995). But, at the other extreme, pure discovery learning, which leaves students to explore and experiment, is identified by both Palumbo (1995) and Dufresne (1996) as time-consuming and we believe is not always desirable within the constraints of the school syllabus. In between the two, Palumbo (1995) identifies discovery learning with some extrinsic intervention to help students reach reasonable conclusions. This has the potential to help students to re-evaluate and restructure misconceptions, with the teacher in a guiding and facilitating role. (Dufresne *et al.*, 1996; Mestre, 1998). With this in mind, we have selected practicals for our Landforms site that aim at including true discovery elements, within our ultimate objective of examining the formation of landforms.

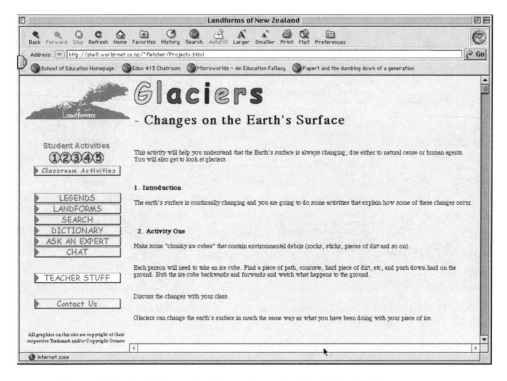

Glaciers
– Changes on the Earth's Surface

Landforms

Student Activities
① ② ③ ④ ⑤
▶ Classroom Activities

▶ LEGENDS
▶ LANDFORMS
▶ SEARCH
▶ DICTIONARY
▶ ASK AN EXPERT
▶ CHAT

▶ TEACHER STUFF

▶ Contact Us

All graphics on this site are copyright of their respective Trademark and/or Copyright Owners

This activity will help you understand that the Earth's surface is always changing, due either to natural cause or human agents. You will also get to look at glaciers.

1. Introduction

The earth's surface is continually changing and you are going to do some activities that explain how some of these changes occur.

2. Activity One

Make some "chunky ice cubes" that contain environmental debris (rocks, sticks, pieces of dirt and so on).

Each person will need to take an ice cube. Find a piece of path, concrete, hard piece of dirt, etc, and push down hard on the ground. Rub the ice cube backwards and forwards and watch what happens to the ground.

Discuss the changes with your class.

Glaciers can change the earth's surface in much the same way as what you have been doing with your piece of ice.

Internet zone

Figure 4: Practicals that emphasise enquiry rather than finding 'the' correct answer facilitate better learning via the Internet

A large range of science activities, practicals and experimentation requires specialist time, outings or equipment. For the study of landforms, field-trips were identified as a valuable component of the study. Simulations and electronic field-trips may serve as worthwhile alternatives, and a large and exciting range exists on the Internet.

Hypermedia

A unique characteristic of Internet-based resources is the ability to link to other information by the use of hyperlinks to create a hypermedium. This may be described as 'a computer-based method of non-sequential reading and writing – a technique with which chunks, or nodes, of information can be arranged and rearranged according to an individual's needs, previous knowledge, curiosities, etc' (Borsook and Higginbotham-Wheat, 1992, cited in Palumbo, 1995). Although advantages may be identified from the explanation, hypermedia also has the potential to deteriorate into a collection of aimless information, losing children in hyperspace (Fletcher *et al.*, 1999). We believe this should be considered when designing sites for young beginner students and the encouragement to 'surf' should be limited to the students' level of confidence. To address this concern we designed introductory yellow button activities focusing on specific questions with limited opportunity for surfing, but at the same time orienting students to an enquiry-based methodology (see Figure 3). We also included higher-order activities, such as the extension activities, associated with the landform pictures for students more confident and competent with the medium. Both these types of activities direct learners and provide some links and direction, but require an enquiry-based and problem-solving approach as the answers are not directly or readily apparent. We suggest that activities should be within the skill levels of the learners to maintain both a positive attitude to the medium, and also to focus the learning on the subject content, rather than navigation and manipulation issues associated with the environment. Familiarity with the Internet environment, and with collaborative and constructivist learning, are likely to develop with practice.

Electronic Field-trips and Webquests

A WebQuest is 'an inquiry activity that presents student groups with a challenging task, provides access to an abundance of usually online resources and scaffolds the learning process to prompt higher order thinking' (March, 1995). The students need to be encouraged to engage in thinking processes. Higher order thinking needs to be incorporated to 'challenge the learner to think, reflect, discuss, hypothesise, compare, classify ...' (IMSENet 1997). Although students may be working through the quest to reach a conclusion, the greater part of the emphasis is on expression of reasoning. This process 'helps students to become aware of their own ways of thinking and of alternative ways of thinking as articulated by others' (Dufresne *et al.*, 1996).

Evaluation of Websites
Factors that affect ease and efficiency of use

Because the Internet is multi-dimensional, there are numerous ways of evaluating sites, and therefore of identifying factors that affect ease and efficiency of use. The search engine Northern Light provided 388,568 references to website evaluation when searched on 29 January 2001. These were proposed by universities, libraries, schools, amateur and professional educators.

For any science site to be useful in achieving curriculum goals, it needs to be student-centred (Ed's Oasis, 1999). It must allow for student action in some form – student communications, person-to-person interactivity, ability to link to additional online resources, opportunity for students to share their work, practical examples to support learning objectives. Palumbo (1995) cautions that 'information usually is considered only in terms of task analyses or media selection' while overlooking learning theories that are best supported by this technology. If the emphasis of a website is not to optimise student learning, the busy teacher must ask, 'What is the point of this site?'

A number of authors have designed evaluation instruments to help teachers. Six factors have been identified as having a major role in contributing to the educational effectiveness of a 'good science site' and each of these is examined in turn. Many of the characteristics identified below are generic to effective websites, but the writers have chosen to emphasise these features as they apply to science sites especially within the junior school curriculum. Whether using websites to retrieve information, or publishing a school website, cognisance should be given to each of these areas. They are:
- content and evaluation;
- source/author and currency;

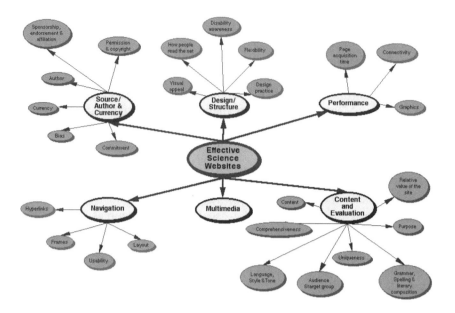

Figure 5: Overview of factors that need to be considered when evaluating science websites

- design/structure;
- navigation;
- performance;
- multimedia.

Factors that children identify as fun or interesting can provide additional insight. Science is after all 'more than memorising facts and formulas' (Leddo, 1997). Science is the study of things around us, and as such it can readily be adapted to study things of familiarity or interest (see Figure 5).

1. Content and evaluation
Purpose

Perhaps the first issue is the purpose of the Web page. Lai (1999) warns against schools rushing in to build their own website without a valid consideration of the reason. He refers to the 'Everest Syndrome'. Due to the ease of Internet publishing, a plethora of home-page type websites are being developed, but many lack quality, because they have often failed to address this aspect.

Audience/target group

Before building a site, the architect must decide who the audience and target group will be (Grassian, 1997; Hoffbauer, 1999). It is better to focus on a select audience and directly target that group, rather than attempt to create a good impression for a wider audience, as a generalised focus will diminish effectiveness for the intended users. In our Landforms website, the target group is New Zealand teachers and their students. It is even more specifically for students who are at Level 3 in science (see Figure 1).

Language, style and tone

Once the audience has been identified, issues of language, style, and tone should be addressed. These need to be consistent with the level of the target audience (Jacobson & Cohen, 1996). In the Landforms site, there is a greater degree of informality when speaking with students, than when speaking with teachers. The level of vocabulary is important. Words that can be readily comprehended by readers reduce the chance of misunderstanding the message. Also relating to style and tone is the choice of font. Those with serifs are better for students than the more informal fonts like Ariel or Helvetica. It is unwise to use all UPPERCASE as this is more difficult to read. Another way of looking at it is to consider the user-friendly aspect, by asking if the user feels comfortable using the site (Schrock, 1998).

Grammar, spelling and literary composition

Basic rules of grammar, spelling and literary composition are also integral aspects of content (Hoffbauer, 1999). It is vital that the site is checked carefully for grammar, spelling and general composition. Failure to do so promotes an impression of casualness that extends to the contents of the site, and may also diminish the integrity of the developer. If developing a website, it is an idea to have someone else check it, as often the person who prepared it will read what he or she thinks is there and not what actually is there.

Content

Schrock (1998) suggests that the most important aspect to consider when evaluating a site is the content. Smith (1997) reinforces the importance of accurate content as one of his criteria for a good site. Harris (1997) sees the goal of accuracy as ensuring information is 'correct, up to date, factual, detailed, exact and comprehensive.' Many people accept what is written on the Internet at face value (Beck 1999; Ferrell 1997; Harris, 1998). They feel that because it has been published on the net it must be true. Kelly in 'Whales in the Minnesota River?' (*New York Times,* 1999) raises the issue of credibility and as a direct consequence, gullibility. She suggests that 'Web surfers must deal with uncertainty: Is the information true, unbiased, and free of hidden sales pitches?' This is often difficult for adults to decide, so designers of science websites need to take even greater care with children. This highlights the responsibility that designers have to ensure that what is published on their site is factual and its veracity can be ascertained, especially when designing sites for students. Is the information being presented fact or opinion? Unless stated as such, there is no room for opinion in a science site. Students need to be furnished with factual information so that they can make informed decisions and develop sound knowledge structures. It is relatively easy for a good science site to be vilified through the use of inaccurate links. In designing a site, every single link needs to be checked to ensure accuracy. The old adage, of 'when in doubt, leave it out' applies here. One way to endorse the accuracy and credibility of a site is to ensure that all references are fully cited and therefore verifiable (Schrock, 1999). That way teachers are free to check the facts for themselves.

Uniqueness

Another content dimension is the unique nature of the site. Is the information being presented freely available elsewhere? Using Northern Light as a search engine, there are 56,614 references to landforms, and 189,980 to volcanoes. Yet there is only one site set up specifically to meet the needs of Level 3 students in the landform requirements of the New Zealand Science Learning Area.

Relative value of the site

The author needs to be aware of the relative value of the site in comparison to the range of other information resources available on the topic. Tillson (1999) believes that a comparison needs to be made with what is available from related sources. The Landform site was developed because it is often difficult for teachers to find everything they need to complete this unit in one place. There are other resources available on landforms – mainly books and videos – but most of these do not address the issue of local landforms. When a person sets up a site, they must ensure that the time that goes into making it is justified in terms of what the audience will get out of it.

Comprehensiveness

While relating to content, comprehensiveness also applies to any associated links. These should be relevant and evaluated in some way. Wallace (1999) refers to the 'one sentence description' for each link. It gives the developer a greater degree of control, but also many users do not have time to search through all links. This is a further sign of a responsible site. A one-sentence brief empowers the user to make an informed choice about whether they visit the site or not. Also adding hyperlinks is a way of catering for the user who requires more information (Wallace, 1999).

2. Source/authorship and currency

Author

Who is the author or producer of this site? It is important in developing a science site that the credibility of the author is established. The teacher who is using a given site will want to know if the author is qualified in the subject contained on that site. The authors of science sites aimed at students may not be university professors in the subject matter but they should have some experience in working with children and in the field of science. Schrock (1998) stresses that the reader should be able to find readily the name of the author/s, where they work, what credibility they have in writing about a given topic, and how to get in touch with them.

Commitment

The integrity and credibility of the author will also be apparent in their commitment to the site. Are they willing to allow students to contact them and ask questions? The authors of the Landform Project put forward their own names as SAE (self-acclaimed experts), showing a willingness to have students or teachers contact them for further support either in content or other curriculum knowledge (see Figure 6).

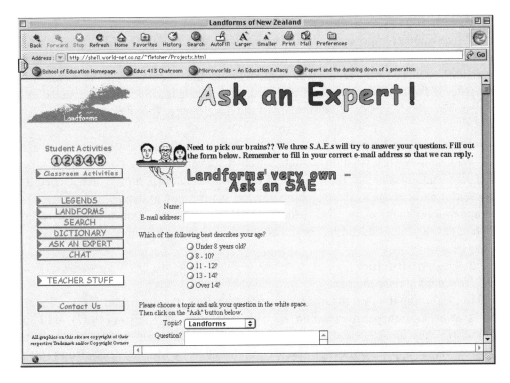

Figure 6: Part of the integrity and credibility of the author(s) will be displayed in their commitment to the site with such components as 'Ask an Expert' or their provision of contact email addresses

Sponsorship, endorsement and affiliation

Sites can be further authenticated by:
- being sponsored by an individual or group who has created other good Web pages,
- having the endorsement of a recognised authority such as University of Otago's New Zealand Learning Network, a scientific organisation such as NASA, government departments, or a reputable site such as *Ed's Oasis* or *Te Kete Ipurangi*, or
- being affiliated to a professional body.

Bias

The author needs to be wary, when seeking sponsorship or affiliation, that they do not become locked into generating a bias commensurate with the sponsor's or affiliate's expectations (White and Chapman 1999). Other dimensions may include gender, racial, or religious bias (ALSC 1997). Schrock (1999) warns against the bias that arises from using words that try to persuade rather than inform. The author may proffer personal opinion without acknowledging it as such. Although often unintentional, such bias can be misleading, especially to younger students. This reinforces the importance of the teacher checking the site first.

Currency

This is another important aspect of a good site (McKenzie, 1997). With knowledge changing so rapidly, it is important that information is kept up to date. Every (good) website should show the date it was created, so that the reader can see the currency of the site. If the site is updated or modified, such changes should also be noted and dated. This reinforces the commitment of the developer to the site.

Permission and copyright

With so much information available, website developers may choose to use other people's ideas on their site; however, much of this information is copyrighted. Generally, there is a willingness to share as long as an effort is made to contact the owner. The original author may ask for a link to their site or for an acknowledgement to be included. When developing Landforms, special attention was paid to gaining such approval.

3. Design/structure
How people read the net

In examining the design and structure of websites, it is important for developers to be aware of how people read on the Web. According to Nielson (1997) and Paul (1999a), 'they don't.' Nielson acknowledges that rather than read, people tend to scan. This is supported through research undertaken by Morkes & Nielson (1997) where 79 per cent of users scanned while only 16 per cent read word-by-word. Authors must learn how to write in this relatively new genre. Suggested hints include highlighting keywords (bold, underline, colour), judicious use of subheadings, bulleted lists, indents and outlines, and reducing the number of words. Traditionally users read right through an article which presented the conclusion at the end (Nielsen, 1996b), but with the Web, and a general reluctance to read (due in large part to information overload) users will often only read the first paragraph. So to compensate for this, it makes sense to put the conclusion or a brief summary statement at the start. Nielsen (1996b) refers to this as 'inverted pyramids'.

Visual appeal

To gain the attention of the reader, a good site must have visual appeal. Science is a subject that lends itself well to visualisation. Exciting photographs and the careful use of animated gifs are options. Charging dinosaurs and erupting volcanoes are topics that appeal to students. However, this needs to be balanced against download time.

The intention of visual appeal must be to enhance information delivery. The site should be clearly presented, avoiding the cluttered look. The developer must be careful about the use of 'obtrusive frills' (IMSENet, 1997). This includes the use of flashy advertisements and the <BLINK> tag. These only distract the user from the true educational significance of the site, weakening its effect. Graphics may be used but should be functional – complementing the text, and enhancing the resource (Smith, 1997) – rather than purely decorative. Landforms has a very limited number of animated gifs, restricted to student pages where they are used purposefully to draw attention and for general appeal. For example, the animated gif on the students' volcano page shows an erupting volcano and serves to draw the students' attention to the site. In addition, these gifs are small.

Design practice

There is a place for creativity, but it must be tempered within the bounds of accepted design practice (Wilkinson, Bennett & Oliver, 1997). Palumbo (1995) warns that the site should be designed so that the learner's perspective is at the forefront. This is of particular importance in science sites, especially when developed as part of the (New Zealand) science syllabus. Curriculum statements, both here and abroad, have a basic philosophy underpinning them, and if the designer is familiar with this philosophy, it can be reflected in the design of the site and activities.

Careful use of fonts, background colours, and patterns will add to the site, but the opposite also applies. The final choices should minimise interference or distractions (Palumbo, 1995). The Landforms site has attempted to use a balanced format, with limited backgrounds and background colours, and a small range of fonts.

Flexibility

Under the constraints of different hardware and software, flexibility for different users needs to be inbuilt. Different options achieved through careful use of HTML or authoring programs can allow for such variation. It is wise to have a number of options – frames versus no frames, text only versus graphics/multimedia browsers, allowance for a range of resolutions, sensitivity to target audience browser and plug-in limitations (Tillson, 1999).

Disability awareness

Serious consideration needs to be given to equity of access. Moock, Trgovac & Paciello (1998) believe that information should be accessible for everyone. The challenge is to change people's attitude and mindset to allow for fair accessibility.

Colour blindness (colour perception deficiency) affects a significant number of people using the Web today and the author should be aware of the effects of certain background/font colour combinations. However, as a general rule younger viewers have less difficulty than older viewers. If the W3C 'Web Accessibility Initiative Guidelines (WAI)' are followed, developers can make their site accessible to all, including disabled users.

4. Navigation

Layout

Sites need a clear layout, and logical organisation so that users can navigate with ease (Jacobson & Cohen, 1996). Maintaining a consistent appearance throughout the website assists navigation. A clear site map should be available so that users know both where they are and where they can go. This can be achieved through a well-labelled table of contents.

The Landforms site makes an effort to keep the student pages distinct from the teacher pages. For example, there is no direct link to the lesson plan from the student page. Classroom activities are accessible from both pages. An overview of the site is appended. Yellow dot activities are a part of the metaphor of this site to assist navigation.

Hyperlinks

One of the benefits of hyperlinks is to help navigation, both within and beyond the site. Links need to be visually obvious. It is wise to conform to the standard set of link colours generally used on the WWW – blue for unvisited links, and purple or red for visited links (Nielsen, 1995). Landforms uses extensive hyperlinks. The main reason is that Web users, especially the young, can more easily track which links have been followed, and which haven't, when a standard system is used. Hill (1998) discovered that low contrast (the difference between two areas of colour) can be fatiguing for young readers and (almost) impossible for older people to read. With this in mind, we made a small adjustment on the volcano page hyperlinks; as the dark blue links did not show up as well on a black background, they were modified to a lighter blue. Suitable links are sometimes embedded deeply within sites and may often take a series of mouse actions to reach usable information. A good example of this is *Volcano World Kids' Door* <http://volcano.und.nodak.edu/vwdocs/kids/kids.html>. When using such links, developers should not waste the reader's time by taking them to the top level. Provide addresses that quickly take the user to the required sub-level (McKenzie, 1995a).

Frames

The question of whether to use frames or not depends to a large extent on personal and historical preference. Nielsen (1995) advocated strongly against their use in his 'Top Ten Mistakes on The Web'. However, by December 1996 he acknowledged that he had changed his opinion (due to Netscape and IE's ability to handle frames) when frames were used by skilful designers. It is recognised that poorly designed frames can be a hindrance and make a site hard to navigate. Weller, Repman, Rooze (1992, cited in Palumbo, 1995) suggest that navigation aids should be included 'to remind users where they are and where they have been.' The Landforms site uses frames to aid navigation. They enable the developer to have a student section and a teacher section as well as to quickly get to other places in the site by use of buttons. In this way the 60-odd pages are readily accessible, using the minimum number of links into the site, while the site outline is always visible and accessible.

Usability

Sites need to be user-friendly (Smith, 1997). Visitors should be able to find their way around readily and within a reasonable number of links. When information is embedded deeply within sites, links should be provided that quickly take the user to the required sub-level (McKenzie, 1995).

Nielsen (1996a) advises against long scrolling pages as most users will not bother to pursue this option.

Landforms has one very long page, the lesson plan, so to get around this problem,

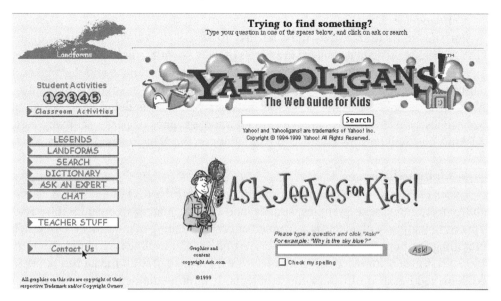

Figure 7: A search engine embedded within a site enhances its overall appeal

internal links have been used and a downloadable copy of the lesson plan has also been made available.

A number of writers suggest caution in the use of plug-ins (Schrock, 1999). On a good site, required plug-ins and other helper applications should be identified (ALSC 1997). This has been done on Landforms, and if the user does not have these, links are provided for their downloading.

It is useful to have a search engine embedded in the website (IMSENet, 1997), (Wilkinson, Bennett & Oliver 1997), but failing that, at least there should be links to a search engine (Smith, 1997) (see Figure 7).

5. Performance

Page acquisition time

This can be a major turn-off for web users. Long waiting periods frustrate the user. Nielsen (1996a) suggests most users will be reluctant to wait for more than 10-15 seconds before abandoning a download. People want more speed. This is why it is so important that sites are not accompanied by large graphic files. If large images are necessary, thumbnails can be used (IMSENet, 1997).

Graphics

Graphics need to be used with caution. Schrock (1998) acknowledges that a 'clearly labelled graphic is worth a thousand words when illustrating a point'. They must help students to achieve the goal of the site. Evaluators have different preferences for the maximum size of graphics files, but less than 50K seems acceptable. If thumbnails are used, it is a good idea to include the file format and size given in brackets after the link (Nielsen, 1995).

Connectivity

For sites to be usable, they must be easy to access. It is noted that some of the NASA sites are difficult to connect to at times of 'new scientific discoveries' (IMSENet, 1997). Also some sites offer only a limited number of connections and this makes it hard to gain access. Other sites are hard to get into as they are extremely popular. Also, there is only a certain bandwidth between New Zealand and overseas, so at busy times all overseas sites are slow. In addition, at times of peak use, many New Zealand sites will be slow because of bandwidth on the New Zealand network.

6. Multimedia issues

Lynch (1997) believes that perhaps the most powerful aspect of the WWW is 'the ability to combine text, graphics, sounds, and moving images in meaningful ways.' This combination of elements is subsumed under the heading of multimedia. Although providing for more options, a greater degree of design discipline is required (Nielsen, 1995). It is also acknowledged that much of the promise of multimedia has failed to be delivered because of bandwidth problems. If multimedia demonstrations do not have a purpose but are merely decorative, they should not be included.

Lynch (1997) also warns of the use of plug-ins for multimedia. More are being developed, and if site developers insist on using the latest plug-ins they may lose many users. Paul (1999b) suggests offering an alternative way of accessing data for those who cannot use the plug-ins.

Conclusion

Developing educationally effective websites involves searching for content on the Internet, examining pedagogy and learning, establishing an aim for this learning, catering for differing learning styles, and using established Web design techniques. For any method of instruction to be effective, students have to be involved in the learning process. The use of the Internet is no exception to this. To make optimal use of the Internet in supporting student learning, there needs to be a shift from a teacher-centred to a student-centred focus. To facilitate this, websites should contain problem-solving activities, enquiry techniques, interpretational-type activities, and questioning that requires analysis and gelling of students' prior knowledge and new information at their level.

However, certain types of activities in science are still best suited to normal classroom learning techniques. While simulations can provide additional insight into scientific principles and problems, data for experimentation, manipulation, and analysis that might otherwise be impossible to achieve in the classroom, and can reduce pedagogical noise, students are more involved in the learning process when actually physically handling the materials and using all of their senses.

Nevertheless, this does not preclude the use of virtual fieldtrips and simulations. Well designed, these are valuable activities in themselves. Their use should be seen as a valuable addition and enhancement to normal experimental techniques.

The Web is unique in that resources can be linked by way of hyperlinks. Hyperlinks are non-sequential, meaning that information can be arranged according to a student's needs and prior knowledge. However, hyperlinking can also compartmentalise knowledge and reduce it to a seemingly chaotic chorus of discrete information. Evidence thus suggests that hyperlinking should be carefully designed with younger students. Opportunities to get 'drowned in the surf' should be minimised, and only a few hyperlinks should be provided with directed questioning. In addition, hyperlinks should be regularly checked for currency and availability.

Site design can also have a dramatic impact on a student's learning. Sites should be designed according to six criteria:

1. **Content and evaluation** – the site should have a clear purpose; a particular target audience; an appropriate language style and tone; proper grammar and spelling; accurate and up-to-date content; be unique; have added value or produce something that is not available elsewhere; and be comprehensive.
2. **Source, authorship, and content** – the site authors should have credibility; a commitment to the site; sponsorship, endorsement or affiliation to a recognised authority; the site should have no bias, whether it be racial, gender or religious, or because of affiliation from an advertising sponsor; it should be current; and it should obey and comply with copyright issues.
3. **Design and structure** – the site should be designed to take account of the user's reading characteristics, it should have visual appeal and design practice, flexibility with differing hardware and software configurations, and awareness of disabilities.
4. **Navigation** – sites should have a clear and consistent layout, a consistent hyperlinking format, be useable and user-friendly, and limit the use of plug-ins unless they add to the site. Frames can be used to aid site navigation. However, if not appropriately designed they can irritate the user and reduce site navigability.
5. **Performance** – when designing a site, careful consideration should be given to the length of the pages, the time they take to load, the use of graphics and their size, and site connectivity.
6. **Multimedia issues** – the Web can combine text, sound, graphics, and video. However, their use should be limited because of connection speeds, bandwidth, plug-ins, and software compatibility problems.

In summary, for a website to be effective, careful consideration should be given to its aim, content, target audience and design. The design involves examining pedagogy and learning, catering for differing learning styles, and using established Web design techniques.

Information and content should be clear, concise, and have a well-defined layout. It should be user-friendly and support learning in the classroom. It should develop enquiry skills while giving direction. It should provide meaningful content. And perhaps most important of all, it should have a purpose and add something to the learning process. One should perhaps not ask which content should be used, but rather, how will designing and using a website further enhance the learning that occurs in the classroom. Only then can a science site be truly effective, and only then can a science site further develop our students for life beyond the classroom.

Note: An earlier version of this chapter was published in *Computers in New Zealand Schools*, March 2000.

References

ALSC (Association of Library Services to Children) (1997). *700+ Great sites – Selection Criteria.* Available at: <http://www.ala.org/parentspage/greatsites/criteria.html>.

Beck, S. (1999). *The Good, The Bad & The Ugly.* New Mexico State University. Available at: <http://lib.nmsu.edu/instruction/evalcrit.html>.

Bowman, J. (1997). *Reshaping Mathematics and Science Instruction Using Real Data.* Department of Curriculum and Instruction. University of New Orleans. Available at: <http://www.uno.edu/~edci/site97/15-sc.htm#Reshaping>.

Dufresne, R.J. Gerace, W.J. Leonard, W.J. Mesre, J.P. & Wenk, L. (1996). Classtalk: A Classroom Communication System for Active Learning. *Journal of Computing in Higher Education,* 7, 3-47.

Ed's Oasis (1999) Evaluation Guide.Available at: http://www.classroom.com/edsoasis/guide2.html>.

Ferrill, K. (1997). *Truth, Lies and the Internet.* Available at: <http://coverage.cnet.com/Content/Features/Dlife/Truth>.

Fletcher, S., Hovell, S., Johnston, L. & Nicholson, S. (1999). How the Internet can be used in an interactive way to support teaching and learning of science. *Computers in New Zealand Schools,* 11(2), 9-18.

Grassian, E. (1997). Thinking critically about World Wide Web. Resources UCLA Library. Available at: <http://www.library.ucla.edu/libraries/college/help/critical/index.htm>.

Harris, R. (1997). *Evaluating Internet research sources.* Available at: <http://www.vanguard.edu/rharris/evalu8it.htm>.

Harris, R. (1998). *Gullibility virus warning.* Available at: <http://www.sccu.edu/RHarris/warning.htm>.

Hoffbauer, M. (1999). *How to evaluate Internet sources – questions.* Available at: <http://www.writeangleconsulting.com/evaluate/question.htm>.

IMSENet (Instructional materials in science education network),

Isernhagen, J. (1999). Technology: A major catalyst for increasing learning. *T.H.E. Journal.* Available at: <http://www.thejournal.com/magazine/vault/A2126.cfm>.

Jacobson, T & Cohen, L. (1996). *Evaluating Internet sources.* University of Albany Libraries. <http://library.albany.edu/Internet/evaluate.html>.

Kelly, T. (1999). *Whales on the Minnesota River: Only on the Web where scepticism is a required navigational aid.* Available at: <http://www1.nytimes.com/learning/general/featured_articles/990304thursday.html>.

Learning Media Ltd. (1993). *Science in the New Zealand Curriculum.* Wellington: Ministry of Education.

Leddo, J. (1997). *Internet-based intelligent tutoring games.* VA: Research Development Corporation. Available at: <http://www.coe.uh.edu/insite/elec_pub/HTML1997/sc_ledd.htm>.

Lynch, P. (1997). *Web Style Guide: Basic Design Principles for Creating Web Sites.* Available at: <http://info.med.yale.edu/caim/manual/contents.html>

March, T. (1999). *What's on the Web? sorting strands of the WWW for educators.* Available at: <http://www.ozline.com/learning/webtypes.html>.

McKenzie, J. (1995). Home sweet home: Creating WWW pages that deliver. Available at:<http://www.fno.org/homesweet.html>.

McKenzie, J. (1997). Comparing & evaluating Web information sources. *FNO,* 6(9) 1997. Available at: <http://www.fno.org/jun97/eval.html >.

Mestre, J.P. (1998). *Cognitive Aspects of Learning and Teaching Science.* In S.J. Fitzsimmons & L.C. Kerpelman (Eds) 'Teacher Enhancement for Elementary and Secondary Science and Mathematics: Status, Issues, and Problems', Washington, DC: National Science Foundation (NSF 94-80). Available at: <http://umperg.physics.umass.edu/physicsEdResearch/reviewPaper >.

Moock, C. Trgovac, K. & Paciello, M. (1998). *Information access: theory and practice.* Yuri Rubinsky Insight Foundation. Available at: < http://128.100.250.10/yuri/aboutsite.html>

Morkes, J. & Nielsen, J. (1997). *Concise, scannable, and objective: how to write for the Web.* Available at: <http://www.useit.com/papers/webwriting/writing/html>.

NCSU (1997). *Evaluating science WWW resources.* Available at: <http://www.ncsu.edu/imse/3/evalweb.htm>.

Nielsen, J. (1995). *Guidelines for Multimedia on the Web*. Available at: <http://www.useit.com/alertbox/9512.html>.

Nielsen, J. (May 1996a). *Top ten mistakes in Web design*. Available at: <http://www.useit.com/alertbox/9605.html>.

Nielsen, J. (June 1996b). *Inverted pyramids in Cyberspace*. Available at: <http://www.useit.com/alertbox/9606.html>.

Nielsen, J. (October 1997). *How users read on the Web*. Available at: <http://www.useit.com/alertbox/9710a.html>.

OTA (1995). *Teachers and technology: making the connection*. US Congress Office of Technology Assessment. OTA-HER-616. Washington DC: Government Printing Office. Available at: <http://www.wws.princeton.edu/~ota/disk1/1995/9541.html>.

Palumbo, D. (1995). *Theory and technology: design consideration for hypermedia/discovery learning environments*. Clear Lake: University of Houston. Available at: <http://129.7.160.115/inst5931/Discovery_Learning.html>.

Paul, F. (1999a). *Nobody wants to read the big picture*. Available at: <http://www.builder.com/Business/Paul/091099/ss01.html>.

Paul, F. (1999b). *Don't rely on plug-ins*. Available at: <http://www.builder.com/Business/Paul/042399/ss01.html>.

Schrock, K. (1998). Separating the wheat from the chaff – how to tell the good sites from the bad; from *Internet Trend Watch for Librarians*. Available at: <http://school.discovery.com/schrockguide/chaff.html>.

Schrock, K. (1999). The ABCs of website evaluation. *Classroom Connect*. Available at: <http://school.discovery.com/schrockguide/pdf/weval.pdf>.

Smith, A. (1997). *Criteria for the evaluation of Internet information resources*. Available at: <http://www.vuw.ac.nz/~agsmith/evaln/index.htm>.

Snyder, J. (1997). *An emphasis on science literacy in pre-service teacher education,* Department of Curriculum and Instruction. University of New Mexico and Sandia National Labs. Available at: <http://www.coe.uh.edu/insite/elec_pub/HTML1997/sc_snyd.htm>.

Tillman, Hope N. (1999). *Evaluating quality on the net*. Babson Park, MA: Babson College. Available at: <http://www.hopetillman.com/findqual.html>.

Wallace, N. (1999). *Web writing for many interest levels*. Available at: <http://www.e-gineer.com/e-gineer/articles/web-writing-for-many-interest-levels.phtml>

W3C *Web Accessibility Initiative Guidelines* (WAI). Available at: <http://www.w3.org/TR/WAI-WEBCONTENT/>.

White, M. & Chapman, J.M. (1999). *Evaluating Internet resources: a checklist*. Available at: <http://books.valdosta.edu/ref/bi/interneteval.html>

Wilkinson, G. Bennett, L. & Oliver, K. (1997). *Consolidated listing of evaluation criteria and quality indicators*. Available at: <http://www.edtech.vt.edu/edtech/kmoliver/webeval/webeval.html>.

Zhao, Y. & Campbell, K. (1996). Refining knowledge in a virtual community: A network-based collaborative project for pre-service teachers. *Journal of Technology and Teacher Education*, 4(3/4) 268-80.

Classroom Adventures: Supporting Technology Integration for Classroom Teachers with Online Collaborative Projects

7

Ann Trewern

In recent years most New Zealand primary and secondary schools have acquired some form of access to the Internet. A recently released ITAG report (2000) indicated that 96 per cent of 2,300 primary schools and 99 per cent of 340 secondary schools had at least one Internet connection available and that a quarter of the nation's secondary schools had up to 80 per cent of their classrooms networked. As schools are rapidly committing themselves to the business of expanding technology hardware and wires and cables to connect to the Internet, teachers are being challenged to take up the technology and incorporate it effectively into all aspects of teaching and learning. The challenge is enormous. For many reasons, effective use of the ICT in ways that provide for dynamic and worthwhile learning opportunities for students has proven to be a difficult task for teachers.

Considering the increasing emphasis being placed on integrating information and communication technology into schools, the lack of supportive structures for teachers to achieve reasonable levels of integration is of some concern. One of the major reasons for the development of the New Zealand Learning Network (NZLNet) was to assist teachers with practical ways to integrate the Internet into classroom practice. The NZLNet is an online support service developed and maintained by the School of Education, University of Otago. In order to provide teachers with some support for using ICT in the curriculum, a variety of online interactive projects for teachers and their students have been developed and conducted as part of the activity structure of the NZLNet. In all, eight projects have been offered to teachers over the last two years. The projects have been offered on a no-cost basis.

Description of the Projects

In order to entice teachers, most projects have had a particular focus on New Zealand places, people and events, or on particularly popular curriculum topics. The intention is to present teachers and their students with a structured learning framework within which a meaningful unit of study could be undertaken that would suit the myriad of ways individual teachers may work with their classes. Projects have been designed to provide a range of opportunities for teachers to experience first hand and alongside their classes a knowledge construction approach to learning in settings where teachers may have minimal access to technology. The projects encourage teachers and students to work in interactive ways with other participating groups; they also encourage interaction within the class. All projects were designed to integrate a variety of learning objectives and essential skills from a number of curriculum areas that included science, social studies technology and language. The activities were designed for upper level primary teachers and their classes and were carried out using email as the primary method of communication and interaction, but several projects have also included computer conferencing options to aid interaction.

- New Zealand Places Game
  < http:// education.otago.ac.nz/NZLNet/projects/NZPlaces.html>
- New Zealand Explorers Project
  <http://education.otago.ac.nz/NZLNet/projects/NZExplorers.html>
- Famous New Zealanders Project
  <http://education.otago.ac.nz/NZLNet/projects/FamousNZers.html>
- Renowned Olympians Project
  <http://education.otago.ac.nz/NZLNet/projects/olympians.html>

All four projects are based on a similar structure. The *New Zealand Places Game* and the *Explorers Project* were developed and conducted during the second and third terms of 1999. The *Famous New Zealanders Project* and the *Renowned Olympians Project* were offered during the second and third terms of 2000. Each of these projects ran for a ten-week school term. The projects were strongly oriented towards a problem-based learning approach and were designed to integrate a variety of learning objectives and essential skills from a number of curriculum areas. The activities were designed for primary teachers and their classes and were carried out using email as the primary method of communication and interaction and with all resources such as instructions, participant lists, and student contributions archived on the World Wide Web.

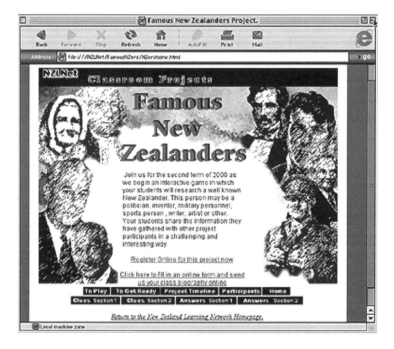

Figure 1: Entry web-page for the Famous New Zealanders Project.

Participating groups were required to choose a place, explorer or a famous New Zealander reasonably local to their school. For the *Renowned Olympians Project* participating groups could choose any athlete who had competed at any Olympiad. Participants were then required to gather information and develop a set of clues that revealed as much about their place or explorer, famous New Zealander or Olympian as possible but without giving away the name of the place or person selected. Games have required participant groups to develop some nine or twelve sets of clues. The creation of clues that provided just enough information to be challenging but without being too difficult for other groups to solve was not an easy task and usually required a lot of in-class research and negotiation about what should be included and excluded before they were submitted to the project moderator.

Once clues were received by the project moderator, the answers were removed and then batches of clues were posted in sets of three, over three or four weeks, to all other game participants. Interaction between participating classes occurred at the clue-solving stage. Active groups were encouraged to ask questions of the other participants by email in order to assist with the process of solving the clues. Interaction occurred between classes and was not part of the project management process. Teachers have reported that these projects have assisted students greatly with developing both their email skills and their research skills. Students utilised various communication and research skills to identify each of the places or people chosen by the other participating groups. Games concluded with participants submitting a list of their solutions to the moderator by email. At the end of the game all participants were awarded a participation certificate.

Numbers of participants have varied for each of these projects with numbers gradually growing for projects as they become better known by teachers. Nineteen classes or groups completed the original *New Zealand Places Game,* twenty-three classes were involved in the *New Zealand Explorers Project,* twenty-eight classes completed the *Famous New Zealanders Project* and forty-one classes completed the *Renowned Olympians Project.* Where larger numbers of participants have taken part in these projects, the project moderator has split the group into two or more sections to limit the number of clue sets participating groups have to manage. An ideal number of participants per section appears to be about fifteen to twenty groups. Groups can solve the clues in more than one section if they are looking for an extra level of challenge.

Rescue Me! A project with a technological twist
<http://education.otago.ac.nz/nzlnet/rescue.me/home.html>

Rescue Me! was a ten-week project where participating groups were required to choose an outdoors location such as a bush area, waterway or mountain terrain that was well known to them and develop a situation where an individual or group had become lost or where one or several members of a group were trapped or had sustained an injury. Scenarios required participating groups to design an open-ended problem allowing for a search and rescue solution that would involve opportunities for children to find out about and include use of technological tools such as GPS systems and two-way radio, among others.

Various potentially difficult situations requiring a rescue were carefully chosen by participating groups and written up by the children in a narrative format. One Dunedin class submitted a scenario that involved losing a group of children who had left their tents one night while on a school camp on St Martin's Island, in Otago Harbour. A class from a school in Northland wrote a scenario about a family boating accident on the Kaipara Harbour. Another wrote a scenario about a school caving accident involving a landslip trapping the children in the cave.

Scenarios submitted to the project moderator were voted on by participants and the five most popular and appropriate were chosen. Participating groups were then required to choose one of the five scenarios, research the situation and create an authentic, viable and detailed search and rescue solution. Researching suitable options involved teachers in using any available school and community resources as well as communicating with the class that developed the problem. Expert search and rescue personnel, community police, army or fire personnel were invited into classrooms to talk to children and answer their questions. Solving groups were able to use computer conferencing options on the *Rescue Me!* website to ask questions of the groups that developed the scenario. One class asked the boating accident group for a map of the Kaipara Harbour area, which was faxed to the moderator and then put online. An advantage of using computer conferencing in this project was that all questions and answers could be seen by all participants. This avoided the need for the class who developed the original scenario to answer the same questions many times. The solutions

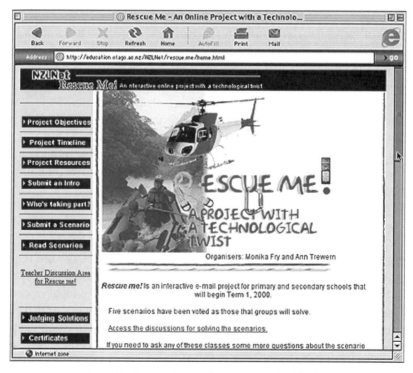

Figure 2: Entry web-page for the Rescue Me! Project

were submitted as word-processed documents, Web pages and PowerPoint presentations, and were published online so they could be shared with other participants groups and judged. Solutions were evaluated for viability by outdoor education personnel and certificates were awarded to all completing participants.

This project was all-encompassing, requiring the integration of a number of curriculum areas including technology, language, and social studies. It required considerable commitment from the participants and flexibility in classroom management. In all, twenty-two participating groups were involved in *Rescue Me!* and nine classes or groups completed the project. The project was designed and developed by Monika Fry and collaboratively managed through its duration by Monika and the author.

Interplanetary Holidays
<http://education.otago.ac.nz/nzlnet/ipholidays/iphome.html>

Interplanetary Holidays was a ten-week project that involved participants in a study of the solar system. The project comprised several phases. In the first phase, participating groups were required to investigate the solar system, choose any celestial body, and submit the name and a description of the chosen celestial body to the project moderator. An expert astronomy educator from the Auckland observatory was available to answer questions or to provide additional information to assist students to write up their descriptions. This interaction was achieved using computer conferencing options and some good discussions on astronomy were established.

Once submitted, the descriptions were separated from the names of the celestial bodies and participating classes were required to decide from their research which celestial body matched which description. The second phase of the project involved participating classes in developing a holiday brochure that recommended the unique aspects of their celestial body to intending space travellers. The holiday brochure could be presented in any digital or paper media. Final versions were shared on the *Interplanetary Holidays* website.

The third phase of the project involved groups voting on the holiday destination of their choice and giving the reasons for their choices. The project was designed to make best use of information and communication technology within the science curriculum and to utilise the vast array of resources available on the Web on this topic. Thirteen participating groups were involved in the *Interplanetary Holidays* Project and some eight groups completed the project. The project was designed, developed and managed by Sharon Nicholson with the author working in a mentoring role.

Water.4.Me

The *Water.4.Me* project evolved as a co-operative venture between the School of Education and the Christchurch City Council Water Education project team known as the Waterlink project. Classes involved in this ten-week project were required to identify and research issues focusing on water in our lives and then to collectively offer a range of creative solutions for a set of authentic waterways and wetlands problem scenarios presented by the *Water.4.Me* team. Like previous projects, *Water.4.Me* involved participants in several distinct phases.

The first phase of the project involved project participants in researching an aspect about 'water in our lives' they wished to find out more about and to develop some research questions which would clarify their area of study. Participants' projects could be broadly based or focus on one aspect that affected a particular waterway such as a river or drainage system quite close to them. These questions were to be shared online with other groups using computer conferencing as the medium of communication. Resource support provided during the early research phase of the project included a number of audio conferencing sessions with water resource experts and regional and national politicians. Class presentations were developed for an exhibition of children's work.

A second phase of the project involved online discussion through the computer conference area of a number of problems and difficult scenarios involving the use of water, and participants' groups needed to suggest ideas based on their research into the area in general.

At the end of the project, groups were to produce a display project based on their research for the GlobalNet event held in Christchurch at the end of October 2000. This could be in any media including a digital display such as a slide show presentation.

This project involved considerable between-class interaction, for instance communication through the computer conferencing areas while research topics were being established, and audio conferencing sessions particularly in the first two phases of the project. Fifteen classes took part in the project, which was designed, developed and managed by Wati Heremaia.

Christmas Packaging Project
<http://education.otago.ac.nz/nzlnet/xmas.project/home.html>

For this eight-week-long single activity project, participating groups were required to take the New Zealand version of the popular song *The Twelve Days of Christmas* and design and construct a Christmas package to send the food or object to a friend or relative. The first stage of the project required participants to select a food item from the song and invent a food product. For example, the kumera mentioned in the song became kumera bread baked into a Father Christmas shape. Participants then selected one of the three most popular food products and created an appropriate package that reflected the Christmas flavour, kept the food item fresh and undamaged, and was simple and recyclable.

Designed as a simple pre-Christmas project, there were no particular class interaction activities woven into the project. However, a great deal of sharing of ideas occurred. For example, although the making of a product to put inside the package was not a requirement of the project, once a school had shared its kumera bread recipe, several schools actually used it as part of the unit. Another school had difficulty locating information about huhu grubs (a chosen food from the song), and sent in information to share with other participating groups. One teacher has also shared the unit of work she developed around the topic (Tait, 2000). Twenty-five groups submitted images of packages for judging. Packages were evaluated for the Christmas design, strength, ability to maintain food quality, simplicity and whether the package was recyclable. Certificates were awarded to all completing participants.

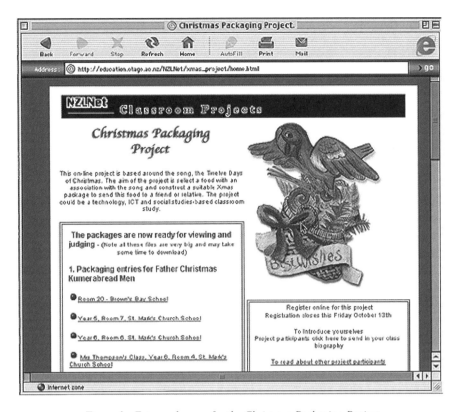

Figure 3: Entry web-page for the Christmas Packaging Project

The Need for Online Projects

These projects were developed to fit snugly with the wider purpose of the New Zealand Learning Network. The intention of the projects was to offer teachers opportunities to take part in activities that would be stimulating for students and let teachers experience integration of information and communication technologies at a practical classroom level with their students. The projects provide supportive structures for teachers and as such can be considered a special and particular form of professional development.

For each project a framework is provided within which teachers and students are responsible for creating a series of questions or scenarios about a designated topic they can take personal ownership of and which is relevant to them. For example, student-developed questions in the *Places Game* and scenarios in the *Rescue Me!* project were required to relate to a place that was local and well known to participants.

The questions, scenarios, or presentations that students develop serve to drive the whole project. The various frameworks allow for a great deal of choice about the content for student research. The framework is also designed to provide considerable latitude for different teaching styles and classroom settings, encouraging teachers to give the activity a go regardless of the specific technological situation in their respective schools.

Activity structures are designed to provide challenging and stimulating activities for students while presenting a light to reasonable workload for teachers and game organisers. Activities need to be demanding for students, but the artefacts students create as a result of their work should require only minimal work to be published in the Web environment, as project organisers can easily become overwhelmed by the quantity of work involved in displaying student work on the Web.

Although there are many overseas curriculum projects available, few New Zealand teachers involve themselves in these projects. There are significant hurdles in successfully joining in with overseas projects. School term times vary from those of northern hemisphere schools. The optimum time for international projects is August to May. Year-long projects are not practical for New Zealand teachers who may be changing year groups in the middle of this time-frame. Shorter term projects occur in the first and last terms of the school year, which can also be difficult when teachers are starting off with new year groups or winding up the school year with its heavy reporting commitments and end-of-year activities. Finding projects that fit well with New Zealand curriculum requirements is also difficult. To provide opportunities for class activities that can be neatly completed within New Zealand term times and relate to the New Zealand curriculum requirements is of great assistance to teachers.

Projects organised by NZLNet focus specifically on the New Zealand curriculum. For example, the *Rescue Me!* and the *Christmas Packaging Project* have been designed to integrate information and communications technology into the new technology curriculum area. Other projects have picked up on commonly taught topics in New Zealand schools and presented new and interesting strategies for delivery. The *New Zealand Explorers* game and the *Famous New Zealanders* game are examples where the library research topic has expanded to become more interactive and more multi-dimensional, widening the skills students require to take part in the projects and enriching and deepening the learning experience (Blumenfeld *et al.*, 1991).

How Are These Projects Organised?

The projects offered have varied tremendously, integrating a variety of content areas, components, participants and activities. Although each project has been different, they nevertheless share some commonalities, as do the stages of involvement for participants.

Getting started

Projects require participants. To attract participants, the project organiser will advertise and call for participants in the *Education Gazette,* online newsletters such as TEACH-IT, listervs such as NZCompEd, and through professional development Web sites such as *Te Kete Ipurangi*. The call for participation would include the goals and objectives as well as a clear and well-structured time-line that provides a description of how the project should be done. Figure 4 shows an example of an initial call for participation.

```
**************************************************
```

Call for Participation – Interplanetary Holidays

```
**************************************************
```

This project has been designed to meet Level 3 of the Planet Earth and Beyond section of the Science curriculum, and would suit participants learning about planets and the solar system.

An imaginary scenario is included as a component of the project to encourage serious consideration of conditions, as they exist in space. Using Earth conditions as a point of comparison would also promote reflection of our own planet – an environment we take so much for granted. We also have an expert on board, who will be available, as a subject expert, to co-ordinate and answer questions from participants.

This game will be played between during Term 2 2000 with registration beginning in the first week of school – Monday May 1st to Friday 5th May.

To get ready:

To participate you will need to send a registration message to:
celestial.trek@stonebow.otago.ac.nz
or register online at http://education.otago.ac.nz/NZLNet/ipholidays/iphhome.html

You need to register by providing the following information:

Class level …

School name …

Contact person name …

Contact person email …

Contact person phone …

School postal address...

During the project:

If you have any inquiries about the project please send these inquiries to the 'Interplanetary Holidays' moderator at celestial.trek@stonebow.otago.ac.nz. You will have a list of each participant's email address from the list sent at the beginning of the project. All participating schools' email addresses will be available from the project web page at http://education.otago.ac.nz/NZLNet/ipholidays/iphhome.html Add the email address to the address book of your mail programme and then it will be handy throughout the game. Using your school name for all participation online will help others identify the source of the messages.

Figure 4: A call for participants for the Interplanetary Holiday project

Figure 4 continued

```
*************************************************
```

Project Timeline

```
*************************************************
```

Week 1: 1–5 May – Registration and Introduction

Groups will be able to introduce themselves online or by email, at Interplanetary Holidays, for posting onto the Internet.

You need to introduce yourselves by providing the following information.

Class level …

School name …

Contact person name …

Contact person email …

Contact person email …

Contact person phone …

School postal address – (We would like to be able to post out evaluation forms at the end of the project)
An introductory paragraph about your class and your school.

Week 2-3: 8-19 May 1 – Orientation

This time is available for classes that need to investigate general features of the Solar System.

Some possible suggestions are available online or email us at : celestial.trek@stonebow.otago.ac.nz

To Do:

- Cover any background information you think would be useful (ideas are available online)
- Ask an Expert when you need help or information
- Send in a choice of three planets (or other Celestial Bodies). We will assign one to you.

Hopefully this will prevent too many participants on one planet.

Figure 4 continued

Week 4-5: 22 May–2 June: General Features of your Planet

Some possible suggestions online are available for your consideration. (Or email us celestial.trek@stonebow.otago.ac.nz)

To Do:

- Ask an Expert when you need help or information
- Submit a description of your Celestial Body by email, or directly on to the site. (Do NOT include the name of this body on your report.)
- Send a separate email to the facilitators, with the name of your Celestial Body.

Week 6: 5-9 June – Identify the Celestial Bodies from the Descriptions

Match the descriptions with the list of Celestial bodies submitted.

To Do:

- Ask an Expert when you need help or information. (Perhaps the Expert can be limited to clues and resources for this week.)
- Match the descriptions with the Celestial Bodies on the list. Submit answers online, or by email.

Week 7-8: 12-23 June – Holiday Brochure

Prepare a Holiday Brochure, that glorifies the unique aspects of your Celestial Body. Some possible suggestions are available online for consideration. (Or email us celestial.trek@stonebow.otago.ac.nz)

To Do:

- Ask an Expert when you need help or information
- Submit a promotion or description. Either by email, directly on to the site, or in HTML format.
- Perhaps you would like to submit a picture (or more)? Pictures need to be postcard size, or A4 maximum. You could also send a digital photo or make an electronic picture, using programmes such as Microsoft Paint or KidPix.
- Ask other people about their planets, if you need to find out more about these holiday destinations.

Week 9: 26-30 June – Final Week

The 'Intergalactic Hospitality Winner' will be announced.

To Do:

Each group places one vote for the Holiday Destination of their choice. A questionnaire will be emailed to you regarding the project. It would be most helpful if you would be prepared to fill it in and return it as soon as possible.

Thank you, Sharon Nicholson

Initial organisation stage

In the ten-week projects that have been offered, up to two weeks are usually allocated at the beginning of the project for registration and online introduction. This long lead-in time serves a double purpose. Firstly, it provides opportunities for the participants to commit to the project or to elect not to proceed further. Secondly, at the beginning of any project, personal introductions will help facilitate future communication between participants.

Activity period

There is a clearly defined period for a major activity or perhaps even two activities to occur, providing for an intensive five to six weeks of involvement by participants. This is the period when students will be most active in the project.

For new participants, online projects may seem quite drawn out in terms of the time they seem to warrant for the amount of activity required. It is important that the project activity structure is suitably paced to allow for access and communication difficulties for teachers and to allow for some flexible timing to be built into the project. Suitable pacing of the project activities for teachers is important in order to ensure continued participant involvement and to maintain student motivation. Too much to do in too short a time-frame can mean unintentional withdrawals from the project where participating groups struggle to match online commitments with normal day-to-day school commitments and expectations.

Although projects offered through the New Zealand Learning Network have a tight overarching structure these are essentially learner-centred environments that are highly generative in nature, where the participating groups collaborate to create the content and then groups proceed to work with that participant-created content. Hannafin (1992) describes typical learner-centred environments as ones where 'students select and sequence educational activities and identify, create, cultivate, or pursue their individual learning needs' (p. 54) and generative learning environments as ones where 'individuals (or groups of individuals) create, elaborate, or otherwise represent knowledge' (p. 58). These projects provide a context within which students interact with curricular content by actively clarifying, manipulating and exploring the context established, and developing both personal ownership and an appreciation of it (Brophy & Alleman, 1991).

Typically these projects require participating groups to first gather information in order to present a problem or series of problems for other groups to study within a particular context. In many of the projects this has meant first gathering information about a place, person, event or object and presenting that information as a series of clues to solve or as a scenario for which a suitable solution needs to be devised. The second stage of the project requires participating groups to select and find solutions for the problems generated by other group members. For example, in the initial phase of the *Rescue Me!* project, participating groups were required to devise a scenario in an outdoors setting in which an accident occurs requiring the possible aid of a search and rescue team. For the second phase, five participant-selected scenarios (chosen by vote) needed to have a solution written for them that met selected criteria.

While these projects are contextualised and scaffolded for teacher and students by providing organised themes or contexts for lesson activities, there is a need to embed aids and support in the form of help and guidance and to provide other resources that can be selected by the student to assist and deepen understanding. Successful student-centred learning systems require the availability of rich resources to enable students to access knowledge and skills as they are needed. Since this is not generally provided in these projects there is a heavy reliance on the support of the classroom teacher that goes beyond the computer activities. The role of the teacher is to provide support for students when knowledge and skills are required and not to be the principal vehicle for the transmission of knowledge. One teacher commented that one of the difficult aspects of the *Places* project was that 'students expected me to know all the answers.' Teachers with limited access to computers will also need to expand the activity in suitable ways in the classroom. These may include students completing individual or group projects relating to the context, bringing in guest speakers, organising audio conferences and so on.

In these projects, teachers are free to organise the day-to-day management in their classrooms in any way they wish. Many choose to work with a whole class on the project, others may choose to involve small groups of students for extension purposes and others may choose to involve the whole class at some stages of the project and small groups at other stages. Many teachers who are new to these projects frequently take up the first project with a small group and will come into the project with the whole class a second time when they are more familiar with the process and know what to expect.

Wrap up
Two weeks are set aside for the project's wrap up and feedback. Some form of judging is undertaken, often by an expert in the field, and project closure is defined by providing feedback to the participating groups and sending out printable certificates for notable achievement and for participation. Judging, feedback and emailing certificates usually takes place before the project participants break for the term vacations.

Teachers' Experiences of the Projects
Very little empirical research has been done to investigate why teachers become involved in telecommunication projects or how they use them in their classrooms. In the following section of this chapter we investigate some of the teachers' experiences with these projects, why teachers become involved, what benefits there are for teachers, and what some of the issues are for teachers.

What are the primary motivations for teachers to become involved in these projects?
The *Renowned Olympians* project saw some forty-one participant groups complete the project. Of the teachers who completed the project, 63 per cent returned an evaluation survey, and 35 per cent who started, but did not complete, also returned a

questionnaire. Results showed that while most teachers had a variety of reasons for participating, the most commonly cited reason was for teachers themselves to experience a way of integrating ICT within a high interest topic, and 75 per cent of teachers indicated this as a primary reason. Other commonly cited reasons included the desire to develop student research skills (66 per cent) and to develop student skills in information and communication technology (50 per cent).

Getting started on a ready-planned project can be an excellent way to learn about the value of this kind of learning environment, as the required tools and resources have been planned for teachers, leaving them the opportunity to safely experience the potential (Campbell, 1999). For 66 per cent of the teachers who started the project, the *Renowned Olympians Project* was the first time they had been involved in an online project. Fewer than one in five teachers indicated they had taken part in other New Zealand-based online projects and no teacher indicated they had taken part in an overseas project.

It is important in designing and planning such experiences that the activity structure is straightforward to implement at the classroom level and yet will provide maximum interest for students and be a worthwhile experience for all. Most teacher participants embarked on the *Olympians* project without help from colleagues. Only a small segment of teachers (15 per cent) indicated they either mentored a colleague or were mentored by a colleague.

It is also important that these first 'testing the water' experiences with Internet integration into teaching and learning are positive for the participants so as to encourage further exploration with the medium. Overall the experience has been positive, with all participating teachers indicating they would definitely consider joining another project.

Teachers will often return to a similarly designed project with altered ideas about how it can be effectively managed within the classroom after they have completed it on a trial basis the first time round. One teacher said that she used the project with only a small group of children but could see ways of using the project with the whole class the next time (*New Zealand Places* project).

What are the benefits of these projects for teachers?
Assisting teachers to 'see' value in classroom use of the technology
Online curriculum projects can allow teachers to experience the power with which combinations of technology tools can motivate students and provide multi-dimensional learning contexts. One teacher commented that experience with the *New Zealand Explorers* project 'strengthened [my] belief in the computer as a tool for learning'.

Experiencing the value in expanding classroom boundaries in purposeful ways
Teachers are often unaware of the value of communications technologies to teaching and learning. These projects provided opportunities for teachers to experience use of ICT in curriculum contexts where increased collaboration occurs with students in the classroom and between participating groups in various places around the country: 'I really enjoyed the contact through email with other schools in the game and like to

see students motivated with a purpose in mind' (Teacher, *New Zealand Places* game).

Another teacher suggested that the projects, such as *Interplanetary Holidays,* 'create a new and different type of learning experience.'

Providing models for ICT integration into other curriculum areas

The lack of provision of good models of practice and support for teachers in the process of integrating interactive technological components into the curriculum is one of the factors that teachers themselves commonly suggest contributes to poor technology uptake. When the onus is put on teachers to come up with solutions for technology integration into classroom practice without much 'expert' support (Harris 1998), the resulting solutions are often skills-based use of the technology. If technology use in the classroom is to move beyond addressing the need for children to learn skills in a range of computer applications, then the provision of opportunities for teachers to experience enhancement of their roles, through ICT use, is essential. To work in supportive and collaborative working structures with other teachers and classes, and to engage in innovative ways of working, is one way of achieving such opportunities. Individually teachers are not in a strong position to generate these opportunities themselves.

Providing situated forms of professional development

Online projects provide opportunities for teachers to personally experience worthwhile models of information and communications technology integration into specific curriculum contexts within their own classroom setting. They can experience the learning successes and pitfalls along with their classes and generally develop familiarity and confidence with the medium in the safety of a pre-planned and organised project. Such opportunities are recognised as offering a particular form of professional development (Harris, 1998). These projects certainly appeared to support teachers in this way. One teacher commented that the *Renowned Olympians* 'was great. I learnt a lot as did my students.'

Developing students skills in realistic learning contexts

What most teachers experience at some stage of these projects is that when employing realistic contexts for developing ICT skills and research skills the students will unexpectedly encounter the need to learn certain skills or understandings that the teacher simply did not expect. One teacher commented that a particularly useful aspect of assessing the project was to find out just 'what children can do using ICT to gather information.' One teacher said of the *Explorers* project: 'Instead of having to make up exercises that are not always relevant, I was able to use the game as a relevant resource.'

Whetting teachers' appetites to do more with the medium

It is hoped that once teachers have experienced successful involvement in local projects, and developed some familiarity with the ways these projects work, they will consider some of the overseas projects that are available. It is also hoped that many teachers will eventually initiate some interclass projects themselves:

I can see there were three major benefits for my class and several more for myself. My class was introduced to ICT skills, we had a context for shared learning and we whetted our appetites for more Internet adventures. My computer skills improved, I opened my eyes to the possibility and value of integrating ICT in the classroom and began looking for more ways to do this. (Teacher, *Rescue Me!*)

How do teachers use these projects in the classroom?

Project frameworks are designed to be flexible enough to allow for varying teacher knowledge and commitment and allow for the complexities of different classroom settings and school structures. The evaluations for various projects have indicated that these activities have been incorporated into a variety of different teaching situations. Evaluation returns for the *Olympians* project indicated that 58 per cent of teachers used the project with their whole class. A common way to manage the classroom information-gathering process was to distribute tasks around different subgroups or pairs in the class and devolve responsibility for finding information to specific small groups of students.

> Initially we would brainstorm the ideas of what the place may be. Then we gave pairs of children a class and it was their responsibility to research more about the clues given, then share with the class, then it was that group's responsibility to email a further question per week. (Teacher, *New Zealand Places*)

Where a single class scenario or presentation has been required, small groups within the class have collaborated to produce a number of versions which have then been voted on to 'pick the best' for final submission to the project participants. Several teachers have reported that the critical review by peers of work to be submitted to a wider audience has induced a very intense process of negotiation within the class. Students need to hone skills of verbal presentation and to use sound criteria to weigh up the merits of different models. One teacher commented on the value of an expanded audience for children's critical thinking processes. In the *Rescue Me!* project, he started his children off by having each write their own rescue story, which had to fit certain criteria. Stories selected needed to be realistic, viable and credible.

> They could see the opportunity to write about blood and guts and nuclear bombs ... but those words 'credible', 'viable' and so on, were great. To be able to tie children's story writing down to reality so that [others] say ... 'Mmmm, I really don't think people would react that way in that sort of situation', or 'when the terrorists burst in … umm ... that's a wee bit out of this world.' Kids were talking about their own writing and each other's writing in that way. Then when it didn't get chosen in the top five [we could then discuss] 'why didn't you think it got chosen?' and we were able to evaluate it that way. This is what I like about these projects, there is so much happening that is so real and so powerful. (Teacher, *Rescue Me!*)

Where smaller groups were used, group size varied but the evaluations showed that projects were most often used as extension activities to deepen thinking for more able students. Reasons for this include ensuring there were enough resources to go around or finding materials at the children's reading level, so they could research themselves.

Some teachers who participated in the projects were in positions of responsibility for ICT in their particular schools and were supporting other staff members through the project. Several needed to co-ordinate activities between more than one teacher. Other teachers were working with their student groups on a very limited basis. Some teachers saw their groups once or twice a week. One teacher even organised the *Olympians* project to be completed by her group of distantly placed correspondence children.

A range of teaching styles have been evident. Some teachers have left small groups of children to work on the project entirely independently. One teacher, referring to the *Explorers* project, stated: 'I left this entirely to the two kids who worked on this project. They selected the explorer and worked out the questions.'

In contrast, other teachers prefer to manage the process quite closely. Several have commented that a lot of preparation had gone into the project, including photocopying and researching relevant information for the children or making all the information available on the school intranet.

Some teachers who used these projects with a whole class found that a major role for the teacher was to disperse tasks and to organise and assist small groups to manage the tasks. Designated groups of students need to develop a system for managing their processes of sending out email questions and ensuring they also answer the questions received from other schools. One teacher commented:

> I only had a small group doing the project, but we spent most of our time organising the responses instead of researching the other clues. We did run into some problems with knowing which [emails] had been replied to and which hadn't. (Teacher, *New Zealand Explorers*)

A frequent method of managing the process in the classroom is to divide the projects so that tasks are shared between groups of children. One teacher commented:

> Allocated pairs of students to one of the other classes that submitted clues. These pairs of children researched the clues and emailed if they required. [We] used our Internet time in reading sessions. A group of five students who were familiar/confident with email were our Helpdesk students. (Teacher, *Renowned Olympians*)

Another teacher said that he chose to

> Start the projects off with just a small group of four kids and they did all the research for our Famous New Zealander (the class were aware of it and they knew what was going on and we told them all about what was going on) but the first time the whole class became involved was when the clues arrived. At that stage I just chopped up the clues and paired up the children putting people together where one may not be a strong reader or researcher with another who was. (Teacher, *Famous New Zealanders*)

The different levels of difficulty presented by sets of clues could also be useful. One teacher commented that harder clue sets were given to groups who liked to be challenged and easier clue sets were given to class members who might struggle with the process a little more.

What are some of the difficulties teachers may encounter in taking part in these projects?

Technical expertise

In the initial project design, the technological expertise required of participants was kept to a minimum as it was not really known just what level of expertise teachers coming into the project would have. Specific email accounts (for communication) and Web sites (for archiving materials) were established for each project. The purpose of minimal technologies was to encourage teachers to become involved for the learning opportunities that were offered rather than have them work their way over insurmountable technological hurdles. There were few difficulties experienced with accessing the project Web pages and the majority of teachers have indicated over several project evaluations that they experienced few technical problems with email.

One of the difficulties for participants, which is often encountered with email-based projects, is the number of different email addresses that can often be accessed by members of the same class, especially in schools where individual children are assigned email accounts. Even teachers can have different home and school email addresses. If simple netiquette rules apply, such as group members indicating which school they come from, then such difficulties are more easily overcome.

Access to technology

Regular and unrestricted access to the technology is essential to the smooth classroom running of these projects. In the *Renowned Olympians* the majority of teachers who completed the project had access to an Internet-connected computer in the classroom. Many teachers indicated they had homeroom access as well as laboratory access.

A far higher proportion of teachers (50 per cent) withdrew from the project where they did not have classroom access. These projects do require regular checking of email to 'keep up' effectively with the pace of the project, track students and avoid being overwhelmed by the volume of information. One teacher said:

> Access to the computers is for one session per week. This was impossible for my class to complete in this time. This is an excellent idea for I.T. and to extend/reward children. Unfortunately the politics of my school let me down. (Teacher, *Renowned Olympians*)

However, on the whole, most teachers probably do not register interest in these projects unless they can be assured of regular access, at least several times a week.

Time

The time required for projects varies and depends very much on the activity structure of the project. 'Tightly framed' projects such as the *Renowned Olympians* are generally more limited in breadth and depth. Teachers in the *Renowned Olympians* project were asked just how much class time it occupied on a daily and weekly basis. Most indicated that the project took about 20–30 minutes per day and between one and two hours per week. These are small and more easily managed projects with generally minimal to moderate workloads for teachers. However, time was one of the most frequently cited reasons as to why teachers did not complete projects.

Other school commitments

Commitment to other projects was also one of the most frequently cited reasons for withdrawal from or inability to complete projects. One teacher commented:

> We did try to run this project co-operatively with junior English/ social studies classes but two school class field trips and a couple of sports visits plus NCEA work caused too many interruptions. We simply didn't have enough time (IT class) with only two periods per week to carry out the necessary research. (Teacher, *Renowned Olympians*)

Seventy-eight per cent of Year 3 and 4 classes completed the project. More Year 7 and 8 classes were unlikely to complete the project than younger levels with only 65 per cent of Year 7 and 8 classes completing the project after starting.

What is the workload for teachers?

One of the reasons many teachers often do not take up the technology is that the Internet and technology use in classroom is seen as another extra on top of an already very busy workload. One of the objectives of these projects was to encourage involvement at the curricular level without adding to teachers' workload. One teacher said of the *Explorers* project: 'It is nice to take part in something NZ and it fits into the SS [Social Studies] curriculum so that teachers are not taking on something extra.'

Project evaluations suggest that overall the workload for teachers has been lighter than expected. However, this does depend on the activity structure of the project. The more open-ended the final requirements of the project, the more work appears to be involved for teachers. It can also depend on how extensively the teacher has arranged for additional supportive activities. Half the teachers in the *Renowned Olympians* reported spending approximately 20 to 30 minutes per day on the project or between one and two hours of school time per week. The majority of teachers have reported that the workload was minimal to moderate.

Teachers' responses to the ease or difficulty of incorporating the projects into long-term planning are more variable. In the *Renowned Olympians* project two-thirds of teachers who responded indicated they had no difficulty and one-third indicated they did have difficulty with long-term planning, with a small number of teachers admitting they planned retrospectively for the project. Where projects involve more cross-curricular activity and a tendency to take unexpected directions, effective prior planning for the project can be problematic.

More broadly conceived projects such as *Rescue Me!* and the *Christmas Packaging Project* allow teachers opportunities to broaden and deepen activity structures in the classroom and can be taken in a variety of interesting directions when opportunities arise (Blumenfeld *et al.,* 1991). One teacher included a visit to the supermarket to study commercial packaging as part of this project. The *Rescue Me!* project provided an example of an all-encompassing project where teachers actively exploited opportunities to enrich the learning environment for their students. One teacher took the students to the scenario site and acted out the rescue. Other teachers involved various people involved with search and rescue skills, such as army personnel and police, in school visits and audio conferences. As one teacher said:

Rescue Me! was really, really hard. I could see the project going two ways. When we read out the scenarios and chose four scenarios, I could see that, sure, we could rescue them. Or I could see it being this huge project, pulling in police people and this person and that person and trying to piece it all together and that's what it became. I guess what's hard about that sort of project, and what scares me and other teachers is that it is almost like you're forced to do retrospective planning which as teachers we feel really uncomfortable with. It's a case of getting to the end and saying, 'Well what objectives did I have to teach? Oh I didn't get that one but I got this one instead.

What Are the Benefits for Students?

Project-based learning can increase student interest because it involves students in authentic problems, in working with others and in building real solutions. It can enhance student motivation and encourage more complex thinking. It has the potential to enhance and deepen understanding because students need to apply information, concepts and principles and the potential to enhance deep understanding because students need to formulate plans, track progress and evaluate solutions. A number of the features of project-based learning have transferred successfully to the online environment.

Fostering cognitive engagement and student motivation

Projects need to be designed in such a way that, with teacher support, they generate and sustain in-depth student engagement with material and foster understanding. A powerful trigger for student motivation is the application of problem-based approaches with Internet delivery mechanisms. The various activity structures employed in different projects have succeeded in providing high levels of challenge and motivation for students. Evaluation returns from the *Renowned Olympians* project in Figure 5 indicate the project sustained high levels of stimulation and motivation for students over a range of age groups.

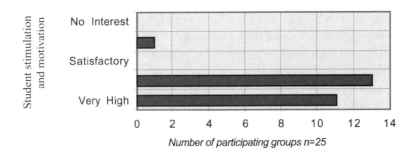

Figure 5: Student levels of stimulation and motivation in the Renowned Olympians Project

Many teachers have commented on the high level of interest the various activities have held for the students. One teacher noted that the *New Zealand Places* project 'created huge interest ... students were very motivated ... increased general knowledge'.

One teacher commented that a benefit for teachers was motivated pupils and pupils learning in a relevant situation. Another teacher commented that there was enjoyment when they thought they had found the clues and even more so when they received confirmation from the class concerned. When they discovered that they had won their section they could not believe it. All went home to their parents with the results and their certificates. The local newspaper even wrote an article on the game with a photograph of the group. (Teacher, *New Zealand Explorers*)

Student ownership of the learning activities

A good project requires that tasks offered will require students to use a wide range of skills, and to interact with curricular content by processing it actively and developing personal ownership and appreciation of it (Brophy & Alleman, 1991). Evaluation of the *Renowned Olympians* project (Figure 6) indicated that teachers considered levels of student ownership of the learning process were, overall, quite high for all age groups.

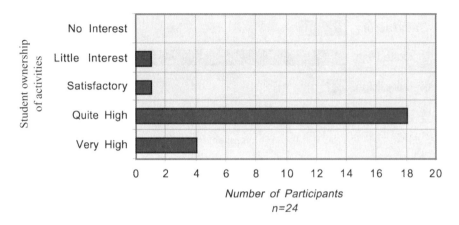

Figure 6: Student levels of ownership of the learning process in the Renowned Olympians Project

However, several teachers also said that ownership of the learning process applied to only a small group within the class. In learning environments where the participants have the task of generating the content for other participating groups to work with, there is room for discrepancies in the quality of the content to emerge. Some clue sets are well designed with a good mix of general and specific questions but formulating fair clues that aren't obvious is difficult for many groups especially when a wide age range of students take part. Many teachers have commented on the tricky nature of the clue sets in the various projects. One teacher commented that the tasks were 'academic for some' while another teacher felt that, in the *New Zealand Places* project, 'some [students] are really struggling to cope with the mental gymnastics required to work with the clues'.

In generative learning environments there are distinct advantages in providing situations where students can submit work for the project, and incorporating an activity structure in which other participants can peer review the content and then choose the particular content they wish to work with.

Self-directed learning

To offer an environment that facilitates student initiative is a primary purpose of these activities. Gaining a clear idea about the extent to which these projects encourage self-directed learning and student initiative is difficult for project managers as the learning process is heavily mediated by the classroom teacher. Evaluations provide an important avenue of understanding. In Figure 7, teachers clearly considered that the level of student self-directed learning was quite high in the *Renowned Olympians* project.

Co-operative learning

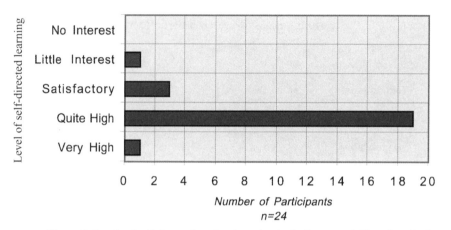

Figure 7: Levels of self-directed student learning in the Renowned Olympians Project

Interaction and collaboration both in the classroom and with classrooms at other sites were important aspects of the activity structure of these projects. Blumenfeld *et al.* (1991) consider that 'working with others requires that students be able to discuss ideas, communicate clearly, consider alternatives, monitor their own understanding, compare their point of view with that of others and ask clear questions' (p. 377). In the evaluation several teachers commented on the 'social togetherness' engendered by the projects and students working collaboratively in the classroom. One teacher stated that she considered the projects were 'an excellent way to foster learning'. Several teachers mentioned the length of time their classes were involved in discussion and that collaboration 'took longer than anticipated'. Many teachers mentioned the way the children worked together as an advantage of the projects. Of the *New Zealand Places* project, for example, a teacher said: 'Co-operative and social skills were reinforced when they worked together without any guidance from me.'

Factors to Consider for Successful Project Design
Instructional contexts for students

Blumenfeld *et al.* (1991) suggest that students perceive interest and value in projects that are varied, where tasks are authentic and have value, and problems are challenging. There needs to be choice about what or how work is done, and opportunities to work in collaborative and co-operative ways with others in the same classroom and in different classrooms. The high levels of stimulation and motivation engendered by the projects as outlined in the previous section, and structures that encourage student ownership of the process and self-directed learning, are an important part of the success of the projects offered.

Context sensitive

The projects reported in this chapter were designed for the New Zealand curriculum and had a New Zealand-wide appeal where schools could also investigate and research a place, person, situation or event of local interest and share that information with others. For example, the *Places* game encouraged interest in geographical regions and heightened interest in diverse and often unusual places of interest that would be hard to achieve in any other way. The *Explorers* project and the *Famous New Zealanders* project encouraged interest in topics quite popular in New Zealand schools but for which little information is available at the appropriate age level to support these topics well. The *Rescue Me!* project offered a cross-curricular theme that firmly located the context of study within the local outdoor environment. One teacher indicated that they had chosen a particular scenario to solve simply because it was local. They knew where the rescue helicopter, police and ambulance services were located, making thinking through a solution a lot easier. The *Christmas Packaging Project* was developed around the theme of the New Zealand version of the carol *The Twelve Days of Christmas.* The *Water.4.me* project encouraged participants to investigate national and international perspectives on the value of water. The *Interplanetary Holidays* project involved working with New Zealand 'experts' and perspectives on our solar system.

While the *Renowned Olympians Project* included an international flavour the majority of participating classes did choose a New Zealand athlete. Just how important topic relevance is in getting teachers involved in these projects can be seen in Figure 8.

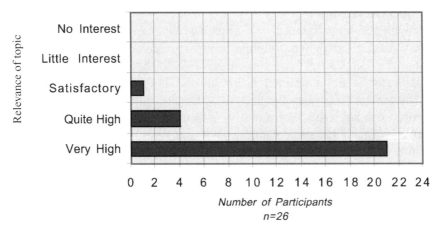

Figure 8: Student interest in the topic in the Renowned Olympians Project

These projects were designed to fit with New Zealand term times and natural teaching cycles, which is often not possible for overseas-based activities, which too often stretch over term or summer breaks for New Zealand students. The instructional context needs to integrate several curricular areas requiring a range of skills from the participants. Both projects covered social studies and language curriculum areas, and incorporated a range of essential curriculum skills such as research, communication and problem-solving.

Well-articulated purposes and flexible processes

Essential to the success of such projects are well-articulated purposes, structure and pacing which need to be clearly stated prior to the beginning of the project and clearly understood by all participants. A flexible approach to keeping to timelines in the game structure is necessary to overcome those difficulties and misunderstandings that can occur when working at a distance. Future projects offered through the *New Zealand Learning Network* need to provide variable project times, so that some are shorter than the standard long-term projects and some are longer. Shorter and more limited projects will be more acceptable to older students and classes.

Levels of commitment

Opportunity to choose various levels of commitment was experimented with in several projects. Providing multiple levels of choice or opportunities for teachers to broaden and deepen the learning experience for their students, if they wish, served to enhance the learning experience for those teachers and students who for various reasons were able to commit more time and energy to the project, or for those student groups who were more proficient. Opportunity for varying levels of commitment is an aspect that needs to be built into the structure of online activities. Instructional activities that allow for groups to safely opt out of parts or sections but still continue their participation in the longer term is another factor that is important to consider for schools participating in these activities.

Project leadership

A committed organiser with time available (about three to four hours each week) and very regular access to an Internet server and interactive online software is also essential. Project leaders have a facilitative role. They need to be very effective communicators in the online environment and need highly effective online organisation and management skills. Leaders need to be flexible thinkers, keen to try new ideas, and prepared to take risks. Collaborative leadership with various teachers from other parts of New Zealand has provided some quite unique opportunities to extend contexts to include a wider range of curriculum areas, and to widen the activity structures and the type of instructional opportunities through the medium.

Learning outcomes first, technology second

Keeping the technological complexity of participation requirements to a minimum is quite important and has worked well. There was, overall, a successful combination of push-and-pull technologies incorporated to overcome those hitches that can occur in the local school network or when children accidentally delete email. In each of the projects, curriculum and instructional contexts take precedence over the learning of technological skills.

Conclusion

This chapter has described some eight collaborative telecommunications projects offered in the New Zealand setting and some ways in which support for integration of technology into the curriculum can be offered to both teachers and students through online collaborative problem-based projects. These projects offer teachers and their classes learning activities that make purposeful use of the communications features of the Internet and the World Wide Web and make pertinent connections to the curriculum. This chapter has highlighted some of the ways teachers are using and managing the projects in their classes, as well as drawn out some of the specific benefits to teachers and to students. Teachers have reported that they have found these projects motivating and challenging for their students and personally stimulating; they have found involvement in these projects a great learning experience for themselves as well as their students. The teacher has a vitally important role to play in the integration of ICT in the delivery of classroom programmes and any assistance that can be given to teachers to foster this process is a part of those all-important steps towards more widespread use.

References

Becker, H. and Ravitz, J. (1999). The influence of computer and Internet use on teachers' pedagogical practices and perceptions. *Journal of Research on Computing in Education*, 31(4), 356-384.

Blumenfeld, P., Soloway, E., Marx, R., Krajcik, J., Guzdial, M., Palincsar, A. (1991). Motivating project-based learning: Sustaining the doing, supporting the learning. *Educational Psychologist*, 26 (34), 369-398.

Brophy, J. & Alleman, J. (1991). Activities as instructional tools: A framework for analysis and evaluation. *Educational Researcher*, 20(4), 9-23.

Campbell, N. (1999). Designing and implementing computer-mediated communication projects in schools. In Lai, K.W. (Ed.). *Networking: Teaching, learning and professional development with the Internet*. (pp.10-121). Dunedin: Otago University Press.

Dimock, K. (2000). Building Relationships, engaging students: A naturalistic study of classrooms participating in the electronic emissary project. Available at: <ftp://ftp.tapr.org/pub/emissary/studies/Dimock.pdf>.

Gray, T. (1997). Does virtual teacher support yield real benefits? In B. Collis & G. Knezek (Eds) *Teaching and Learning in the Digital Age: Research into Practice with Telecommunications in Educational Settings* (pp. 69-85). The Texas Center for Educational Technology and International Society for Technology in Education.

Gray, T. (1998). Online Class: *Comprehensive online learning experiences. A formative evaluation*. Available at: <http://www.edsoasis.org/TGuild/Resources/EvalOC.pdf>.

Hannafin, M. (1992). Emerging technologies, ISD, and learning environments: Critical perspectives. *Educational Technology Research and Development*, 40(1), 4-63.

Harris, J. (1998). Wetware: Why use Activity structures? *Learning and Leading with Technology in Education*. Available at: <http://ccwf.cc.utexas.edu/~jbharris/Virtual-Architecture/Foundation/index.html>.

Harris, J., O'Bryan, E. & Rotenberg, L. (1996). It's a simple idea but it's not easy to do: Practical lessons in telementoring. Available at: <ftp://ftp.tapr.org/pub/emissary/studies/LLT.Oct96.pdf>.

ITAG, (March 2000). *ICT in Schools 1999*. Report prepared for information technology advisory group (ITAG). Available at: <http://www.med.govt.nz/pbt/infotech/ictschools1999/ictschools1999.html>.

Kumari, S. (1998). Teaching with the Internet. *Journal of Information Technology for Teacher Education*, 7 (3), 363-377 .

McGee, P. (1997). Collaboration and unintentional teacher learning in telementoring contexts. Unpublished manuscript. University of Texas San Antonio. Available at: <ftp://ftp.tapr.org/pub/emissary/studies/McGee.pdf>.

Tait, M. (2000). *The Twelve Days of Christmas, Golden Bay High School, Year 9 Information Technology Packaging Assignment*. Available at: <http://education.otago.ac.nz/NZLNet/xmas_project/GBHS-UnitPlan/packaging_home.html>.

The Wired School: Legal, Ethical and Social Issues

8

Anne Elliot

The number of schools connected to the Internet has grown considerably in the last few years. A report about ICT use in New Zealand schools by the Information Technology Advisory Group (ITAG) indicates that 96 per cent of primary and 99 per cent of secondary schools are connected to the Internet (ITAG, 2000). In half of the schools, 'significant numbers' of staff are regular users, while fewer than 30 per cent of schools report significant use by students. This is an increase of almost 50 per cent since 1998. A New Zealand Government Executive press release (Swain, 2000) stated that the Ministry of Education spent $7 million on cabling for schools and estimated that 60 per cent of all classes would be connected to the Internet by the end of 2000. This increase in access has caused uncertainty, confusion and concern by many schools about students' safety when using the Internet. The concern is related to the unhindered access and exposure to information hitherto unavailable in schools. Many of these issues are new to schools and, in spite of an increase in professional development opportunities, the problems teachers and schools can run into are not always apparent, nor is it clear how to prepare safe access for students. The concerns are related to legal, ethical and social issues. This chapter will discuss some of the issues schools should be aware of and suggest ways teachers and schools can make Internet use in schools educationally appropriate and safe. These issues include concerns about Internet content, censorship, privacy and copyright, hacking, spam, harassment and other inappropriate uses of the Internet as well as the implications for schools of the so-called 'digital divide'.

The Diverse Nature of Internet Content

The Internet mirrors society in that it reflects the worst and the best society has to offer. It is not a utopia of sanitised information waiting to be discovered, but a rich environment representing the breadth and variety of 'the human condition'. Some consider this richness the very asset of the Internet, but the unprecedented diversity of material available has brought with it new issues and responsibilities for schools.

Internet pornography, for example, has received a great deal of attention in the media and it does appear to be prolific. According to Hunter (2000), there were an estimated 800 million World Wide Web (WWW) pages in 1999, but others put that figure much higher. No one knows exactly how many of these sites have pornographic content, but their profitability may hold a clue. DataMonitor reported that in 1998, US$1 billion was spent online on 'adult content'. This constitutes 69 per cent of the total Internet content sales (cited in Hughes, 2000). By 2003, such spending is predicted to reach US$3.1 billion, half the anticipated revenue of total online content sales (Hughes, 2000). This income is generated from a membership or subscription fee charged for access and excludes revenue from merchandise and advertising.

While it is clear that pornographic sites are indeed prolific, the media portrays the Internet as if you are likely to stumble upon pornography wherever you go. This is not so. Most pornography sites are visited because people make the deliberate choice to go there. A news item in the *Otago Daily Times* (ODT), for example, reported that the Internet address 'sex.com' could attract a sale price of up to $US85 million ($NZ193.4 million) and was claimed to be a virtual 'licence to print money' (ODT, 2001).

Is the media attention given to pornography an example of 'moral panic' (Goode & Ben-Yehuda, 1994) or 'Net hysteria' (Graham, 1997)? It is obvious that the media have a vested interest in issues that are likely to attract attention. However, in the process of sensationalising the issue of pornography, little distinction appears to be made between adult-intended pornography, much of which is perfectly legal, and paedophilia, which is both abhorrent to most people as well as a being a criminal offence in most countries when it involves the sexual abuse of children. This confusion is illustrated in a Select Committee business summary (Select Committee Office, 2000), which includes the following comment from a submission to the Prohibition of Child Pornography Amendment Bill:

> There was also widespread support for a comprehensive review of censorship laws in New Zealand particularly given *the proliferation of pornography arising from the growth of the Internet* [italics added]. (Select Committee Office, 2000, paragraph 21)

It is clear that the important issue of protecting children from sexual abuse was merged in the minds of those making submissions with a worry about the general increase in pornography on the Internet, when the two are very separate issues (see the illuminating article *The nature and dimension of child pornography on the Internet* (Taylor, 1999) accessible online at <http://www.stop-childpornog.at/pa_taylor.html>.

Censorship and the 'dark side' of the Internet

In New Zealand, access to pornography has historically been regulated by censorship. Section 3 of the Films, Videos and Publications Classification Act 1993 defines as 'objectionable', i.e. illegal, that which depicts or promotes 'sex, horror, crime, cruelty, or violence in such a manner that it is injurious to the public good' <http://rangi.knowledge-basket.co.nz/gpacts/public/text/1993/an/094.html>. Objectionable material includes that which depicts:

1. exploitation of children or young persons for sexual purposes;
2. sexual conduct with or upon the body of a dead person (necrophilia);
3. bestiality (sex with animals);
4. acts of torture;
5. promotes or encourages criminal acts or acts of terrorism.

The Act, then, refers not only to material we may normally associate with the concept 'pornography,' but also to a much greater variety of material, such as sites promoting 'cyber terrorism' or anti-Semitism (see, for example, the Anti-Defamation League's site at <http://www.adl.org/>).

Internet industry self-regulation

In 1996, the Department of Internal Affairs clarified their interpretation of the Films, Videos and Publications Classification Act 1993 and outlined newsgroups which are objectionable under the Act. This resulted in the removal of some of the worst offending newsgroups by ISPs (Watson & Shuker, 1998). While access to offensive material, including pornography, is available through all New Zealand Internet Service Providers (ISP), the Internet industry has a vested interest in promoting itself as responsible. To this end, an Internet Code of Practice was developed by the Internet Society of New Zealand (ISOCNZ) to give 'the industry the chance to demonstrate to government and the public its commitment to high standards' (ISOCNZ, 1999). One of the society's objects is 'to liaise with other organisations, New Zealand Government authorities, and the general public for co-ordination, collaboration, and education in effecting the above objects' (ISOCNZ, 1998, Article 2.10). While some ISPs are not members of ISOCNZ, they all operate within the same general guidelines. However, as the ISP Xtra explains,

> No one could possibly sit down and look at the millions and millions of files available on the Internet – files that can change daily or even more frequently. This is the nature of the Internet. Even if Internet Service Providers could keep tabs on all newsgroups – which they can't – it is simply not possible to uncover all offensive material that may be disguised or hidden under seemingly innocent guises. <http://www.xtrasite.co.nz/info/terms/>.

In spite of industry self-regulation measures and provision of user-education and client acceptable-use agreements, legal and ethical Internet use is ultimately up to the user.

'Policing' the Internet

The Censorship Compliance Unit of the Department of Internal Affairs is charged with ensuring that publications considered objectionable are not made available to members of the public. It also investigates complaints and may call on the police to help (all police are Inspectors of Publications). The activities of the Department of Internal Affairs were explained by the previous chief executive:

> Internal Affairs has been quite active in terms of censorship on the Internet recently, and we have quite a few prosecutions pending ... a search warrant can be issued, but simply possessing these materials is not enough to allow a warrant. By entering into public chat groups such as pre & teensexpics, our inspectors are able to find people who are supplying objectionable materials. With evidence of this they are able to obtain a search warrant which allows them to get the name and address from the Internet service provider. Once they have this information they are then able to obtain a search warrant to search the person's home (Blakeley, 1997).

The unit's activities are reported regularly in the news media (see, for example, <http://www.nzherald.co.nz/storydisplay.cfm?thesection=news&thesubsection=&storyID=143973>).

Slevin (2000) suggests that we must be careful not to let the media's negative reporting about the Internet prevent us from engaging with it. While its impact may cause anxiety, ICT is becoming fundamental to how we live. If we are to develop of using the Internet, we need to acquire a more informed understanding develop paedagogically appropriate ways of using it in schools. Relying on say or being convinced by the media that the Internet is too dangerous a place to let children visit will deprive children of some great opportunities to learn about the medium and about the world.

Guiding Internet Access in Schools

As the Internet cannot readily be intercepted at New Zealand's gateway to Cyberspace, schools are faced with several challenges when making the Internet available to students and staff. One is to make surfing legal, another is to make it appropriate in relation to the ages of the children. A system for indicating age appropriateness of legal material is used in the classification of films and videos (Table 1).

Table 1: The classification system for films and videos

'objectionable'	illegal to view or possess
restricted	18 – restricted to persons 18 years and over 16 – restricted to persons 16 years and over R – specified restrictions
unrestricted	G – suitable for general audience PG – parental guidance recommended for younger viewers M – suitable for mature audiences 16 years of age and over

It would not be practical to evaluate each Internet site as if it were a film, nor could this take into account the various contexts for access. However, the classification system does indicate how we as a society seek to protect children while acknowledging that young people should gradually have access to more challenging material commensurate with their stages of maturity.

What schools can do
Teacher professional development in ICT

Schools have many options for making Internet access an appropriate and legal experience for children. First, schools and teachers should become informed about the issues by becoming familiar with the Internet. Second, they should become acquainted with the Act and how it relates to the Internet. In a research study in 1999 (Lai, 2001), teachers were asked if they knew about the Films, Videos and Publications Classification Act 1993. Twenty-two per cent of secondary respondents said they knew about the Act, but when asked what they knew about it, very few could describe what the Act was about. Only when teachers and schools are informed can they make educationally appropriate decisions about how to manage children's Internet access.

Familiarisation with the Internet for teachers could include:

• **Providing time and assistance for teachers to explore the Internet.** Schools must ensure that teachers who are not familiar with the Internet are given time and assistance to explore what the online world is like and what content is available. A good start would be to access the excellent educational resources available for both students and teachers. These could include the resource centre for New Zealand teachers, *Te Kete Ipurangi* <http://www.tki.org.nz>, *The New Zealand Learning Network* <http://education.otago.ac.nz/NZLNet/home.nclk>, *Sunshine Online* <http://www.sunshine.co.nz/nz/index.html> for junior teachers, the *Education Gazette Online* <http://www.edgazette.govt.nz>, and the Ministry of Education <http://www.minedu.govt.nz/>. Having a personal email address would also support teachers in becoming personal users and gaining contextual experience. As Internet use is a cost to the schools, limits to use should be discussed, and access should suit teachers' schedules. In addition, acceptable use standards such as those included in the *Draft Corporate Code Of Practice For Organisations* (available from the Department of Internal Affairs' website – see *Resources for Schools* below) should also be discussed. Support in the form of staff peer tutoring could also be explored.

• **Using search engines.** Searches for educationally appropriate as well as dark-side sites could be tried. This would reveal the vastness of material available on the Internet and provide a context for discussing potential issues for student use. Search strategies, for example using boolean operators, should be tried and the results examined to demonstrate the importance of effective search strategies. Another useful strategy is to read the descriptions carefully to determine what would be an appropriate and useful link. A New Zealand search for 'sex' and 'women' might, for example, include the following two results:

Writers Workshop: Free Stuff
People get very embarrassed about sex. Perhaps with reason. It's a good idea to use the word 'gender' when you are talking about …

Welcome to the Kiwi Guide!
Sex Guide! Tell the girls what you want! 24/7 unlimited LIVE video conferencing with hot girls for free! You have to check these …

Which would be an appropriate site to access for information about the term 'gender'?

• **Exploring newsgroups.** Newsgroups, mentioned above, are a form of electronic discussion lists. There are many thousands of newsgroups (ClearNet state that they have access to more than 35,000) covering an enormous range of subjects. Because anyone can participate in newsgroups, the quality of the discussions varies a great deal. To find newsgroups on a particular topic, search in one of the news directories, for example Liszt <http://www.liszt.com/news/>. There are many newsgroups of interest to teachers covering such topics as using technology, curriculum and classroom-to-classroom projects. An example is *k12.ed.math*, where discussions on mathematics education take place. Postings can be read by everyone, but to participate in a discussion, you need to configure your newsreader program by entering your ISP's news server details (see, for example, ClearNet's news tutorials at <http://www.clear.net.nz/documentation/howto/mac/tutorial/news/>). There are numerous dark-side newsgroups. This is one of the places where objectionable material, such as paedophilia, is said to be exchanged, because of the ease with which images can be attached to postings and circulated to a worldwide audience.

- **Chat groups.** Chat is a popular activity with Internet users of all ages. It is a very social activity and mostly not very serious. While schools may choose not to make chat available, teachers could familiarise themselves with it. Xtra's chat area, <http://www.xtrachat.co.nz/>, has helpful tips for new users. A comprehensive and up-to-date Australian review of chat options and their implications for schools is at <http://www.sofweb.vic.edu.au/Internet/chat.htm>. While chat groups provide a social outlet for many people, this is also an area of the Net where children and young people can be tempted to divulge personal information or be frightened. This can happen when chat participants pretend to be someone else by changing their age and gender. While certain chat groups are monitored by the police and the Censorship Compliance Unit for potentially illegal activities, most chat groups give great pleasure to many people.

- **Explore WWW content.** There are types of WWW content, which may be of concern when accessed by children and young people. These include sites that promote racism, for example:
– *Stormfront* promotes 'white pride' at <http://www.stormfront.org/> and features a children's section.
– *Future Generations* at <http://www.eugenics.net/> promotes eugenics.
– *Resistance* at <http://www.resistance.com> is a magazine for 'white power' music, where music and its lyrics are used to promote racist values and attitudes.
    While these sites may not incite violence or cruelty, they do promote hatred of others in a manner most people would find offensive.

Educational solutions
- **Teaching children about the Internet.** The most powerful way to manage Internet access with students of all ages is to apply the same educational principles to it as teachers do to other areas. Online safety and responsibility should be an ongoing and thought-provoking topic. Use the 'teachable moment', but also plan actual sessions, where issues are integrated into curriculum areas. Teacher ICT professional development sessions, in-school discussions or syndicate planning sessions are opportunities for brainstorming ideas and developing collaborative units. Topics teachers could choose include:
    Free speech – what is it? Why do we value it so highly? Has there always been free speech? Are there international conventions about freedom of expression? What would it be like if we did not have free speech? What are the limitations to free speech? Is free speech always a good thing?
    Anonymity – a characteristic of online communications that may change the way we behave. How may anonymity change how we act?

How can we deal with challenging online experiences? What should we do if we accidentally access inappropriate sites? Brainstorm ideas.

Discuss the dark side of the Internet. Students need to know that there are sites which are considered harmful. They also need to know why. Dependent on the age of the students, explain that some sites contain pornography and other profane and obscene materials, hate and racist material, and information about dangerous or unhealthy activities. Explain that such sites reflect the negative side of human nature and are based on the values of people who do not share a vision of the world as a peaceful place, where all people and other living things are treated with caring and respect (based on Willard, 2000).

- **Acceptable use policies (AUP).** A student policy for Internet is usually referred to as an Acceptable Use Policy (AUP) and establishes what a student may and may not do with computers at school (see AUP template in Appendix B). The policy seeks to protect the student, teacher and school from legal liability and moral responsibility. Schools usually require students and a parent or caregiver to sign an actual agreement before access is made available. An AUP can also establish the consequences of inappropriate Internet use, but having an AUP is unlikely in itself to provide safe and responsible Internet access for students. First, an AUP needs to be kept up-to-date. Second, it needs to reflect the collective vision of the school and staff as well as the school's ICT plan. Third, an ongoing programme should be in place, where students can increasingly learn about the online world. Developing an AUP can be a useful way for a school to focus on the educational use the Internet will be put to and the issues involved in this. It is also likely to highlight the need for a staff Internet policy, which would indicate staff responsibilities and rights as employees, procedures for dealing with breaches of copyright and privacy and 'netiquette'. The *Draft Corporate Code of Practice for Organisations*, mentioned above, would serve as a useful model. It should be noted that the Department of Internal Affairs states: 'The draft is only a guideline. Having a Code of Conduct will not protect you from prosecution action so organisations should always consider getting their own legal advice' <http://www.censorship.dia.govt. nz/DIAwebsite.nsf/URLindex/DF667AB0DC96F927CC2568F7007CB1D1>.

- **Promotion of safe sites.** A school can promote sites known to provide access only to appropriate content. Such sites can be bookmarked in the browser so that children can visit or search independently. There are many sites entirely devoted to making children's online experiences appropriate, fun and educational. They include: *Ask Jeeves for Kids* <http://www.ajkids.com/>, *Launch Site* <http://www.launchsite .org/english/index.html> and *Yahooligans* <http://www.yahooligans.com>.

- **Passwords.** Internet access requires a password to be entered at the beginning of a session and teachers can ensure this is not given out to children. To keep passwords confidential, it is recommended that they are changed frequently, and that they are noted somewhere to allow access for other staff members.

• **Supervision.** Children could be permitted to use the Internet only under supervision. For classroom computers, this is usually not a problem. If a library, for example, does not have an adult present at all times, access may need to be restricted to those times when supervision is available. Some schools allow Internet access at lunchtimes in a suitable location where supervision is provided.

• **Placement of computers.** Computers can be placed in such a way that teachers can see the monitor from most places in a classroom or library. When students know that teachers can see the monitor, they are more likely to go only where it is appropriate to go.

Technical solutions
• **Intranet.** Schools are increasingly installing network cabling (ITAG, 2000). With the addition of a web server (a dedicated computer which can store and retrieve HTML documents) a private network using Internet software and standards can be created. An intranet allows for the storage of material for offline browsing (see below), student-created material to be available to everyone in the school and the monitoring of students' activities when they access the Internet. This form of monitoring often ensures greater compliance with Acceptable Use Policies.

• **Offline browsing.** Schools can save web pages as well as whole sites for children to use offline.
Netscape has three ways of saving individual pages:
1. To save only the text, use the *Save As* command and then choose to save as *Text*. Such pages can later be opened in a browser but the images will be missing, and text and background will be black and grey. Some characters may also have changed.
2. Pages can also be saved as HTML by choosing to save as *Source*. This enables the colours and layout of the page to be retained, but the images will be missing.
3. If using the *Communicator* version of Netscape, open the page in the composer by choosing *File* from the menu bar, then *Edit Page*. Save the page in a separate folder, which will contain the actual page as well as any associated images.
In *Internet Explorer*, pages can be saved not only as plain text or HTML files, but also as a 'Web Archive.' In the menu bar, go to *File* → *Save As*, then choose *Web Archive*. The *Options* button gives a choice of downloading images, sounds, movies and links as well as how many levels (pages) deep. A warning is given about the time such downloads may take, especially if several levels are required.
Where better management of saved/downloaded pages is required, special software can be used to save the entire page, including images. Such software programs can, for example, be found at DaveCentral's *Offline Readers for the PC* at <http://www.davecentral.com/offline.html>, and the Tucows collection at <http://tucows.ihug.co.nz/offline95.html> for PC and <http://mac.tucows.netc.on.net.au/offlinemac.html> for Macintosh.
WebWhacker is one of the offline browsing programs available from the sites mentioned above and a review can be found at TeacherNet.com at <http://www.teachnet.com/how-to/organization/webwhacker031599.html>.

Using software for offline browsing brings with it a number of advantages, for example, saving on online costs, speedy access to downloaded pages, increasing the ability for parents and others to be involved in finding resources, and being able to transport pages and sites by disk to a classroom computer not connected to the Internet. However, copyright issues have to be considered. Schools should contact Web owners for permission before downloading whole sites. Schools should also bear in mind that information can quickly become outdated.

• **Filtering or blocking of Internet content.** Filtering either permits access only to predetermined sites (inclusion filtering) or excludes access to sites with content considered inappropriate (exclusion filtering). Inclusion filtering is based on so-called 'white lists,' which include only sites that have been vetted for the appropriateness of their content. It is based on self-reporting, where the authors or publishers of websites choose to have their content rated. It can be very effective if the person or organisation compiling the list shares the same set of values as the Internet user. The disadvantage of inclusion filtering is that a relatively small portion of the World Wide Web (WWW) has been rated. In 1999, for example, 100,000 websites were using RSACi to self-rate (cited in Hunter, 2000). *Yahooligans* <http://www.yahooligans.com> is based on an inclusion list of over 3,000 websites (CSIRO, 1999). Exclusion filtering is more common and is based on 'black lists' of sites considered objectionable. 'Black lists' are claimed to be unreliable, because, for example, many new websites are published each day making it is impossible for organisations to keep up their review of sites.

Web pages can be rated and labelled by the website publishers or authors to indicate the nature of their content. Several organisations offer ratings systems; for example, the Recreational Software Advisory Council of the Internet (RSACi) as shown in Table 2.[1]

Table 2: The RSACi rating system

	Violence	**Nudity**	**Sex**	**Language**
Level 4	Rape or wanton gratuitous violence	Provocative frontal nudity	Explicit sexual acts or sexual crimes	Crude, vulgar language or extreme hate speech
Level 3	Aggressive violence or death to humans	Frontal nudity	Non-explicit sexual acts	Strong language hate speech
Level 2	Destruction of realistic objects	Partial nudity	Partial nudity	Clothed sexual touching
Level 1	Injury to human beings	Revealing attire	Passionate kissing	Mild expletives
Level 0	None of the above or sports related	None of the above	None of the above or innocent kissing; romance	None of the above

If content of a site is rated at Level 0 in all four categories, a label may be added to that site.[2]

Filtering with dedicated filtering software. Filtering software interacts with other programs installed on a computer and uses certain keywords to monitor, screen and block access to any material whether the computer is connected to the Internet or not. Filtering software works in the background and is invisible to the user. There are many different filtering programs available, both shareware and commercial programs. Shareware programmes can, for example, be found at DaveCentral's *Kid Safe Surfing* pages <http://www.davecentral.com/kidsafe.html>, at Tucows *Parental Control* section, <http://tucows.ihug.co.nz/parent95.html> for the PC and <http://mac.tucows. netc.on.net.au/parentmac.html> for Macintosh. Commercial programs include *CyberPatrol* <http://www.cyberpatrol.com/>, *CYBERSitter* <http://www.cybersitter. com> and *NetNanny* <http://www.netnanny.com/>. Each program has slightly different categories and rating levels, which can be chosen to suit the environment in which the computer is used. A password controls access to the settings which, for example, can prevent personal information from being given out on the Internet; mask inappropriate words, phrases or language; prevent certain specified sites from being accessed (based on black lists); and keep an event log, which records all sites visited by the user. Filtering software companies provide updates to the list of bad sites at various intervals. These can be downloaded from the companies' Internet sites by subscription.

Setting up your browser to block access to Internet content. Internet browsers can also be set to block access to websites. *Internet Explorer* for the PC, version 4.0 and up, has a built-in filter, which is located in *Internet Explorer's* menu bar under *Tools → Internet Options → Content → Content Adviser.* The filter uses a ratings standard based on the RSACi rating system, mentioned earlier. The filter settings are accessed with a password, can be changed at any time, and can be turned completely off. Comprehensive instructions about how to set up the filter is available at <http:// www.rsac.org/>, by clicking on the link *Parents – How to use ICRA. Internet Explorer* for the Macintosh has a simpler, built-in filter found in the menu bar under *Edit → Preferences → Web Browser → Ratings.*

Netscape for both the PC and Macintosh uses a feature called *NetWatch* to block access to unwanted sites. To set up *NetWatch,* go to the menu bar in the *Netscape* browser and choose Help → NetWatch. This takes you to the *NetWatch* information page at <http://home.netscape.com/comprod/products/communicator/netwatch/>. Click on the 'NetWatch setup process' link and follow the instructions.

Divided opinions on filter software. Filter software has generated a lot of discussion. One argument against is that filtering simply makes invisible that which children will be able to access at home and in the wider community. Willard (1998) suggests that the use of filtering to limit children's access can lead to a deceptive sense of security. This may in turn result in complacency in supervision; lack of enforcement of AUP agreements; less emphasis on the importance of students being equipped to use the Internet safely and responsibly; and less emphasis on students acquiring information literacy. Another argument against the use of filtering software is that it cannot be guaranteed to prevent access to all. Furthermore, it can also block access to sites which may contain no objectionable material at all. A light-hearted 'Foil the Filters' competition organised by Digital Freedom Network <http://www.dfn.org> illustrates how unreliable 'censorware' is (Brown, 2000). Examples of winners include:

- a secondary student, who was unable to access his own high school's website from his own school's libary, because the filtering software blocked access to sites containing the word 'high';
- a person called Hillary Anne, who was unable to register her name because it included the word 'aryan', and someone called Heather, who was unable to register her name because it contained the phrase 'eat her';
- a company website called 'Surplus Exchange' could not be reached by its customers because it contained the word 'sex' (http://dnf.org/focus/censor/contest.htm);

To decide whether to filter or not, schools will need to become informed about the pros and cons (see the *Resources for Schools* section below).

Copyright

Copyright automatically applies to all creative work. No special protection is needed for the author or creator to be regarded the owner of that copyright, for example by displaying a copyright notice. However, many people do display a copyright notice on their work to ensure that their work is understood to be protected. Sometimes authors may grant other people permission to use their material by stating that their work may be freely used or distributed. Such permission is usually granted in a restricted way, i.e, stating where and how it can be used. Copyright expires fifty years after the creator's death. The Copyright Act 1994 states that creative work made available via a computer network is considered a form of publishing and is therefore protected against copying for other than the purpose of research or private study (sections 10 and 43 of the Act, available at <http://rangi.knowledge-basket.co.nz/gpacts/public/text/1994/an/143.html>).

Plagiarism

Plagiarism is claiming the work of others as one's own. While plagiarism has always been a problem in schools, computer use has greatly increased the ease with which students can plagiarise. With CD-ROM encyclopedias now a common source of information for children, 'cut-and-paste' has never been easier. The Internet has added to this ease.

There are three ways plagiarism may occur in schools: unintentional, where students do not know what plagiarism is or that acknowledgements need to be made by citing the sources used; intentional 'cut and paste'; and a new form of 'wholesale' plagiarism, where entire essays on any topic can be downloaded from the Internet. The are more than 80 sites, so-called 'paper mills' (see http://www.coastal.edu/library/mills2.htm), which offer essays for download. An example is *School Sucks* at <http://www.schoolsucks.com>. This new form of plagiarism has caused software to be developed that can, for example, identify, create and compare keyword profiles between electronic documents.

What schools can do

- Whether students have access to computers or not, research skills should be taught from an early age and are usually part of a school's information literacy skills programme. In smaller schools, where specialist school librarians may not be available, information literacy programmes often rely on the expertise of the individual classroom teacher.
- Teach students how to acknowledge other people's work in their references, both print-based and electronic (see, for example, *Citing Internet Resources* <http://connectedteacher.classroom.com/newsletter/citeintres.asp> and *Plagiarism & Referencing Electronic Resources* <http://www.sofweb.vic.edu.au/Internet/research.htm#reference>.
- Focus less on students being required to find discrete facts and more on students building new understandings, so that they become producers of insights and ideas rather than mere consumers (McKenzie, 1998).
- Teachers could discuss both the practical and ethical implications of intellectual property rights by examining websites. An example of a website where children may find material that interests them is the *National Institute of Water and Atmospheric Research* (NIWA) at <http://www.niwa.cri.nz/>. Here copyright is clearly indicated:

Copyright © 1998, 1999, 2000 NIWA. All rights reserved.
Graphics and page construction by Greg Lowe.
Last modified 22 December 2000.
Please address all queries and comments to WebMaster@niwa.cri.nz.

Discuss how students are permitted to quote from such a site by acknowledging the source, but that one cannot use the material in any publicly published work, for example on a website, without permission. Permission could be sought by emailing the web master and is often granted, specifying the limit of the permitted use. This can serve as a model of appropriate behaviour. (*Citing Internet Resources*, mentioned above, explains how to reference electronic images.)
- Discuss what 'fair use' is.

Copyright on Software

Section 80 of the Copyright 1994 Act explains how copyright applies to computer programs. The Act states that it is illegal to make a copy of a program except as a back-up for one's personal use (see <http://rangi.knowledge-basket.co.nz/gpacts/public/text/1994/an/143.html>).

It is often assumed that when one buys a software program, one owns it. What is owned is the licence to use that software, usually on just one computer. One cannot, for example, sell a computer at a higher price by pretending also to sell the installed software without providing the original disks.

Many software programs can be downloaded from the Internet, both freeware, shareware and commercial programs. Freeware programs are, as the name indicates, able to be used without a fee. Shareware, however, requires a small fee to be paid. This is usually not paid for at the time of downloading, as programs are offered for a try-out period. Users are expected to pay a small fee to continue using that software. Registration and payment are usually be made by email with a credit card. An 'activation key' is then returned. As upgrades become available, registered users can download these free.

The difference between shareware and commercial software is that shareware often continues to be functional after the expiry of the trial period, albeit with a reminder showing up after each restart. Commercial software is often save disabled and will cease to function after the trial period.

With the popularity of CD-ROM writers, copyright is easily infringed on all manner of material, including MP3 music files. It has been reported, for example, that 4,000 pirated CDs were seized during 2000 (Independent Newspapers Ltd, 2000b) and more than 200 counterfeit operations closed down with six criminal convictions (InfoTech Online, 2000). In Auckland, 3,000 counterfeit computer games were crushed at a public event to demonstrate the loss of $20–30 million per year to piracy (Independent Newspapers Ltd, 2000a). Recently, an incident of a 'bootleg' CD, given to a child for Christmas, shocked many parents because it contained images of child pornography and had links to Russian pornographic sites. The CD had been made from content downloaded from the Internet and was bought at a flea market (Independent Newspapers Ltd, 2000b). CDs of pirated software or music, including illegal compilations of MP3 files downloaded from the Internet, may be offered for sale amongst students without the school being aware of this.

What schools can do
- Model appropriate ethical behaviour by ensuring that all software, including shareware, is used according to the licence agreements. This entails having a sufficient number of licences for installed software. It also entails ensuring either that the required fee is paid at the end of a trial period, or that such software is uninstalled. Having a pop-up reminder window appear at every start-up does not send the right signal to students. Modelling appropriate software use reinforces the legal and ethical position taken by a school in other computer use.
- Look at software packages with students and discuss the copyright notices. What do users agree to?
- Compile a list of justifications people may use to excuse copyright infringement and discuss their moral and ethical validity. What are the legal implications of positions taken?
- Discuss with senior students that ethically significant problems in computer use are acknowledged by many professional organisations, which have developed codes of behaviour for their members. Visit, for example, the *Online Ethics Center* at <http://onlineethics.org/>.

Privacy

It is easy to assume that we are anonymous and retain our privacy on the Internet. This is far from the truth. A search of the archives of *Privacy Forum*, <http://www.vortex.com/privacy>, will reveal the numerous ways our online privacy is compromised and *JunkBusters*, <http://www.junkbusters.com/ht/en/cookies.html>, demonstrates how users can be tracked from their mouse clicks by the use of 'cookies' (small codes invisibly placed on your computer). Under 'What your browser tells them', click on the link to the demonstration page to see what information about you can be detected by others.

Children are not immune from invasion of their privacy. Online marketing and advertising target children and young people by luring them with branded environments. *Sesame Street*, <http://www.sesamestreet.org>, for example, uses their colourful and personable characters to combine children's games, stories, music and art with merchandising and advertising. By the seamless integration of advertising and content children can be manipulated to divulge information sought by advertisers and marketing organisations. Examples include the mail room, where children are invited to send email to a Sesame Street character, and a sweepstake activity, which involves entering your personal details such as name, email address, postal code, age, gender and number of children in the household. An opportunity to 'Tell me more' is also offered with a further seventeen pieces of personal information requested. Comprehensive and detailed privacy statements are included on the site and these state, for example, that no information provided by children under thirteen will be used without prior parental consent. However, a sense of unease may prevail when the following statements also occur:
- Under the link 'Advertising':
  Alliances with the most powerful partners on the Web, such as AOL, Excite and Netscape, mean the Workshop is the #1 source for family fun, learning, and resources. Check out how you can make Sesame Workshop work for you! <http://www.sesamestreet.org/advertising/0,4228,,00.html>.
- Under the link 'Affiliates':
  Earn Commission: Add Sesamestreet.com links to your Web site and earn .03 cents per click through. The more clicks, the more money you earn!
  < http://www.sesamestreet.org/affiliates/0,5414,,00.html>.

An article, 'Web of deception: Threats to children from online marketing' examines the marketing and data-collection practices on the Internet targeted at children (Montgomery & Pasnik, 1996). In the US, the Children's Online Privacy Protection Act (COPPA) came into effect in 1998. It regulates the collection of personal information from children under age thirteen in order to protect children's privacy on the Internet.

What schools can do

There are many interesting and educational things schools can do to teach children about privacy online.
- Children will, for example, be fascinated by cookies and, depending on the age of the children, they could investigate how cookies work and if any are stored on the

classroom computer. (For further information about cookies, see <http://www.kidsprivacy.org/terms.html>)

- Investigate the Privacy Act 1993. Visit the Privacy Commissioner's website at <http://www.privacy.org.nz>. A variety of resources is available. It also features some very amusing and thought-provoking cartoons, which could be used as starting points for discussions.
- Subscribe to the Privacy Commissioner's newsletter (see <http://www.privacy.org.nz/privword/pwtop.html>).
- Check if the school's website has a privacy statement which informs visitors what the school does with information it collects from visitors. If not, draft one and present it to the ICT co-ordinator for feedback (see the sample privacy statement in Appendix B).
- Visit Kidsprivacy.org and check out the *Tips for Guiding Children Online* at <http://kidsprivacy.org/tips.html> or *Rules to Surf By: Teach Your Kids to be Privacy-Wise* at <http://www.getnetwise.org/safetyguide/privacy/>. (For a definition of what a privacy policy is, see <http://www.kidsprivacy.org/terms.html>)
- Discuss with students what personal information actually means. (For an explanation of personal information, see <http://www.kidsprivacy.org/terms.html>.)

Schools' Online Publishing

Previously, many schools have produced school magazines with photos of children and examples of their school work. With schools increasingly having their own websites, new privacy, copyright and safety issues have arisen. Schools will already be well acquainted with the Privacy Act 1993, which has as one of its main purposes the promotion and protection of individual information privacy. The Act contains twelve information privacy principles dealing with the collection, holding, use and disclosure of personal information and with the assigning of 'unique identifiers' (Privacy Commissioner, 1998). This means that students have the right to privacy in their personal information, including their photos. Students also have copyright on their school work and schools may be breaching copyright if school work is published without consent. To ensure that students' rights are not breached, the Ministry of Education has issued a *Guidelines for Schools for the Online Publication of Student Images and Schoolwork* (Ministry of Education, 2000).

What schools cannot control is what students publish privately outside of school. Recently, an American student published a website about what he thought of a particular teacher. This was not complimentary. Although the page was created and put on the Internet from home, it demonstrates the ease with which what should be private can be broadcast to the world.

What schools can do

- Schools should adopt a policy for the publication of students' images and school work on a school website.
- In primary schools, written consent should be obtained from each student's parents or legal guardians, and in secondary schools also from each student, before

publishing any information about the student (including photographs) or any of the student's copyright material on the Internet.

- The consents should be sought when they first enrol or, for students already enrolled, when the issue of publication first arises for that student.
- Before publishing a student's material on the Internet, the school should check that they have the appropriate consent and be aware that publication may have legal consequences, i.e. schools should ensure the material does not infringe copyright, does not defame, is not objectionable from a human rights point of view, and is not obscene.
- Schools should discuss what the purpose of their website is. How will children's work and images enhance that purpose? Is the material better shared on a school intranet?
- When using photographs of teachers or children, choose those where identification of individuals is not possible. Images can also be blurred in an image manipulation program such as PhotoShop.
- Teachers should discuss with students what responsibility publishing on the Web carries with it. Discuss what defamation is. What purpose does proof-reading serve? Is plagiarism an issue? What would it feel like to discover *your* idea on someone else's website?
- Personal information about either students or staff, such as addresses and telephone numbers, should never be published. Email links on a school website should always be to a general school mailbox and not to an individual's email address. All such mail should be checked first by teachers.

Online Manners: 'Netiquette', Computer Ethics, Hacking, etc.

'Netiquette' is a broad term describing what is deemed to be appropriate behaviour on the Internet. It denotes, for example, the conventions that have developed online to convey the manners we use in real life. 'Smileys' are symbols one can use to communicate emotions, for example, ☺ for saying things of a light-hearted nature and ☺ for 'just kidding'. Acronyms are also in common usage, for example 'BTW' for 'by the way.' Netiquette also refers to responsible behaviour, which does not annoy or inconvenience others, in email, mailing lists and newsgroups. WRITING IN CAPITAL LETTERS, for example, indicates shouting and is frowned upon (see ClearNet's netiquette page at <http://www.clear.net.nz/netscape/services/netiquette.html> for more information).

We are all guided in our everyday conduct by our personal ethical standards. Computer and Internet use can produce a sense of anonymity, which may lead some to change their usual ethical standards subconsciously. The computer industry is aware of the temptations that exist within the industry to behave in ways that are unethical and/or illegal. The Computer Ethics Institute, for example, developed the *Ten Commandments for Computer Ethics* to bring attention to the issue:

- Thou shalt not use a computer to harm other people.
- Thou shalt not interfere with other people's computer work.
- Thou shalt not snoop around in other people's files.

- Thou shalt not use a computer to steal.
- Thou shalt not use a computer to bear false witness.
- Thou shalt not use or copy software for which you have not paid.
- Thou shalt not use other people's computer resources without authorization.
- Thou shalt not appropriate other people's intellectual output.
- Thou shalt think about the social consequences of the program you write.
- Thou shalt use a computer in ways that show consideration and respect.

(http://www.brook.edu/ITS/CEI/CEI_HP.HTM)

Students' natural curiosity and stage of moral development may tempt some to engage in inappropriate computer use.

More unusual uses of the Internet include 'hacking',[3] 'spamming'[4] and the planting of 'viruses'.[5] These serve no educational purpose. Most ISPs require clients, including schools, to sign user agreements that protect other users from these behaviours. Possible computer-related misconduct is, therefore, a real issue for schools, especially among older students.

Hackers gain access to other people's computers for various purposes, for example to 'test' the level of security or to get free Internet access. A hacker was reported to have gained access to a number of Xtra customer's passwords and, hence, to their Internet accounts by circulating a 'Trojan horse' virus by email (*New Zealand Herald Online*, 2000b). Virus attacks occur with monotonous regularity. Hoax virus warnings also circulate by email with monotonous regularity and can cause a great deal of unnecessary anxiety. Some hackers promote the free flow of information and consider their illegal actions ethical, because they 'help' people (see for example Wired News' *Crackers attack China on rights* at <http://www.wired.com/news/politics/0,1283,15857,00.html>).

Spam is another form of Internet abuse, where unsolicited junk email is sent, often in large quantities. It is annoying, because the recipient pays to download it and spends time dealing with it. Most spam consists of advertising. Often recipients have inadvertently subscribed to or agreed to be willing to receive information about products, for example when joining a free email program. Mail bombs involve sending volumes of emails so large that it may overload someone's email box and possibly bring down an ISP's entire service. Some spam contains information about how to make money quickly. The Ministry of Consumer Affairs operates a *Scam Watch* page <http://www.consumer-ministry.govt.nz/scam_alert.html>, where current Internet scams can be checked. It also provides advice on what to do when you have been spammed.

A Crimes Amendment Bill (http://www.isocnz.org.nz/crimes-sop.html) is under consideration, and would make 'cyber crime', such as hacking, a crime.

What schools can do
- Schools should ensure that their computer systems are as secure as possible. This is a specialist area and involves getting professional technical advice.
- Schools should also ensure that their systems are protected with virus protection software. Such software needs to be updated regularly to protect against new viruses. Virus tips and prevention, as well as links to many useful resources about viruses,

can be found at <http://www.tki.org.nz/r/ict/interact/virus_info_e.php>

- An AUP will usually include the consequences of behaving in ways that are illegal, annoying and that infringe the rights of others. Most of the more extreme antics students may engage in can be avoided if schools are aware of the potential problems; protect themselves with user agreements which spell out what acceptable computer use is; create a school computer culture which is respectful of the rights of others; provide interesting and engaging learning experiences; and believe students to be capable of making the right choices.
- Use the *Ten Commandments for Computer Ethics* as a discussion starter. Discuss why the computer industry has found it necessary to develop guidelines such as these. Invite students to revise the list or add to it on an ongoing basis.
- Discuss how to deal with spam. Develop a list of spam do's and dont's (see <http://www.arachnoid.com/lutusp/antispam.html#overview_dos_donts>).
- Visit the Ministry of Consumer Affairs' *Scam Watch* page, mentioned earlier. Discuss what may tempt people and how one can avoid being drawn in.

Social Issues

New social issues have also arisen with the advent of the Internet. These range from concern about the different levels of access expressed by the term 'digital divide,' to addiction and alarming online behaviour, for example 'hate speech'.

The digital divide is a worldwide phenomenon and the term illustrates the disparity between the 'haves' and 'have nots'. In Britain, for example, a Social Exclusion Unit was established to smooth out the differences between the information-rich and information-poor. One of its Policy Action Teams announced a £252 million initiative to establish 1,000 telecentres in the community to provide greater access to ICTs, for example in sports clubs, TABs and schools. In New Zealand, the government has recognised the growing disparity in ICT access, use and skill, and the Cabinet Economic Development Committee stated its vision for closing this digital divide in June 2000:

> All New Zealanders … have the opportunity to access and effectively use current and emergent information and communications technologies … to participate fully in the economic, social, educational, cultural and democratic opportunities available in an information society (quoted in Maharey & Swain, 2000).

To promote this goal, the government published a substantial paper, *Closing the Digital Divide* (Maharey & Swain, 2000), which documents what is already known about the digital divide, the problems associated with equitable access and what further work is required. It notes nine groups deemed more likely to be disadvantaged in relation to ICT access and skills. They are Maori and Pacific peoples; those on low incomes; solo parents; the elderly; people with lower educational attainment; the unemployed; people in rural areas;[6] women;[7] and the disabled. These groups are not mutually exclusive, but give an indication of the complexity of issue. In education, the success of the *Computers in Homes* project is mentioned. This is an initiative undertaken by the 20/20 Trust to make available an Internet-capable computer to families unable to buy one themselves. The families are also offered a telephone line, if necessary, six months' free Internet access, and technical support. They must also attend five training sessions. In return, parents are required to teach at least one family member, friend or neighbour what they have learnt, and to let their children have supervised access to the Internet for up to one hour per school day. So far, projects have operated in Panmure Bridge School, Auckland, and Cannons Creek School, Wellington. The scheme is being assessed by Victoria University and has been so successful that it is set to expand. The project is operated in tandem with the selected decile one schools.[8] Cannons Creek School, for example, has updated its website, <http://sites.tki.org.nz/cannonscreek/>, to include online resources for students to use for homework, especially targeting literacy and numeracy skills (20/20 Communications Trust, 2000).

The *Closing the Digital Divide* paper also notes that *National Guidelines for Library and Information Services in Schools* will be developed by June 2001 (point 76). These will cover issues of access to and use of ICT, including the development of ICT-related information literacy.

The disparity in access is also noted in the Education Review Office (ERO) report, *The Implementation of ICT in New Zealand Schools* (ERO, 2000). The report points out that schools are faced with several challenges. One is how to integrate school-based learning with ICT use at home (the haves);[9] another is how schools can help reduce the gap between students with access at home and those without (the have-nots). ERO notes that only 11 per cent of schools surveyed demonstrated an awareness of the need to link school and home ICT learning. Furthermore, many schools did not know how many students had access at home. This suggests that schools now have the additional task of considering their role in bridging the gap between the 'information-rich' and the 'information-poor'.

The ERO report also observes that students have access to the Internet for teaching and learning in just 46 per cent of schools. There was little variation between the decile of the school in this regard, but while the report found little difference in the availability of computers in the classroom, there were significant differences in the extent to which computers were networked, with higher decile schools more likely to be networked. The report concludes with the observation that many schools need to change their focus from getting ICT in place to using ICT to improve outcomes for students.

What schools can do
Educational solutions
- As teacher professional development programmes progress and teacher confidence increases, schools can ensure that students have access to the Internet.
- Schools should work towards an emphasis on integrating ICT across all curriculum areas.
- Schools need to be aware of student access to ICT at home to be able to address equity issues. Surveys to this effect need to be updated regularly.
- A policy could be considered stating how schools will integrate school learning with ICT access at home.

- Schools may need to consider ways they can remove barriers to learning for those students who do not have access to ICT at home. This could be achieved by providing supervised Internet access after school. While issues of time and resources are involved, schools often provide extra-curricular opportunities. Another option that may be considered is to use ICT-savvy community volunteers.
- Schools could consider providing ICT education programmes for parents, as children are going to benefit more when parents are informed.
- As demonstrated by Cannons Creek School, a school website could be updated to include appropriate sites that would be useful for homework and for current topics, as well as providing material for parents to help their children develop numeracy and literacy skills.
- A school-wide information literacy programme will greatly enhance students' capacity to benefit from ICT as well as other computer use.

Technical solution
- Ensure that networking is a priority in the school's ICT plan.

Harassment, Abuse and Excessive Internet Use

Warning signs about the excessive use of the Internet have begun to appear. Such use is most often associated with prolonged engagement in chat rooms and email use. While this behaviour is usually not the result of computer use at school, it is nonetheless an issue of which schools should be aware. A survey on the impact of the Internet found that too much time spent on it may make people reclusive and less likely to interact with others face to face (reported in Harris, 2000). One warning given is that the changed social dynamic in email and chat may cause frequent users to seek out only like-minded people. This was, however, dismissed by others, who suggest that definitions of what constitutes contact, for example, need to be more clearly defined (Harris, 2000).

Normally we experience a clear separation of our public and private domains. Our behaviour may change in an online environment, as mentioned earlier, where a sense of anonymity prevails. Young people may, for example, experiment with taking on multiple personae as they engage in virtual experiences that would not normally be part of their real-life experiences. They may also be drawn towards sites that are set up for the specific purpose of influencing their values and behaviour, for example racist or hate sites. As yet, we have not in New Zealand experienced the extreme behaviours reported in, for example, the US, Germany and Israel (see for example the Anti-Defamation League's website at <http://www.adl.org>). However, harassment in the form of derogatory or inflammatory language was reported in an incident of 'cyber bullying' (*ODT*, 2000). Unsigned emails with inappropriate language were sent to students at a Dunedin high school. Such experiences can leave the recipients powerless and humiliated. As an anonymous remailing service[10] was used, the emails contained no known sending address. However, the ISP was able to trace the sender to students from another local high school.

Willard (1999) warns about how some young people, whom she describes as 'social outcasts' may use the Internet. She suggests that peer influence may cause young people to engage in activities that are contrary to their values. Some young people may also establish dark-side sites themselves. However, little is known, so far, about how interactive technologies may affect young people's moral and social development.

What schools can do

- Note behaviours that may be associated with excessive or unhealthy Internet use as part of their monitoring of students' well-being. Behaviours include atypical antics, students suddenly doing poorly in their school work, extreme tiredness or behaviour which is of general concern. Loners and others who do not fit into existing peer groups may be at particular risk.
- Cover irresponsible speech in the school's AUP.
- Discuss defamation, harassment and flaming or abusive language and its effect on others.
- Discuss how actions in cyberspace create the impression that actions or words have no significant effect, because users are distanced from the harm they may cause.
- Discuss the use of remailing facilities that disguise the source of speech. Is there a time when anonymity may be appropriate?
- Integrate discussion, where appropriate, with the Health syllabus.
- Incorporate 'respect for self' issues in discussions. These include activities that generally do not have an impact on others, but can be injurious to oneself; for example, addiction and 'garbage' activities (Willard, 1999).
- Occasionally focus on 'undesirable' sites that contain violence with students, label the behaviour such sites may foster. This is likely to have more impact on young people than simply dismissing such sites as being 'unsuitable'.

Conclusion

While becoming familiar with the Internet and deciding on the perimeters for its use may seem a daunting task, the Internet offers immense opportunities. This potential can be realised when schools are clear on their educational purpose in using the Internet, have well-developed ICT plans, support teachers in their efforts to embrace the medium, and are focused on the integration of ICT across the curriculum.

The dark side of the Internet can indeed seem intimidating, but as we acquire an informed understanding of the issues its use raises, we can develop educationally appropriate ways to deal with these. Depending on students' ages, these will include using it as a rich resource to promote discussions relating to values, the law, personal and social ethics, and the limits to individual freedom. Many opportunities exist for schools to focus on the positive benefits of a global community, but with the unregulated nature of the Internet, responsible use in the form of informed self-regulation is becoming an important educational goal. Students would, thus, be equipped to safely face an increasingly complex world, which is likely to be networked.

Notes

1   Now renamed Internet Content Rating Association (ICRA).

2   In addition to this actual label, the rating organisation generates a Content label (a short piece of computer code), which the authors add to the site's source code. The following is an example of such a code for a page rated with RSACi:<META http-equiv="PICS-Label> content='(PICS-1.1 "http://www.rsac.org.ratingsv01.html" 1 gen true comment "RSACi North America Server" for "http://www.ggetnetwise.org" on "1999.08.02T18:41-0800" r (n0s0v010))'>. The numbers at the very end of the code, n0s0v010, indicates that the content of this site is as 0 in all categories, where *n* is nudity, *s* is sex, *v* is violence and *l* is language.

3   An exhaustive definition of hacker can be found at *Dictionary.com,* <http://www.dictionary.com>. See also *The Jargon File,* <http://info.astrian.net/jargon/>.

4   To learn about spam, see *Spam!* <http://www.research.att.com/~lorrie/pubs/spam/>, a full-text article from *Communications of the ACM,* 41 (8), 1998. Available in html or pdf format and *Coalition Against Unsolicited Commercial Email* <http://www.cauc http://www.cauc e.org/>. The New Zealand Spam Fighter site is at <http://www.2x2.co.nz/picks/stopspam.html>.

5   A virus is a small program, often distributed via email, which embeds a copy of itself in other programs. When these programs are executed, the virus is executed, too. Viruses may then attach themselves to outgoing email attachments. For a definition on virus, see <.http://www.dictionary.com/cgi-bin/dict.p1?term=virus>.

6   The recent *Ministerial Inquiry into Telecommunications* reported on the numerous difficulties experienced by rural residents, including schools, in their access to the Internet (see the website of the *Ministerial Inquiry into Telecommunications* <http://www.teleinquiry.govt.nz/>).

7   ACNielsen eRatings' *Internet Audience Measurement Results* report that in New Zealand the balance between male and female Internet use is 55 per cent and 45 per cent respectively (<http://eratings.com/news/20000504.htm>).

8   In 1995, all schools were assigned a decile rating based on the socio-economic level of the community, with decile 10 being the highest. Schools are funded in relation to their decile rating with decile 1 schools (the lowest 10 per cent on the socio-economic scale) receiving $333.70 per pupil in addition to the base operations grant.

9   Almost half of New Zealand homes have a computer (ERO, 2000, section 9.5).

10   An anonymous remailer is a program that runs on a computer somewhere on the Internet. When you send mail to the remailer address, the remailer strips your name and address off the email message and forwards it to its next destination. The recipient gets mail that has no evidence from where the original email came.

Resources for schools

Acts of Parliament

<http://rangi.knowledge-basket.co.nz/gpacts/actlists.html>

Acts relevant to schools are:

Copyright Act 1994

<http://rangi.knowledge-basket.co.nz/gpacts/public/text/1994/an/143.html>

See section 80 for copyright information on computer programs.

Crimes Act

<http://www.isocnz.org.nz/crimes-sop.html>

This is a copy of a Supplementary Order Paper from 7 November 2000 containing the proposed amendments of the Crimes Amendment Bill (No 6), which will make 'cyber crime' such as hacking illegal.

Films, Videos, and Publications Classification Act 1993

<http://rangi.knowledge-basket.co.nz/gpacts/public/text/1993/an/094.html>

See sections 2 and 3 for a definition of 'publication' and 'objectionable.'

New Zealand Bill of Rights Act 1990
<http://rangi.knowledge-basket.co.nz/gpacts/public/text/1990/an/109.html>

Privacy Act 1993
<http://rangi.knowledge-basket.co.nz/gpacts/public/text/1993/an/028.html>

Censorship Office and Censorship Compliance Unit
Department of Internal Affairs, PO Box 805, Wellington.
Tel: 04-495 5317. Fax: 04-494 0656. Email: censorship@dia.govt.nz
Web address: <http://censorship.dia.govt.nz>

From Now On – The Educational Technology Journal
<http://fromnowon.org>
An excellent online journal about IT and IT use in schools. Free email subscription available.

New Zealand Safety Kit
Hardcopy sent to all schools. Also available online at <http://www.netsafe.org.nz>

Online safety in New Zealand schools
<http://education.otago.ac.nz//NZLNet/safety/home.nclk>
Website resulting from research carried out by the School of Education, University of Otago.

Internet Acceptable Use Policies
For Staff
Draft Corporate Code of Practice for Organisations, Department of Internal Affairs
<http://www.censorship.dia.govt.nz/diawebsite.nsf/
c7ad5e032528c34c4c2566690076db9b/
d25a4919d180d176cc25683a00734800!OpenDocument>.
Covers topics in a general way that schools could adapt and amend for their own purposes.

For Students
Pakuranga School's AUP
<http://www.pakuranga.school.nz/info/Internet.html>

Yahooligans: Teachers' Guide: Acceptable Use Policies
<http://www.yahooligans.com/tg/aup.html>
Explains what an AUP is, what to include as well as providing a sample AUP.

Responsible Netizen Model Internet Use Policy
<http://netizen.uoregon.edu/templates/model_policy.html>
An American sample AUP. Also available in pdf format.

Netiquette
The Internet 'Twelve Commandments'
<http://www.isocnz.org.nz/principl.htm>
Principles for use of the Internet: Legal responsibilities, Responsibilities to yourself and Netiquette by the Internet Society of New Zealand.

Privacy
Office of the NZ Privacy Commissioner
<http://www.privacy.org.nz/>
A comprehensive site which deals with the practical implications of the Privacy Act. Subscribe to the Privacy Commissioner's newsletter, *Private Word.*
Resources are also available from the Canadian Privacy Commissioner's website <http://www.ipc.on.ca/english/>

Computer jargon
Free Online Dictionary of Computing (FOLDOC)
<http://foldoc.doc.ic.ac.uk/foldoc/index.html>
Glossary Of Computer Terms
<http://www.odintech.com/beginners/glossary.html>

Chat
Running Educational Online Encounters
<http://www.spirit.com.au/Dreaming/chat/chathome.htm>

Note: These links as well as further resources are available at:
<http://education.otago.ac.nz//NZLNet/safety/resources.nclk>

Appendix A
Acceptable Use Policy (AUP) Template
- **Rationale**
  Reasons for the school implementing an computer/Internet AUP
- **Charges**
  Are there any costs to be met by the user?
- **Netiquette**
  What online behaviour will be expected?
- **Guidelines/terms for use**
  What the school expects/does not expect from their users. This should include expected legal and ethical behaviour.
- **Monitoring**
  Explain what monitoring, if any, will be carried out on user Internet use.
- **Repercussions**
  What are the consequences of breaching this policy?
- **Disclaimer**
  Inform users/parents/caregivers what liabilities school does and does not accept.

- **Legislation**

  If any statutes are referred to in the rules/guideline section above, reproduce the relevant sections here. Not everyone is aware of the contents of these statutes.
- **Glossary**

  Include a glossary as some computer and Internet terms may not be known to users/parents/guardians.
- **Permission/acceptance**

  To be signed by both parents/guardians and students:

  Students – Provide space for the student to sign, indicating they have read, accept and agree to the terms of the AUP.

  Parents/guardians – Provide space for the parents/guardians to sign, indicating that they have read, accept and give permission for the student to use the Internet. Provide space for staff members to sign.

(Adapted from AUP Template, Online Safety in New Zealand Schools at <http://education.otago.ac.nz//NZLNet/safety/template.html>.)

Appendix B
Sample privacy statement for a school's website

All personal information collected by _____ School is protected by the Privacy Act 1993. We will only record your email address if you send us a message. Your personal information will only be used for the purposes for which you have provided it and your email address will not be added to a mailing list. We will not use your personal information for any other purpose, and will not disclose it, except where authorised or required by law or with your consent.

Note: When you send email to _____ School, or submit feedback using our feedback form, the content as it is transferred across the Internet may not be secure. Contact us by telephone, facsimile or post if you have concerns about the security of your message.

The staff who operate _____ School's website are subject to the Privacy Act 1993. This Act lays down strict privacy safeguards which New Zealand Government departments and agencies must observe in handling personal information. More information about the Privacy Act can be obtained from the Privacy Commissioner's website at: http://www.privacy.org.nz/. The Act itself can be viewed at http://rangi.knowledge-basket.co.nz/gpacts/public/text/1993/an/028.html

The data we collect

When you look at this website, our server makes a record of your visit and logs the following information:
- the user's server address,
- the user's top level domain name (for example, .nz, .com, etc..),
- the date and time of visit to the site,
- the pages accessed,
- the type of browser used.

Reasons for collecting data

The data listed above are collected for the following purposes:

- website and system administration, including monitoring to prevent security breaches;
- enhancement of the web-site to the user's needs.

No attempt will be made to identify users or their browsing activities except, in the unlikely event of an investigation, where a law enforcement agency may exercise a warrant to inspect the Internet Service Provider's logs.

References

20/20 Communications Trust. (2000). *Computers in Homes Project.* Available at: <http://www.2020.org.nz/projects/computersinhomes/>

Blakeley, R. (1997, April). *Governance in cyberspace.* Speech to the NZIPA. Available at: <http://www.dia.govt.nz/press/speech/governance.html>

Brown, A. (2000, September 28). Winners of the Foil the Filters Contest. *Digital Freedom Network.* Available at:< http://dfn.org/focus/censor/contest.htm>

CSIRO (1999, December). *Access Prevention Techniques for Internet Content Filtering.* Report prepared for the National Office for the Information Economy, Australia. Available at: <http://www.noie.gov.au/publications/noie/consumer/csirofinalreport.html>

ERO (2000, June). *The implementation of information and communications technology (ICT) in New Zealand schools.* Available at: <http://www.ero.govt.nz/Publications/pubs2000/implementationICT.htm>

Goode, E. & Ben-Yehuda, N. (1994). *Moral panics: The social construction of deviance.* Blackwell: Oxford.

Graham, I. (1997). *The danger: Net hysteria in the mainstream media.* Available at:< http://www.libertus.net/liberty/media.html>

Harris, R. (2000, March 2). All Net and no play makes Johnny a social recluse. *Black Issues in Higher Education,* 16 (27), p.42.

Hughes, D. (2000, Spring). The Internet and sex industries: Partners in global sexual exploitation. *IEEE Technology and Society Magazine,* pp. 35–42.

Hunter, C.D. (2000, Summer). Internet filter effectiveness – Testing over- and underinclusive blocking decisions of four popular web filters. *Social Science Computer Review,* 18 (2), 214-222.

Independent Newspapers Ltd. (2000a, October 4). *Software crushed.* Available at: <http://www.stuff.co.nz/inl/index/0,1008,411462a1896,FF.html>

Independent Newspapers Ltd. (2000b, December 29). *Porn find 'no surprise' - experts.* Available at: <http://www.stuff.co.nz/inl/index/0,1008,569548a11,FF.html>

Infotech Online. (2000, October 12). *Crushing blow for piracy.* Available at: <http://www.stuff.co.nz/inl/index/0,1008,427414a1899,FF.html>

ISOCNZ (1998). *Articles of Association.* Available at: <http://www.isocnz.org.nz/articles.htm>

ISOCNZ (1999). *Internet Code of Practice.* Available at: <http://www.isocnz.org.nz/code.htm>

ITAG (2000, March). *ICT in Schools 1999.* Available at: <http://www.med.govt.nz/pbt/infotech/ictschools1999/index.html>

Lai, K.W. (In press). Internet in the classroom: Teachers as custodians? In H. Taylor & P. Hogenbirk (Eds). *Information and Communication Technologies in Education: The School of the Future.* Boston: Kluwer, pp. 49-60.

Maharey, S., & Swain, P. (2000, December 5). *Closing the digital divide.* Available at: <http://www.executive.govt.nz/minister/maharey/divide/index.html>

McKenzie, J. (1998, May). The new plagiarism: Seven antidotes to prevent highway robbery in an electronic age. *From now on: the educational technology journal,* 7 (8). Available at: <http://

fromnowon.org/may98/cov98may.>

Ministry of Economic Development. (1999, December). *The social impact of information technology.* A Briefing to the Minister for Information Technology. Available at: <http://www.med.govt.nz/pbt/infotech/bim_social_inclusion.html>

Ministry of Education. (2000). *Guidelines for schools for the online publication of student images and schoolwork.* Ministry of Education: Wellington. Available at: <http://www.tki.org.nz/r/governance/curriculum/copyguide_e.php>

Montgomery, K. & Pasnik, S. (1996). *Web of deception: Threats to children from online marketing.* Center for Media Education. Available at: <http://kidsprivacy.org/deception.pdf>

New Zealand Herald Online. (2000, August 23). *Money-saving plan reveals hacker.* Available at:<http://www.nzherald.co.nz/storydisplay.cfm?thesection=news&thesubsection=&storyID=148734>

Otago Daily Times (ODT). (2000, November 1). *Cyber bullies beware – you can be traced.* Available at: <http://www1.odt.co.nz/cgi-bin/getitem?date=01Nov2000&object=KUE41H5585UR&type=html>

Otago Daily Times (ODT). (2001, January 19). *A 'licence to print money' by selling Sex.com on the Internet.* Available at: <http://www1.odt.co.nz/cgi-bin/search-display-story-online-new?PATH=19Jan2001/editorial/content/CIH14C2597EM.html&WORDS=sex.com&DB=Editorial>

Privacy Commissioner. (1998, January) *Privacy Commissioner's newsletter,* 21. Available at: <http://www.privacy.org.nz/privword/newpw9.html>

Select Committee Office. (2000, December 1-8). *Select Committee Business.* Available at: <http://www.scoop.co.nz/archive/scoop/stories/01/76/200012080044.6caac9c8.html>

Slevin, J. (2000). *The Internet and society.* Polity Press: Cambridge.

Swain, P. (2000, March 24). *Survey of NZ schools connected to the Internet.* Press Release, New Zealand Government Executive.
Available at: <http://www.executive.govt.nz/speech.cfm?speechralph=30681&SR=0>

Taylor, M. (1999, September 29 – October 1). *The nature and dimensions of child pornography on the Internet.* Paper presented at the International Conference, 'Combating child pornography on the Internet,' Vienna. Available at: <http://www.stop-childpornog.at/pa_taylor.html>

Watson, C. & Shuker, R. (1998). *In the public good?: Censorship in New Zealand.* Dunmore Press: Palmerston North.

Willard, N. (September,1998). *Statement presented to: House Commerce Committee, Related to House Resolution 3177.* Available at: <http://netizen.uoregon.edu/opinions/hr_statement.html>

Willard, N. (1999, September 18–19). *The social dimensions of the use of interactive technologies by young people: A research agenda.* Responsible Netizen Project. Available at:< http://netizen.uoregon.edu/pdf/sduityp.pdf>

Willard, N. (2000, December). *Choosing not to go down the not-so-good cyberstreets.* Available at: <http://netizen.uoregon.edu/documents/nwnas.html>

Dealing with Inappropriate Materials on the Internet: Strategies for Teachers and Parents

9

Kwok-Wing Lai

As teachers have increasingly been expected to use the Internet as an educational tool, the opportunities for professional development in information and communication technology (ICT) have expanded, both overseas and in New Zealand. However, many of these professional development programmes (e.g. the New Zealand ICTPD programmes) are still very much skill-based and oriented towards developing teachers' confidence and competence in technology use. In general, little attention is given to cultural, social and ethical issues related to Internet use (Lai, 2001a).

These are important issues to consider. For example, one major concern is that young people may be accessing materials, at home or at school, that are not only unlawful to have in their possession but also may be harmful to them. Under present New Zealand legislation (the Films, Videos, and Publications Classification Act 1993), it is unlawful to possess 'objectionable' materials (information, pictures, moving images and sound). While the Ministry of Internal Affairs (through its Censorship Compliance Unit) is charged with ensuring that objectionable materials are not available in the country, intercepting and controlling the materials accessible through the Internet is difficult. In providing students with access to the Internet, school principals and teachers therefore have to address some major custodial and educational issues associated with online access. For example, increasingly teachers have to interpret what constitutes 'objectionable material', both from a legal and a custodial point of view. Schools are faced with the need to impose some form of restriction or censorship on Internet use in their classrooms to keep students safe from material inappropriate for their age. Very often, teachers have to make ad hoc decisions on practices and strategies to deal with these issues. Professional development to inform teachers of these issues is urgently needed.

To make informed decisions, teachers need to understand their legal and custodial role in the information age. Information about what good practice is already occurring is needed to provide teachers with guidelines as to what should be included in a professional development programme. The problem has become even more complex as more and more students are now accessing the Internet from home, and the amount of time they spend on the computer at home is far greater than that spent at school. More informed decisions will be made by teachers if they have a better idea of how parents deal with similar issues at home.

The significance and practical implications of these issues in the school setting have been outlined in the previous chapter of this book. This present chapter will discuss more specifically how teachers as well as parents perceive their ethical and legal responsibilities as well as the strategies they use to deal with these issues. The following discussion is based on findings gathered from two research projects (Lai, Elliot, & Trewern, 1999; Lai, 2001a, 2001b; Lai & Pratt, in preparation). The first

Dealing with Inappropriate Materials on the Internet 183

study (the School Study), undertaken in 1999, focused on strategies primary and secondary teachers used to deal with objectionable materials on the Web. There were three stages in this study. In the first stage an online questionnaire was administered to about 300 primary and secondary schools; in the second stage a follow-up questionnaire was completed by these schools; and in the final stage ICT co-ordinators/managers of 16 secondary schools, plus 65 students, were interviewed in 1999. The second study (the Home Study), undertaken in 2000, was focused on the use of the Internet at home. About 160 parents/care-givers and 170 secondary students were surveyed in this study.

Ethical Responsibilities

In the School Study, we were interested in finding out the extent to which teachers were aware of their ethical and legal responsibilities when they used the Internet with their students. An open-ended question was asked in the online survey with regard to the perception of teachers' ethical responsibilities. Findings from this survey showed that, by and large, teachers perceived their primary role as custodian or gatekeeper, and considered themselves responsible for keeping students from unwanted materials by providing them with a safe environment to learn. As can be seen from Table 1, the majority of the teachers believed that they should supervise and monitor students' access to the Internet, and restrict access if necessary. However, two major differences between the views of primary and secondary teachers should be noted: how students' responsibilities were perceived and the extent to which students should be taught to become responsible users.

Table 1: Teachers' perception of their ethical responsibilities in Internet access

	Primary (n=169)	Secondary (n=87)	Overall (n=272)
Supervising and monitoring	40%	22%	35%
Restricting access to sites	28%	30%	30%
Educating and guidance	9%	23%	15%
Protecting students	8%	7%	9%
Acting as parents	7%	10%	8%
Students' own responsibilities	0%	14%	5%

Note: percentages don't add up to 100% as multiple responses were given and some responses were not included in this Table.

Strategies Adopted by Teachers

Supervising, monitoring, and restricting access. From the School Study it is clear that teachers were very concerned that their students might access materials they should not be accessing. The concern was particularly evident in primary schools. Teachers saw that it was their responsibilities to supervise and monitor their students' Internet activities. The following comment was typical:

We do not allow unsupervised access or 'surfing' the net without direction. We believe that school Internet users should have a purpose before implementing it. We control the access … (A primary school principal)

Teachers have reported ways of restricting access, such as: (a) using filtering software such as NetNanny or CyberPatrol to screen materials; (b) creating an intranet; and (c) bookmarking sites.

Protecting students. Teachers also felt it was necessary to provide students with a safe environment. The following comments were typical:

To protect children from manipulation … (A primary school principal)

Students should be monitored at all times to ensure they are not at risk. (An associate primary school principal)

We must be sure that children only access 'safe' sites. I believe they should be supervised while using the Internet, but this obviously limits its use. (A teacher of Years 6–8)

Playing a parental role. Primary teachers in particular took account of the views expressed by parents when considering issues related to Internet censorship. Many teachers also adopted a similar role to that of a parent, when they used the Internet with their students.

Our parents have strong views that our Internet access is for information communication and educational use only at this stage. (A primary school principal)

We feel that we should only be allowing students to access the material that their parents would be happy with. (A primary school principal)

Teachers indeed have to consider parents' views as it is clear from the Home Study that many parents had little tolerance of website materials that were considered inappropriate. In the Home Study parents and caregivers were asked to rate the level of inappropriateness of the language as well as the images presented on the websites. In general, over 60 per cent of the parents considered as unacceptable low to moderate levels of inappropriateness of the language or content, as listed in Table 2.

Table 2: Percentages of parents who considered websites to be inappropriate

Language:	
Racist	65.5
Violent	50
Gender-biased	68.4
Profane	65.6
Related to crime	64.1
Content:	
Explicit sex	62.3
Nudity	66.5
Terror/horror	64.4
Violence	64.8

Educating students. It is surprising to note that very few primary teachers (9 per cent) have considered the need to educate their students about how to deal with objectionable or inappropriate materials responsibly. Even in secondary schools, fewer than one quarter (23 per cent) of the teachers have given ethical guidance to their students. Views such as the following were rare:

> The children need to develop a knowledge of the appropriate use for the Internet and [be] able to [get] the necessary information but they need to be aware that facts change and what they read may not be correct. They need to [be] taught to monitor their usage of the Internet and use it effectively. (A primary senior ICT teacher)

> To help them develop skills in finding out, explore with assistance the range of information in specific areas they are studying and be discriminating in selecting info to answer their questions. Developing personal integrity in what they choose to view and access, understanding that the validity and content of many sites is very suspect – yet not denying the vital tool it is becoming to find out fast … (A teacher librarian)

In secondary schools, there was a view that at the end of the day teachers could not really do a lot about censoring:

> Secondary students are old enough to know what they should and should not be accessing … ultimately we can no more stop them accessing some sites if they are really determined than we can prevent them bringing a porn mag [magazine] in from home … (A computer network administrator)

Students' responsibilities. While primary teachers placed greater emphasis on supervision, their counterparts in secondary schools placed more emphasis on the responsibilities of the students:

> Students are ultimately responsible for their choices and it is helpful for them to sign usage contracts upon entry to the school. These contracts can state clear consequences for abuse of Internet usage.

As a result, more secondary schools have developed acceptable user policies (AUP) or contracts for students to sign with regard to appropriate usage of the Internet. They have also developed school-wide policies and protocols to regulate access to the Internet. For example, in the School Study survey, 77 per cent of the secondary schools have developed an Internet usage policy, while 42 per cent of the primary schools had similar policies. Overall 55 per cent of the schools had a policy.

Legal responsibilities

With regard to legal responsibilities in gatekeeping Internet materials, nearly one-third of the schools (31 per cent) either believed that they had no additional legal responsibilities or they were not sure what their legal responsibilities were. Responses of primary and secondary school teachers were similar. For example, both groups considered the use of the Internet similar to that of other learning technologies.

> None [no legal responsibilities] outside of normal teaching situations. The Internet can be treated as a reference book in this regard … (A primary IT support teacher)

> Unsure [about the legal responsibilities] but feel it would be the same as any video or TV programme we watch. (A primary assistant principal)

Same as applies to any other information source we have available to students. (A secondary school librarian)

Other teachers believed that they were legally accountable, but had superficial understandings of what their responsibilities were. Most schools believed that they had acted appropriately if students were supervised and guided (as they would be at home) to make sure that they had no access to objectionable material. According to one respondent,

> The ages, abilities and experience of the students in using the technology dictate to a large degree the teachers' legal responsibility in relation to Internet access. At the primary level (Years 1-6) I believe that if the teacher has previewed the site, is present, supervising, and has the students' screen in view then all practical steps have been taken to ensure safe access … (A deputy principal of a primary school)
>
> We should protect ourselves. All information is stored on our computer system for which we are responsible, it must therefore be appropriate.' (A secondary computing teacher)
>
> The school is accountable if students access inappropriate sites or materials. (A principal of a primary school)

Some teachers believed that they had fulfilled their legal responsibilities as long as their students and parents had signed an AUP. Again, secondary teachers put more emphasis on policy documents:

> As this can involve uncharted waters, we have parents sign a consent/disclaimer form as a legal protection for the school. (ICT tutor and resource manager)
>
> I think we are covered by only allowing supervised access. Apart from this I have no idea what or if there is a legal position. (A primary IT co-ordinator)

It seemed to teachers that they had relinquished responsibility once the parents and students signed the agreement:

> Parents accept the END responsibility via an Agreement. (A primary IT teacher)
>
> None [no legal responsibilities] – the form [AUP] we use shifts all the responsibility onto the student. (A secondary school network supervisor)

Dilemma for the teacher

In restricting students' Internet access, teachers are faced with a dilemma. As many teachers begin to subscribe to the increasingly popular constructivist learning framework, they are encouraged to develop a learner-centred approach to teaching. For example, they are asked to take up the role of facilitator to support students in exploring and conducting research independently, in authentic learning situations. When using the Internet as an educational tool, students are encouraged to hypothesise, problem solve, and make decisions. However, with unrestricted access to the Internet, students will inevitably access unscrutinised and irrelevant materials, as well as potentially objectionable or inappropriate materials. How to maintain a balance of giving students freedom of access, while at the same time providing a relatively safe environment for them to learn in, is a challenging task, as can be seen from comments gathered from the School Study:

We want to provide as big a range of resources as possible … Most students use the Internet as a research tool … I don't want to restrict or stop this because of the few who abuse the system … and we know to keep an eye on them … (A secondary school teacher)

We must be sure that children only access 'safe' sits. I believe they should be supervised while using the Internet, but this obviously limits its use.' (A teacher of Years 6–8)

Maintaining a balance between restricting access and trusting students is difficult. The following principle, adopted by a secondary school, is enlightening:

We believe that students need to learn discriminatory behaviour when using the net. We attempt to operate within an environment of trust … The Internet and other evolving communications technologies will be a central part in the lives of our students, and we have a duty to help in preparing our students for this. We also have a responsibility to educate those students about the dangers and pitfalls those technologies present. We believe that a balanced approach of opportunity and protection is appropriate and we strive to find this balance. (A network administrator)

Teachers may need to teach their students how to evaluate information gathered from the Web, and to encourage them to reflect on the implications and consequences of the information-gathering process, rather than to simply acquire the skills of generating more information (Postman, 1992). Teachers are now under pressure from parents and the community to increase usage of the Internet for school work. But they should be aware that gathering information from the Web requires guidance previously not available to themselves and their students.

Strategies Used by Parents

No matter how hard schools try to restrict students' access to objectionable or inappropriate material from the Web, and no matter how successful schools' monitoring strategies are, teachers should be aware that students use the Internet very differently at home. Parents also use different strategies to deal with Internet access. There is no doubt that most students spend more time using computers at home than in school. For example, the Otago Technology Project (Lai, Pratt, & Trewern, 2001) reported that senior students (Forms 5–7) spent 56 minutes per day at home using computers, compared to only 32 minutes in school. Junior students (Forms 3–4) spent 55 minutes per day at home and 36 minutes in school using the computer. Our Home Study also confirmed that students spent a lot of time at home surfing the Internet. For example, nearly a third (32.6 per cent) of the students in that study used the World Wide Web at least daily or more than once a day. Nearly a quarter (23.9 per cent) used it for more than one hour (6.4 per cent between 2 and 4 hours) per day, and another quarter (27.9 per cent) between 30 and 60 minutes.

While schools predominantly impose restrictions on students' access to the Internet, the strategies adopted by parents are rather different. Findings from the Home Study (Lai & Pratt, in preparation) showed that students had little supervision of Internet use at home, with close to half (43.2 per cent) reporting that they had never been supervised when using computers. An additional 28.4 per cent of the students reported that they were seldom supervised. In total nearly three-quarters (71.6 per cent) of the students in that study were largely free of control over how they used the Internet at home.

When parents were asked why they did not monitor or supervise their children, knowing that there were objectionable or inappropriate materials easily retrievable from the Internet, they used the word 'trust' frequently. The following comments are typical:

> There is an element of 'trust' – I believe it is important for him to know how to deal with this material whether I am there or not as sometimes it is totally unexpected.
> Son and I have good honest communication – he trusts me that I am not trying to stop him using the Internet but showing them the consequences/pitfalls of Internet use.
> Same as judging TV, music, etc. is dependent on his age, understanding of the issues after discussion with us (as parents) also his understanding that what is acceptable to a certain degree at home, is not acceptable elsewhere.

Students also had similar responses:

> My parents believe I am responsible – unlike the school. (aged 14, Year 9, male)
> My parents trust me more than the school trusts other kids. (aged 13, Year 9, female)
> The school has many rules that we have to follow otherwise we get banned but at home my parents just trust me. (aged 14, Year 10, female)

Students understood that parents and teachers had differing legal responsibilities:

> School has a legal obligation and responsibility, parents have their own opinions and responsibilities that differ. (aged 15, Year 10, female)

Students' Perceptions of Control Imposed on Them

How effective are the monitoring and censorship strategies used by teachers? It is interesting to note that in the School Study teachers' perceptions of the effectiveness of Internet censorship were quite different from those of students. For example, the majority of teachers (primary, 77 per cent; secondary, 82 per cent) in the School Study perceived supervision as highly effective. But when students were interviewed, they generally perceived that there was too much control on Internet use by their teachers and many students felt that their privacy had been invaded. For example:

> You have people watching over you and you go into something and one of the teachers might say, hey you're not supposed to go into that kind of thing because so and so, it's too much to download, or something like that … (female, aged 16)
> It's pretty stink because like, they're always like, your shadows sort of thing. Don't rely on us and have faith sort of thing … it would be better if people relied on us, like, responsibility and trusted us … (female, Form 3)

Even with the monitoring and restricting strategies imposed, students could still do things on the computer without being caught by the teachers if they wanted to. For example, one student made the following comments:

> In the library computers I hooked them up to the Internet and surfed the Internet and downloaded a 36 megabyte game for free, without anybody knowing it was me. Hacked into the library computers and sent messages to everybody on the admin network … (aged 16, Form 6, male)

With regard to the level of control of Internet access, findings from the School

Study were generally supported by the Home Study. For example, two-thirds of the students in the Home Study reported that their schools had a tight control over how they used the Internet. The control at home, however, was minimal (see Table 3).

Table 3: Control of Internet access between schools and homes (in percentages)

	Low	Moderate	Extreme
School	12.6	20.8	66.7
Home	41.1	30.1	28.2

Comments from students included:

My parents don't check all the sites looked at and mail received like the school. (aged 16, Year 11, Female)
At home I just ask, at school I need 3 signatures and a teacher walking past me every few minutes. (aged 12, Year 7, male)
There is always an adult near at school and often there is no parent in the room at home. (aged 12, Year 7, male)
Well at home it's really my time to look at my favourite websites. (aged 11, Year 7, male)
At school every website we go [to] is recorded and there is always a teacher present. At home we go on the Web whenever and the websites aren't recorded. (aged 13, Year 7, female)

Although most students in the Home Study believed that it was due to their parents' trust that they were free to use the Internet at home, a few were less positive about the lack of supervision:

The school cares if we use the internet and my parents don't. (aged 15, Year 11, female)
School can check up on you but at home no one bothers. (aged 15, Year 11, female)

Students generally reported that their patterns of Internet usage at home were quite different from their usage in school:

At school you're on the Internet to work, not play like home. (aged 12, Year 8, male)
At school we aren't allowed to go onto any website except school work stuff. At home I can go to any leisure items. (aged 12, Year 8, female)

Only 39 per cent of the students in the Home Study reported that they frequently used the World Wide Web for school work, while 63 per cent reported that they frequently used the Web for leisure activities.

Different Exposure to Objectionable Materials

Teachers had a tighter control on students' access to the Internet, not only because they perceived their ethical and legal responsibilities differently from parents, but because they had a deeper exposure to objectionable or inappropriate materials. Data collected from both the School and Home Studies indicate that teachers have more often come across inappropriate materials than parents and students, as can be seen from the following table.

Table 4: Percentage of respondents reporting that they had come across websites with the following contents:

	Primary Teachers (n=124)	Secondary Teachers (n=72)	Parents (n=151)	Students (n=175)
Violence	22	24	11	17
Explicit sex	52	65	17	18
Racism	13	18	3	6
Profanity	17	31	11	10
Horror	13	14	7	11
Crime	6	17	2	6
Cruelty	8	15	2	4
Cult	11	26	3	5
Drugs	10	21	3	7
Gambling	15	17	9	18
Bomb-making	4	21	3	7

Also, both secondary teachers (69.1 per cent) and primary school teachers (29.6 per cent) said their students had come across inappropriate sites. Interestingly, nearly half (45.2 per cent) of the parents in the Home Study had never seen any websites they considered to be inappropriate for their kids to access (67.1 per cent had never come across any illegal sites). As teachers have more experience in accessing inappropriate or objectionable websites, they do have a reason to be more concerned about the safety of their students.

Concluding Remarks

At present most professional development programmes are underpinned by constructivist and situated learning models which encourage teachers to adopt a student-centred approach to teaching. Teachers are encouraged to become knowledge facilitators instead of knowledge providers. As such, students are asked to use the Internet as an educational tool to facilitate research and problem-solving. Unfortunately, ethical and social issues relating to the process of accessing information and its subsequent use are seldom addressed in the curriculum.

In this chapter we have reported some findings collected from two research projects on ethical use of the Internet in New Zealand schools. Primary teachers' conception of their ethical and legal responsibilities differed markedly from secondary teachers. Most primary teachers saw themselves as gatekeepers, keeping their students away from objectionable materials. Secondary teachers placed a greater emphasis on educating their students and having them take greater responsibility for using the

Internet. Teachers and parents have adopted different strategies in dealing with issues of monitoring and censoring Web-based materials and students also have different responses to these strategies. Although teachers in general considered their strategies to be effective, they were only effective to the extent of restricting Internet access in schools. As students have far greater freedom in accessing the Internet at home, it may be important for teachers to educate their students to be responsible and ethical Internet users at home as well as at school.

Acknowledgement

The author would like to thank Anne Elliot for providing valuable comments on an earlier draft of this chapter. He also wishes to thank Dr Keryn Pratt for assisting in data collection in the Home Study project.

References

Lai, K.W., Elliot, A. & Trewern, A. (1999). *Ethical use of computers in New Zealand schools: A preliminary study.* In Proceedings of ICCE '99, 7th International Conference on Computers in Education, Vol. 1, pp. 648-651.

Lai, K.W. (1999). Teaching, learning, and professional development: The teacher matters most. In K.W. Lai (Ed.) *Net-Working: Teaching, Learning, and Professional Development* (pp. 7-23). Dunedin: University of Otago Press.

Lai, K.W. (2001a). Role of the teacher. In H. Adelsberger, B. Collis, & J. Pawlowski (Eds). *Handbook on Information Technologies for Education & Training.* Springer-Verlag.

Lai, K.W. (2001b). Internet in the Classroom: Teachers as Custodians? In H. Taylor & Hogenbirk, P. (Eds). *Information and Communication Technologies in Education: The School of the Future* (pp. 49-60). Boston: Kluwer.

Lai, K.W. & Pratt, K. (in preparation). *Ethical use of the Internet at home.*

Lai, K.W., Pratt, K. & Trewern, A. (2001). *Learning with Technology: Evaluation of the Otago Technology Project.* Dunedin: Community of Otago Trust.

Postman, N. (1992). *Technology: The Surrender of Culture to Technology.* New York: Alfred A. Knopf.

Professional Development Needs for Health and Safety: Issues with Computer Use

10

Kwok-Wing Lai

Although computers have been used in schools for over twenty years, it was not until recently that teachers and educators began to pay attention to the health risks associated with their use (Lai, 1995; Grant, 1998). Increasingly, health and education professionals have suggested that teachers and students need to be ergonomically conscious when using computers (Laeser, Maxwell & Hedge, 1998; Atencio, 1996; Gross, 1998, McMillan, 1998). The health risks they are concerned about range from discomfort (such as eyestrain, wrist and shoulder pain), and overuse syndrome to musculoskeletal injuries. The advent of laptop computers in schools, where students are expected to use a small keyboard, trackball, or some pointing device for extended periods of time, has already posed a greater risk of developing occupational overuse syndrome (OOS) (Ministry of Education, 1998). For example, a recent study (Bell, 1999) surveying 314 children in three Australian schools shows that 60 per cent of the participants suffered some kind of back, neck, head and shoulder pain when using and carrying laptop computers. As both teachers and students are increasingly spending more time on the computer for their work, schools cannot ignore the health risks associated with its use. This chapter discusses briefly some of these risks and, based on the findings of a recent study (Lai, 2000), examines teachers' awareness of these issues and the strategies that can be used to deal with them.

Eye Problems

One common problem experienced by frequent computer users is visual fatigue and eyestrain, leading to sore and burning eyes, headaches, double vision, and even to nausea (Dillon & Emurian, 1995). Working with the computer screen is significantly different from reading print-based materials. Unlike print-based materials, which reflect light, the computer monitor (the visual display unit, VDU) is a self-illuminated object. Looking directly at the computer screen is somewhat like looking into a light source. Less surrounding light may be needed or the VDU may create discomfort to the eyes (Anshel, 1994). As well, the flicker or flashing effect generated from the computer screen creates a very distressing and distracting experience for some computer users. Flickers may be created if the refresh rate of the VDU is too slow. At present, images on most computer screens are generated by cathode ray tubes, as they are on television monitors. The computer monitor (the cathode ray tube) creates images on its screen by firing electrons from a gun across the inside surface of the screen, which is coated with chemical phosphors. As the phosphors will glow when hit by the electrons, patterns of illuminated and dark spots can be created by turning the beam of electrons on and off. The scanning is done horizontally from the left to the right, and starts from the upper-left corner of the monitor and scans downward. When the whole screen is scanned, the beam will return to the upper-left corner and begin its second round. The vertical scan rate (called the refresh rate) has to be sufficiently rapid in order for the phosphors not to fade away before the next pass. If the refresh rate is too slow, it will create a flashing effect, or flicker, similar to what we experience from old fluorescent lights (Poor, 1993). To minimise discomfort, it is important to use non-interlaced monitors (scanning is done in every single line in one pass) which have a refresh rate of around 70Hz (the whole screen is scanned 70 times per second).

To reduce eyestrain, the work environment should be properly lit. The New Zealand Department of Labour recommends a background lighting of between 200 to 300 lux (a lux is roughly the amount of illumination given by a candle in a square metre) if a room is solely used for computer-related work. More background lighting should be provided (between 200 and 500 lux) for a general-purpose room (e.g. a classroom). Local lighting should be provided as necessary. Inadequate lighting may produce reflections from the glass surface of the computer screen, which create eyestrain or headaches for frequent users. To minimise glare, computer monitors should be put at right angles to windows and anti-glare screen filters may have to be used. Poorly designed work environments may accentuate the development of Computer Vision Syndrome, defined by the American Optometric Association as 'the complex of eye and vision problems related to near work which are experienced during or related to computer use' (Anshel, 2000). This is poised to become a big problem for children.

Anshel (1994) has recommended a 3B (Blink, Breathe, and Break) approach to reduce eyestrain for frequent computer users.

- **Blink.** Computer users tend to blink fewer times when they concentrate on their tasks. Anshel (1994) recommends that frequent computer users keep up the normal blink rate to allow the eyes to rest and clean and rewet the surface of the eyes.
- **Breathe.** Computer users (particularly kids) tend to hold their breath when they complete an exciting task (e.g. playing a video game). Since breathing can control muscle activities, holding one's breath may tighten the eye muscles and create discomfort. Even and steady breathing can therefore help relax the eye muscles.
- **Break.** Our eyes are not designed to focus on something at a close distance for an extended period of time. Since working in front of a computer screen requires intense concentration, we tend to forget to take regular breaks. Anshel (1994) recommends microbreaks (10 seconds every 10 minutes, look away 20 feet from the computer monitor), minibreaks (5 minutes every hour, stand up and stretch), and maxibreaks (a coffee or lunch break, every few hours).

Body Posture

Maintaining a good posture is extremely important for computer users if the computer is to be used for an extended period of time. Poor body posture, as well as poor design of the workstation, may lead to muscle pain, particularly in the shoulders, neck, lower arms and wrists, which, if not attended to, may develop into what are commonly called Repetitive Strain Injuries (RSI). To maintain a good body posture, it is important to set up a computer workstation which can accommodate different body dimensions. A good workstation should have an adjustable desk and chair, and it should be possible for the keyboard and mouse to be put sufficiently far away from the monitor (about 30 inches) to allow the hands to rest in a relaxed position. There should also be a foot rest for shorter people to support their feet. No doubt ergonomically designed furniture and workstations could mitigate some of the 'at risk' postures when teachers and students are using computers (Oates, Evans, & Hedge, 1998). Maintaining a good posture and forming good work habits (e.g. having frequent breaks) are equally important. As teachers and students increasingly have to use the computer for instructional and administrative purposes, they need to understand these issues and to form good work habits as early as possible: bad habits, once formed, are usually difficult to unlearn later. There is a need for teachers and school administrators to be more ergonomically conscious.

Overview of Health Issues

To what extent are teachers and administrators aware of the health risks involved in computer use, as discussed in the previous sections, and to what extent have they successfully dealt with these issues? At present very little research has been conducted on health and safety issues associated with computer use in schools, although ergonomic research in the workplace in other settings has been undertaken by organisations such as the International Labour Office (Rosskam & Baichoo, 1997). To fill this gap, a study was undertaken in 1999 in New Zealand to investigate the awareness of teachers and school administrators of the health issues related to computer use. Three sets of questionnaires were sent to the (a) principals; (b) administrators (secretaries); and (c) computing teachers/computer co-ordinators of all the schools in the Otago and Southland regions. A total of 852 questionnaires were posted to 284 schools (246 primary and 38 secondary schools), and 362 questionnaires (43 per cent) from 207 schools (73 per cent) were returned. The overall response rates for principals, teachers, and administrators were 56 per cent, 30 per cent, and 41 per cent, respectively. The response rates for primary school principals (59 per cent) and secondary school teachers (71 per cent) were particularly high. In the following sections some of the findings gathered from this study provide an overview of the health issues related to computer use in this country. More details about this study can be found in Lai (2000).

Taking Breaks

Not surprisingly, New Zealand principals, teachers and administrators did spend a lot of time using computers in school. Principals in both primary and secondary schools spent a similar amount of time on the computer (on average 1.55 hours per day) but secondary teachers and administrators spent nearly double the amount of time on the computer compared to their counterparts (primary teachers = 1.1 hours, secondary teachers = 1.9 hours; primary administrators = 2.9 hours, secondary administrators = 5.1 hours).

Health professionals suggest that frequent short breaks are needed to reduce the risk of eyestrain and developing OOS if users spend an extended period of time on the computer. It seems that New Zealand teachers and administrators have not yet formed such a habit. Findings from this study show that only 5 per cent of the respondents reported having breaks regularly. It is interesting to note that nearly one-quarter (24 per cent) of the respondents could not provide a specific answer to this question, showing perhaps they did not pay adequate attention to this issue. For those respondents who answered this question, on average principals took breaks most often (every 37 minutes), followed by teachers (every 43 minutes). However, administrators, who indicated they spent far more time on the computer, took breaks least often (every 46 minutes).

Awareness of Health Risks

In the study respondents were asked whether they were aware of six kinds of health risks associated with computer use. They are: (a) back pain; (b) lower arm pain; (c) neck pain; (d) shoulder pain; (e) wrist pain; (f) headaches; and (g) eyestrain. Overall, the respondents' awareness was rather high, with between 69 per cent and 91 per cent of them aware of these health risks. Teachers and administrators also seem to be well informed about ergonomic products (e.g. adjustable desks and chairs), particularly in secondary schools, where over 90 per cent of the respondents had knowledge about ergonomic furniture and equipment. In primary schools, the percentages were lower (76 per cent of the teachers, 84 per cent of the principals). Their knowledge about computer software which would help them to reduce the health risks of computer use were also much lower. In primary schools, the highest percentage came from the principals (11 per cent), and in secondary, it was from the teachers (26 per cent).

High levels of awareness, however, did not translate into preventive strategies. For example, only 54 per cent of the teachers reported that they watched their posture when using computers and 60 per cent of them paid attention to the lighting of their rooms. As for principals, they paid even less attention to their posture (49 per cent) and lighting (57 per cent). The majority of the respondents did not have any purpose-built furniture either. Although 95 per cent of the administrators had an adjustable chair, fewer than half of them (42 per cent) had an accompanying adjustable computer desk. Very few of the teachers and principals had other ergonomically designed furniture. The school administrators were also asked whether they had requested any specific items which would make their use of the computer safer. In primary schools 49 per cent of the administrators and only 33 per cent in secondary schools had requested such items.

Health Problems Affecting Teachers and Administrators

It is surprisingly common for teachers, principals, and administrators to experience health problems with computer use, with nearly half (47 per cent) of them having done so. Of the 117 administrators who returned their questionnaires, 71 (61 per cent) reported they had experienced some kind of health problems and this was more significant in secondary schools (73 per cent) than in primary schools (57 per cent). Five of these respondents had already developed RSI. Thirty-three (28 per cent) administrators had experienced eyestrain, nine of them reporting a deterioration of their eyesight and as a result having to wear prescription glasses. Other health problems included hand and wrist pain (37 per cent), neck pain (30 per cent), shoulder and lower arm pain (41 per cent), and back pain (13 per cent). A third major problem was headaches (27 per cent). As school administrators worked much longer hours on the computer than the other two groups, it is not surprising that they reported having more health problems.

As for teachers, 45 (52 per cent) of the respondents reported having health problems related to the use of computers at work. The two most widespread problems were wrist pain (49 per cent) and eyestrain (44 per cent). The following are some of the health problems teachers experienced:

> 'Wrist … when doing a lot of mousing & editing a school magazine – kept me awake at nights. Also lifted some chairs & a computer monitor during room refurbishment. Lifted badly & was off work two and a half weeks with pinched nerve. Could not sit at computer for 4-5 weeks.'
> 'Back – too tense when working against clock. Arm & wrists – pain after stretches at keyboard. Headaches – at end of every working day. Eye strain – tired, burning eyes.'

Forty-five principals (28 per cent) reported having experienced similar health problems related to computer use as teachers, with wrist pain (45 per cent), eyestrain (33 per cent), and neck pain (31 per cent) being the most common.

The Need for Information and Policy Guidance

Very few teachers and principals were aware that the New Zealand government had developed guidelines on health and safety issues for those using computers at school. Although a package which includes guidelines on ICT safety issues was sent out by the Ministry of Education in 1998 to all schools, only 17 per cent of the primary schools and 14 per cent of the secondary school principals were aware of these guidelines. They were keen to have information about ergonomics:

- 'Information re harmful properties in the air from this electronic gear. How close to sit to monitor screen to avoid exposure.'
- 'Furniture/equipment at the primary end of education – what's a good height for screen? Are chairs available for "wee ones"?'
- 'How much time I should sit at the computer before having a break, what exercises I should do and what other equipment would help to counteract some of the problems …'

Principals were particularly interested in legal issues related to the health risks of computer use. As suggested by Cameron (cited in Bell, 1999), the public liability health insurance risks have not yet been clearly calculated and could be a major concern for school management in the near future.

Surprisingly, not a single participating secondary school in this study had a policy on health and safety issues associated with computer use. While primary schools fared better, only about 6 per cent of them had a standing policy. However, 85 per cent of the primary and 86 per cent of the secondary school principals felt the need for some kind of policy and guidelines. A number of them preferred that policies be developed by the Ministry of Education as 'it would be easier for one organization to carry this out rather than every school or institution reinventing the wheel by producing their own'. Some principals felt that since 'computer use is being imposed upon schools' and the 'new curriculum initiatives require that schools be equipped with computers', the Ministry of Education should be responsible for developing and disseminating guidelines for computer use in schools. Principals preferred practical and systematic information, provided by experts, and enforced by an outside body such as the Ministry of Education.

The Need for Professional Development

It is now well established in the literature that professional development is a key factor if an innovation is to be successfully implemented in the classroom (Fullan, 1990). However, health and safety issues are seldom included in ICT professional development programmes. For example, in our study, only 10 per cent of the primary and 21 per cent of the secondary schools had organised professional development related to health issues with computer use for their staff. It is clear that health and safety issues were not emphasised in professional development in most schools. When organised, they were considered as part of the overall professional development, 'included in … training for staff on computer skills' and they usually involved some form of inspection from the Occupational Safety and Health Authority (OSH).

Professional development for the respondents meant gaining knowledge of ergonomic products or measures to prevent OOS. Topics such as psychological stress related to computer use, as well as the feeling of incompetence when using computers with their students due to inadequate training and professional development were seldom included.

Unfortunately, some principals had doubts about the need for professional development in this area:

'Our teachers are not using computers during school hours but children are.'
'Very few school personnel use computers for extensive periods so I'm not sure how great the need is.'
'Not interested at this time … It is not a concern to me. I know of problems. But until it affects me I sail on without concern.'
'Time has to be spent on training for teaching and computer use. Health and safety are important but not the driving force for in-service training.'

The lack of professional development in this area may explain why health issues associated with computer use were seldom discussed with students. In this study, it is reported that only 34 per cent of the primary teachers and 59 per cent of the secondary teachers have discussed these issues with their students. This is rather unfortunate as, increasingly, students will spend more time using computers in school as well as at home. In this present study 12 per cent of the primary and 11 per cent of the secondary schools have already indicated that their students were using a laptop or notebook computer at school. Students need to be aware of these health risks and preventive measures need to be instigated urgently if a safe work environment is to be provided for them.

What Should We Do?

Although computer use in the classroom or in the school office is usually very different from that in an office setting where people can spend all day working on a computer, health problems in the school setting are more widespread than expected, particularly with school administrators. It seems that there is a lack of depth in the understanding of these health risks as well as an inability to come up with some strategies to deal with them, at least partly due to the lack of efficient dissemination of information and national guidelines as well as to the lack of professional development and discussion of these issues in schools. What, then, should we do?

1. *Considering health risks as a matter of priority*. It should be noted that parents and educators are not wilfully ignoring the health risks of having poorly designed computer furniture or the importance of professional development. At present they are more preoccupied with the educational opportunities offered by the burgeoning technology, and the computer hardware and software needed to meet educational needs. Ergonomically designed furniture is not a priority compared to hardware and software purchase as 'by the time a school purchases hardware and software [it] seems little [is] left over in [the] budget for ergonomic furniture' (teacher's comment). Schools simply cannot afford it. These problems will certainly get worse if they are not treated as a priority.

2. *Providing professional development*. It is clear that at both national and school levels there is an urgent need for professional development on the ergonomic aspects of computer use to heighten the awareness of these issues as well as to deal with them proactively.

3. *Considering the school–home link*. The school–home link cannot be ignored when discussing issues related to the health risks of computer use, as it is increasingly common for students to have computers at home and typically students spend a lot more time playing computer games and chatting on the Web than using computers at school. It is important to promote healthy computer work habits not only at school but at home as well. Unfortunately, many parents are more concerned about how fast their kids can search the Internet than forming good work habits.

4. *Adopting a broader perspective*. So far we have confined our discussion to the physical health risks associated with computer use. However, the lack of professional development in ICT has created huge psychological stress for many teachers. As one teacher said, the computer has imposed 'a great anxiety whenever I have to use it as my inadequacies are likely to be exposed …' The inadequacies referred to by this teacher reflected the lack of training on computer use as well as on how to use a computer as a teaching and learning tool. Health risks teachers should be aware of ought also to include the anxiety and psychological stress they have to deal with in using computers in their classrooms.

Final Remarks

In the final analysis, the computer users themselves have to take responsibility for their own well-being. They have to examine their work environment and culture, as well as their work habits, from an ergonomic perspective. To deal with the health risks mentioned in this chapter, teachers need to have a deeper understanding of the issues and an ergonomically conscious work culture, created and supported by the school as well as the wider community both locally and at the national level. As a starter, perhaps teachers should ask themselves the following questions (adopted from Dillon & Emurian (1995)):

- After working with a computer, do you feel your eyes are sore or strained?
- Do you feel mentally fatigued after working with a computer for an extended period of time?
- After working with a computer for a while, does your vision seem blurry when you look at distant objects?
- Do you feel any discomfort or pain in your back, neck, wrist, etc. after working with the computer for a while?

If your answer to any of the above questions is positive, perhaps you should be alarmed. Not to make things worse, remember the ABC of computer use:

- **A**lways maintain a good body posture.
- **B**link, breathe, and break.
- **C**hoose ergonomic furniture and equipment, and make informed purchases.

Some Resources

A collection of resources on health issues associated with computer use is available at the New Zealand Learning Network, administered by the University of Otago <http://education.otago.ac.nz//NZLNet/safety/health_and_safety.html>
This website has been developed specifically for teachers and has some very useful resources and links on health and safety issues associated with computer use.

Computer software available on the Web can remind users to take breaks periodically. Here are some of the sites:
<http://www.acypher.com/Restie/>
<http://www.publicspace.net/MacBreakZ/>
<http://home.earthlink.net/~thomasareed/shareware/coffeebreak/index.html>

Acknowledgements

The research project mentioned in this chapter was supported by an Otago Division of Humanities Research Grant (LAMJ21). The author also wishes to thank Alison Grant, Anne Elliot, Philip Munro, and Nicola Elliot for their support in data collection and the preparation of this chapter.

References

Anshel, J. (1994). Visual ergonomics in the workplace: How to use a computer and save your eyesight. *Performance and Instruction*, 33(5), 20-22.

Anshel, J. (2000). Kids and Computers: Eyes and Visual Systems. Available at: <http://www.ctdrn.org/rsinet>.

Atencio, R. (1996). Eyestrain: The number one complaint of computer users. *Computers in Libraries*, 16(8), 40-43.

Bell, J. (1999, March 2). Laptops download a hi-tech malady, *The Bulletin*, 26-27.

Dillon, T. & Emurian, H. (1995). Reports of visual fatigue resulting from use of a video display unit. *Computers in human behavior,* 1(1), 77-84.

Fullan, M. (1990). Staff development, innovation, and institutional development. In B. Joyce (Ed.). *Changing school culture through staff development* (pp. 3-40). Alexandria, VA: ASCD.

Grant, A. (1998). Information technology in the New Zealand curriculum and occupational overuse syndrome. *Computers in New Zealand Schools*, 10(2), 37-41.

Gross, J. (1999, March 15). Missing lessons in computing class: Avoiding injury. *The New York Times*.

Laeser, K., Maxwell, L. & Hedge, A. (1998). The effect of computer workstation design on student posture. *Journal of research on computing in education*, 31, 173-188.

Lai, K.W. (1995). Computer use and potential health risks, *Computers in New Zealand Schools*, 7(2), 43-47.

Lai, K.W. (2000). Health risks with computer use in New Zealand schools. *In Proceedings of the 8th International Conference on Computers in Education/International Conference on Computer-Assisted Instruction 2000* (vol. 2, pp. 1019-1027). AACE.

McMillan, N. (1998). *Ergonomics in Schools: Some Issues*. Paper prepared for New Zealand Accident Rehabilitation, Compensation and Insurance Corporation, Wellington.

Ministry of Education. (1998). *Safety and technology education: A guidance manual for New Zealand schools*. Wellington: Ministry of Education.

Oates, S., Evans, G. & Hedge, A. (1998). An anthropometric and postural risk assessment of children's school computer work environments. *Computers in the schools*, 14(3/4), 55-63.

Poor, A. (1993, July). The perfect display. *PC Magazine*, pp.147-181.

Rosskam, E. & Baichoo, P. (1997). Preventing workplace injuries and illnesses through ergonomics. *World of Work*, 21, 5-8.

Contributors

Ross Alexander has worked as a primary school teacher for the past thirteen years, the last five as deputy principal at Houghton Valley School in Wellington. He has used computers in education for many years, and has a special interest in the development of school intranets as a communication medium, and in the use of administrative software for assessment. He is currently working as Site Manger for Te Kete Ipurangi (TKI) – The Online Learning Centre. Ross is completing a Postgraduate Diploma in Teaching (ICT) at the University of Otago. His email address is: ross@tki.org.nz

Anne Elliot is currently a Teaching Fellow in the School of Education, University of Otago. She was a primary teacher and has been involved in using computers in schools and for postgraduate studies for more than 10 years. She has published in *Computers in New Zealand Schools* and *Net-Working: Teaching, Learning & Professional Development with the Internet* on rural schools and legal and ethical issues when students have access to the Internet. In her spare time she is the webmaster of several websites. Anne's email address is: anne.elliot@stonebow.otago.ac.nz

Stephen Fletcher is a teacher in charge of information technology at the Taumarunui Campus of the Taranaki Polytechnic. He has been teaching and learning science and information technology in the primary, secondary, and tertiary education sectors for the last eight years, as well as undertaking educational contract work in the private sector during his spare time. He has published in *Computers in New Zealand Schools*, and is interested in the potential use of ICT in the development and delivery of education in rural New Zealand. He is currently completing a Postgraduate Diploma in Arts (ICT in Education) at the University of Otago. Stephen's email address is: fletcher@taumarunui.com

Stephen Hovell is principal of Pamapuria School in the Far North. He has been working with children on computers in rural classrooms since 1986. He enjoys science teaching, has a special interest in astronomy and believes in the potential of the Internet to support teachers in implementing the New Zealand curriculum. He is currently studying towards an M.Ed. in information and communication technology at the University of Otago, and is interested in the pedagogical value of virtual field trips. He has published in *Computers in New Zealand Schools*. Stephen's email address is: srh@xtra.co.nz

Dr Kwok-Wing Lai is an Associate Professor in the School of Education, University of Otago. Wing has a keen interest in studying and researching the use of computer-mediated communication in the school curriculum, teacher development, and also the social and ethical aspects of ICT use in education. He is currently the editor of *Computers in New Zealand Schools*. His sixth book, titled *Learning with Technology: Evaluation of Otago Secondary Schools Technology Project* (co-authored with Keryn Pratt and Ann Trewern) is to be published in June 2001. Wing's email address is: wing.lai@stonebow.otago.ac.nz

Philip Munro is currently working in the School of Education, University of Otago, as a Research Assistant and Teaching Fellow in the Distance Learning Unit. He has been working on a number of ICT-based research projects in the last few years. Philip's email address is: philip.munro@stonebow.otago.ac.nz

Sharon Nicholson has taught science to a range of students – at secondary level, at tertiary level to support vocational training, and at primary level. She has taught in South Africa, New Zealand and in the UK, where she is at present a teacher at Gainsborough Primary School in East London. Sharon is interested in identifying factors that facilitate and encourage active engagement by learners in the learning process. For the research component of her Masters degree, completed at the University of Otago, she researched factors that contribute towards successful online Internet projects. She has published in *Computers in New Zealand Schools*. Sharon's email address is: ESNicky@aol.com

Dr Keryn Pratt is a Junior Research Fellow in the School of Education, University of Otago, where she is currently the Project Manager of seven research projects in information and communication technology in education. Her current research projects include evaluating the current distance education progamme at Otago, evaluating the effects of a hardware grant on Otago schools, censorship issues regarding students' home Internet use, ICT in teacher education, ICT professional development and the effectiveness of assistive technology for students with special needs. Keryn's email address is: keryn.pratt@stonebow.otago.ac.nz

Ann Trewern is a Lecturer in the School of Education, University of Otago. She teaches a number of web-based postgraduate and professional development programmes in information and communication technology in education. Ann has particular research interests in the use of information and communications technology in the classroom, and in the role of the Internet in enhancing professional development and in curriculum delivery. Ann's email address is: ann.trewern@stonebow.otago.ac.nz

Janice Wilson is Faculty Leader of Technology at St Oran's College in Lower Hutt. Janice has had many years' involvement in the use of computers in education and is interested in finding ways in which her school can seamlessly integrate ICT into every area of the curriculum. Janice has completed a Postgraduate Diploma in Teaching (ICT) from the University of Otago. Her email address is: janraywilson@paradise.net.nz

Index